Sun Jan 25 2004

The item below is now available for pickup at designated location.

San Jose State
King Library

Saint Mary's
CALL NO: 362.82 G862
AUTHOR: Greif, Geoffrey L
When parents kidnap : the families
BARCODE: 351510011133081
REC NO: i1591873
PICKUP AT: King Library

KEIKO CHARIF
5293 JOSEPH LN
SAN JOSE CA 95118

408-267-6664

33:18

PAGING SLIP - The item/s listed below have been
requested. Please retrieve from the stacks.
Place this slip in the item and give it
to a Circulation supervisor. Thank you.

Saint Mary's College
Library
P.O. Box 4290
Moraga, CA 94575-4290

Book Stacks: 2nd floor
CALL NO: 362.82 G862
AUTHOR: Greif, Geoffrey L
When parents kidnap : the families
BARCODE: 3515100113301
REC NO: i1591873
PICKUP AT: King Library

KEIKO CHARIF
5293 JOSEPH LN
SAN JOSE CA 95118
INSTITUTION: San Jose State
LOCATION: SJSU
PATRON TYPE: LINK+ Graduate

408-267-6664

WHEN
PARENTS
KIDNAP

WHEN PARENTS KIDNAP

The Families Behind the Headlines

GEOFFREY L. GREIF
REBECCA L. HEGAR

THE FREE PRESS
A Division of Macmillan, Inc.
NEW YORK

Maxwell Macmillan Canada
TORONTO

Maxwell Macmillan International
NEW YORK   OXFORD   SINGAPORE   SYDNEY

The Free Press
A Division of Macmillan, Inc.
866 Third Avenue, New York, N.Y. 10022

Maxwell Macmillan Canada, Inc.
1200 Eglinton Avenue East
Suite 200
Don Mills, Ontario M3C 3N1

Macmillan, Inc. is part of the Maxwell Communication Group of Companies.

Printed in the United States of America

printing number
1   2   3   4   5   6   7   8   9   10

Library of Congress Cataloging-in-Publication Data

Greif, Geoffrey L.
    When parents kidnap: the families behind the headlines.
        p.   cm.
    Authors, Geoffrey L. Greif and Rebecca L. Hegar.
    Includes bibliographical references (p.   ) and index.
    ISBN 0-02-912975-3
    1. Kidnapping, Parental—United States.   2. Kidnapping, Parental—United States—Psychological aspects.   I. Hegar, Rebecca L.
    II. Title.
    HV6598.G735   1993
    362.82'97'0973—dc20   92-23855
                                                                 CIP

The authors acknowledge permission to use material abstracted from Rebecca L. Hegar, "Parental Kidnapping and U.S. Social Policy," *Social Service Review* 63 (September 1990): 407–421. Copyright © 1990 by The University of Chicago. All rights reserved.

CONTENTS

PREFACE

When we first became interested in learning about parental kidnapping, we were surprised at how little systematic social science or psychological research had been undertaken on the topic. Having completed this book, we have a better understanding of why that is so. Researching and writing about why parents kidnap their children is a daunting and complex task for many reasons.

First, it is difficult for professionals engaged in research to find and make contact with people who have experienced the abduction of a child by a parent, especially if they are not involved with the criminal justice system and do not seek mental health services for themselves or their child. Therefore, very little has been published about the parents or children who may be most representative of the families in which abductions occur.

Second, abduction of children by their parents is a subject many people might prefer to avoid. It has been painful to hear the stories of hundreds of left-behind parents whose children have been missing for periods of time ranging from a few weeks to many years. These mothers and fathers being cut off from their children, not knowing their whereabouts, doubting their well-being, fearing their children have been turned against them—have experienced any parent's worst nightmare. For parents who are still searching, there is the constant hope that some clue will turn up that will result in recovery of the child, that he or she will telephone, or that the abducting parent will return. At the same time, and particularly if the child has been missing for a long period, the parent left behind must begin to construct a life that may not include the child. How much time can a parent spend searching?

Although approximately half of the 371 parents we came to know had recovered their children by the time of our survey, emotional damage had been done to the family in many cases. Many of the parents who had recovered are wary of another abduction. Their vigilance must be constant. To protect their privacy—and, in some cases, their safety—the names of people involved in the case studies we recount, as well as their locations and other identifying information, have been changed.

The third reason that investigation of this topic is difficult concerns the children. Parents often wish to protect their children from remembering and talking about the abduction, and in most cases we have not asked to speak directly with young children. Our perspective about the children's experiences comes from the children we did interview and occasionally provided services to, from the recollection of young adults who volunteered to talk with us about the events of their childhoods, from parents, and from other professionals. Regardless of their ages, it has been painful to interview the victims of abduction and to learn about their pasts and their fears. Often confused and hurt by the experience, sometimes emotionally shattered and never untouched by it, the children who have been recovered carry the double legacy of a failed parental relationship and the stress of life on the run. How they cope with the abduction varies with age, relationship with the abductor and the parent left behind, and experiences while missing.

We have been fortunate to be able to add the important perspective of a number of abductors, none of whom were on the run or in violation of a custody order at the time of our interviews. (To have sought out those who were in hiding would have placed at risk the confidentiality we were able to provide to all who cooperated with us.) Most of the abducting parents we met believed their actions were justifiable. They often presented themselves as anguished parents who were attempting to protect their children from the other parent. Some had sought help from the courts first, but when they perceived assistance was not forthcoming, they acted. We have gained other perspectives on abducting parents from those who have sought them for violating the law, represented or prosecuted them in court, given them shelter, or undertaken research about them. These perspectives are often less flattering. The resulting mosaic is a complex picture, sometimes indistinct, sometimes showing intriguing patterns.

As we listened and learned, we had to place the multifaceted and often competing stories we heard from family members into a context and, as social workers, make recommendations based on our understanding of the issues. Parental kidnapping goes beyond the pain of the individuals involved. It takes place in a societal context that is shaped by changing family patterns, public perceptions of abduction by parents, and a legal system that attempts to prevent and resolve abductions. We were assisted by experts throughout the country in the formulation of our recommendations concerning how society should respond to abductions by parents. We heard from experts in family law, fathers' rights advocates, advocates for women, and staff from shelters for battered women. Our research took us into some of the ongoing debates about the roles of mothers and fathers and the treatment of women and men in legal disputes. Naturally, some of the people we consulted thought our recommendations did not go far enough in various ways whereas others thought we had gone too far.

With estimates of the number of parental abductions running into the hundreds of thousands annually, and with abductions taking such a personal toll, changes clearly are needed. The legal responses to abduction need to be more uniform nationwide, as well as fine-tuned to offer a range of resolutions based on the circumstances and effects of each case.

As coauthors, we bring to the complex topic of parental kidnapping nearly 40 years of experience in working with families and children as social workers in school systems, child welfare offices, and mental health services. In addition, we have written extensively about issues of divorce and child custody, child protection and placement, and social policy affecting families and children. Some of the research undertaken for this book has been reviewed by our academic peers and published in professional journals (see bibliography). We have attempted to offer a balanced view and provide suggestions for policy changes that are possible to achieve.

We hope this book will be helpful to those working in the area of parental abduction and related issues, that is, to mental health and child welfare professionals; attorneys and judges in civil, criminal, and juvenile courts; legislators and other policy makers; law enforcement personnel; staff in missing children's organizations; and advocates for families and children. This audience can benefit from an in-depth description of what happens when parents abduct. By having an understanding of the complexities of these situations, responses from those in a position to help can be more effective. Most important, we hope this book will provide comfort and support to those in greatest need of it, the parents and children themselves. If parents whose children are missing or who have had an abduction resolved learn about the similarities between themselves and others who have had this experience, they will be able to cope better with their situations. Learning about those similarities will go a long way toward helping them heal.

ACKNOWLEDGMENTS

In completing the research and writing of this book, we find that there are many people to thank. Early in our project Jan Russell of the State's Attorney Office of Cook County, Illinois, shared with us a survey of parental kidnapping that she had authored. Carolyn Zogg of Child Find of America, Inc. gave us information and helpful cooperation. Many missing children's organizations also helped with pretesting by distributing questionnaires to parents who had contacted them for help: Missing Children of America, Inc., Anchorage; Find the Children, Los Angeles; Adam Walsh Child Resource Center, West Palm Beach; Missing Children Help Center, Tampa; Exploited Children's Help Organization, Louisville; Missing Children–Minnesota, Minneapolis; Services for the Missing, Gibbsboro, New Jersey; I.D. Resource Center of Albuquerque; Child Find of America, New Paltz, New York; National Missing Children's Locate Center, Gresham, Oregon; Children's Rights Northeast, Columbus; The Society for Young Victims (Massachusetts and Newport, Rhode Island); Childseekers, Rutland, Vermont; Operation Lookout, Mountlake Terrace, Washington; Missing and Exploited Children's Association, Lutherville, Maryland, and Child Find, Quebec, Montreal. Christopher

Hatcher at the University of California Center for the Study of Trauma has been supportive in a multitude of ways, both in sharing his data and in opening up doors for us.

Others have provided us with background information: Carol Alexander and Judy Wolfer from the House of Ruth in Baltimore; Eric Foretich and Faye Yager; Detective Gregory Kovalenko of the Baltimore County Police; Howard Merker of the Maryland State's Attorney's Office; and JoAnn Lippert, Ph.D, of Reno. Ken Lewis, Glenside, Pennsylvania; Jim Levine, our literary agent; and Ruben Rodriguez of the National Center for Missing and Exploited Children also have been helpful.

A number of experts read and gave us indispensable feedback on earlier versions of the final two chapters. These include the following: Linda Girdner, Ph.D., Patricia M. Hoff, Esq., and Miriam Rollin, Esq., of the Parental Abduction Research Project, American Bar Association Center on Children and the Law; Karen Czapanskiy, Esq., and Jana B. Singer, Esq., of the University of Maryland School of Law; Eva J. Klain, Esq., American Prosecutors Research Institute, National Center for the Prosecution of Child Abuse; Michael Knipfing, Esq., Jeff Muise, and Carolyn Zogg of Child Find of America, Inc.; and Len Faseler, Esq., of Austin, Texas. These people have been generous with their time and ideas in reacting to our proposals and recommendations. Their ideas have made this a better book; however thanking them does not imply that they or their organizations endorse what we have written, for which we alone are responsible.

We would also like to thank the students at the University of Maryland at Baltimore School of Social Work who spent countless hours on this research project coding information, helping to get it ready for the computer, and telephoning parents from all over the country who took part in the survey. Their names also deserve mention: Amy Applebaum, Nancy Bellon, Nancy Booker, Debra Campbell, Ronit Climan, Rachel Cohen, Harry Congdon, Larissa DeGraffenried, Hetty Fanfani, Lee Goldman, Andrea Halman, Mary Lou Hobbs, Denise Hoffman, Judi Holland, Pat Hosinski, Cheryl Johnson, PeggiAnne Joy, Sue Keil, Cathy Latham, Valerie Lester, Joanne Lindsay, Sarah Montgomery, Linda Moran-Main, Linda Natoli, Karen Radich, Wendy Ann Rosenbaum, Heidi Simmons, Mary Sopato, Faye Sundry, Sara Tinkcom, Jill Weinstock, Louise Whiteside, Mary Ellen Wivel, and Robbyn

Zimmerman. Most of all, we would like to thank the parents and children who opened up their lives to us and answered hours of questions. They gave a great deal of themselves so that we could understand and help other parents and children in similar situations. We dedicate this book to them and to our own parents, Ann and Leonard and Lucille and Joe, who first showed us how much parents can care for their children.

CHAPTER 1
Parental Kidnapping in Context

Joan believed her visitation rights as a noncustodial mother slowly were being chipped away by Jerry, her ex-husband. It was becoming more and more difficult for her to see her seven-year-old daughter, Alice, because of scheduling conflicts with Jerry's new job. In addition, Joan was convinced that Jerry and his new wife were turning Alice against her by pointing out to Alice all of Joan's bad traits. The day Joan was given notice by her employer that she was being let go in a wave of company cutbacks, she emptied her bank account, picked up Alice after school for their biweekly evening together, and went on the run. Jerry was in shock. After calling Joan's parents and getting no assistance, he called the FBI, the police, and the local missing children's organization. Losing his child, he would say later, was the worst thing that ever happened to him.

Mary came home from work one day and found a note from Chuck, her husband of 7 years, saying he had left with their two children. Chuck abducted them as a way of getting revenge upon Mary. Their marriage had been on the rocks for years, and after Chuck refused counseling, Mary began talking about leaving. He suspected she was having an affair, although she was not. When he took the children, he was convinced that Mary would realize how important he and the children were to her and that she would feel some of the pain he had been experiencing. Mary cried uncontrollably for days after they left and found it impossible to sleep at night. When Chuck called a week later to report that they were living in another country, she begged him to come home. He said he'd think about it but did not call again for two months.

Linda was a battered wife and blamed herself for years for her husband's outbursts. Her friends finally convinced her that she did not have to live with the mortal fear that had become almost a part of her. Linda had not believed her daughter was in danger until she read that children who witness violence between their parents are being emotionally abused. After one particularly bad beating, Linda took her daughter and hid in a women's shelter.

Nancy and Jesse's marriage and family life had been marred by their alcoholism. After years in and out of treatment, Jesse began a prolonged period of abstinence. Nancy continued to drink. The healthier his life became, the more unhealthy hers grew. Jesse took over the primary care of their six-year-old son, while Nancy withdrew from the family by staying out late at night and sleeping until noon. The couple's arguments increased and frequently spiraled into violence. One day Nancy took off with their son, leaving Jesse with a furnished apartment but no money and no credit cards. When Jesse turned to the police and a local missing children's organization to help with the search for his son, he also reentered counseling, since he feared he was going to start drinking again to cope with the stress and sudden loss of his family.

John lived 200 miles from his three children, his ex-wife, and her new husband. He visited only sporadically. But when he heard from his oldest daughter (then age six) that she was being abused by her stepfather, he sprang into action. With his ex-wife's tacit support (she had a history of emotional problems and did not feel she could protect her children from their stepfather), he arranged an abduction during which he and his brother threatened the stepfather with criminal charges if he pursued them.

Roseanne, who was abducted when she was seven and was on the run with her father for one year before returning to her mother, sees the experience as a turning point in her life. Now 22, she has trouble forming close relationships and distrusts men.

Out of all the events that stress a family that is breaking up, parental abduction is one of the most disruptive. When a child is snatched by one parent and deprived of contact with the other, an already-strained family is put at further emotional risk: For the parent left behind, feelings of rage, loss, anxiety, and helplessness are common. For the child, life on the run means moving from one house to the next, avoiding close ties with anyone, and hearing distortions about the other parent. To the abductor, frequently an anguished and desperate parent, the abduction seems the only way to right a perceived wrong, to recapture the affections of the other parent, to get revenge, or to hold on to someone dear. For the public, the first awareness of abduction comes in the form of faces on milk cartons.

Although abductions often begin as private family events, privacy soon is shattered by the need for help in searching for the child. The context of parental abduction soon shifts to the public arena, where an array of legal and volunteer efforts exists for the purpose of resolving abductions. Some of these efforts are more effective than others. For example, many police departments and district attorneys' offices have investigators who specialize in resolving parental abductions. Other jurisdictions hardly consider it a crime and do little to help the searching parent. The National Center for Missing and Exploited Children, a publicly funded clearinghouse that provides information and assists in searches for missing children, is linked with a number of publicly and privately funded missing children's organizations throughout the United States. A handful of the local organizations are quite sophisticated in terms of their ability to help parents locate missing children. Others are one- or two-person operations, often started by parents who suffered the trauma of having their own children abducted by a stranger or by the other parent.

The social context of parental abduction extends beyond these public and private efforts to assist individual searching family members. All 50 states and the District of Columbia have enacted civil and criminal laws that apply in parental kidnapping cases. Congress also has become involved in parental abduction by passing the Parental Kidnapping Prevention Act (PKPA) to mandate cooperation between the states in enforcing child custody decrees and instituting other measures to resolve abductions. In addition, the United States has joined a growing number of other countries in signing the Hague Convention on the Civil Aspects of International Child Abduction, in which participating nations agree to return abducted children to their countries of residence.

With estimates of the number of parental abductions in this country running as high as 350,000 a year,[1] parental abduction is a family, social, and legal problem that cuts across many of our institutions, affecting young and old, rich and poor, and all racial and ethnic groups. While the number of children estimated to be the victims of parental abduction in the United States is high, other countries seem to be struggling with a smaller problem. One Canadian study reports that about 375 cases a year are reported to the police,[2] and an estimate of parental kidnapping in the United Kingdom places the number at approximately 500 annually.[3] This book, based on a study of 371 parents left behind in abductions, as well as on numerous interviews with children who were abducted and with abductors, describes the circumstances leading up to the abduction, the pain that family members experience following it, and the location and recovery of many of the children. The different experiences of parents and children are explained in part by a typology of five patterns of parental abduction. The final chapters of the book consider what society can do to prevent abductions and to resolve them when they occur.

ABDUCTION IN HISTORICAL PERSPECTIVE

Abduction of children probably has been a part of family life since the beginning of history. Among the first child abductions to enter European awareness were the biblical story of King Solomon deciding custody of a child that one mother had taken from another[4] and various tales from classical mythology. In one Greek myth the mother of Apollo's illegitimate son intends to kill the child, so Apollo arranges for Hermes to abduct the infant Ion and hide him with a priestess.[5] When Ion is older, his mother and a stepfather regain custody, but confusion about Ion's identity and misunderstandings among the family members persist until he finally is acknowledged by both of his parents. Since early times, children have been both economic commodities and emotion-laden targets for revenge by abductors. They have been snatched for a wealth of reasons by both relatives and nonrelatives. Recall the story retold by Shakespeare of the two little princes snatched from their mother and imprisoned in the Tower of London by their uncle because their claim to the English throne thwarted his own ambitions.[6]

One sociologist classifies the abduction of children into at least five broad categories: (1) those that occur for domestic relations reasons (the major focus of this book); (2) those that result in hostage situations; (3) those motivated by intended rape or other sexual abuse; (4) those that accompany nonsexual assault or murder; and (5) those motivated by the possibility of ransom.[7] These reasons reflect the range of ways that children have been used and abused in a process where they become objects of adult manipulation.

The kidnapping of children has been a documented part of the American psyche for well over a century. It was of sufficient interest in 1875 that an account of a false charge of parental kidnapping was reported on the front page of the *New York Times*. In that account, Henry Schreiner, a Savannah father, was accused by the children's grandfather of kidnapping his own children, aged four and six. For reasons not specified, the grandfather wanted to prevent the father and children from leaving the country. After being detained in Baltimore for two separate investigations, the father and children finally sailed to Europe.[8]

Three years later, a Mrs. L. A. Blackstone, a socialite who was described as having previously been an actress and the mistress of a prominent merchant, was charged on the front page with having kidnapped her child from the arms of the child's nursemaid. The marriage was reported to have dissolved due to marital infidelity, with the father retaining custody. The *Times* went on to report:

> The whole city is greatly excited over the event. Public sympathy is generally with Mr. Blackstone, and very harsh language is used in connection with the woman. A few persons, however, . . . say that if the domestic life of the divorced couple could be known it would be found that the woman had been sadly abused. It is the popular belief that she captured the child . . . in order to secure money for its return.[9]

Mrs. Blackstone responded to the charges two days later in an open letter to the *Times,* writing that she never had been a mistress, that she had been an actress for only two weeks, that her character was "unsullied," and that taking her child was prompted by the universal feeling that mothers have toward children.[10]

How much interest was there in parental abduction cases? It appears that the media brought the problem to the public's attention fairly frequently—at least once a year—and probably only prominent cases were reported. The *New York Times,* by one estimate, reported more than 30 domestic kidnapping cases between the time of the Schreiner case and the beginning of the 20th century.[11] In fact, in the 1990s the *New York Times* was still reporting cases of parental kidnapping.[12]

The most famous child kidnapping of this century, although not a parental abduction, galvanized the public and legislators to begin thinking about prevention as well as criminal prosecution. When the 20-month-old Lindbergh baby was abducted in early 1932 and held for a ransom of $50,000, Americans were horrified. Charles "Lucky" Lindbergh, the aviator hero, and his family were being victimized. The ransom was paid, but the baby was never returned alive. The body was found on May 11 of the same year. Bruno Hauptmann was convicted and executed for the murder four years later.

In part as a reaction to that infamous case, as well as to the growing number of abductions, kidnapping by nonparents was made a federal offense, and the Federal Bureau of Investigation was founded a year after the Lindbergh baby's death.[13] Since then, the FBI has been the federal legal institution most closely associated with locating missing children.

Other kidnappings also have attracted the attention of the public. In 1963 Frank Sinatra, Jr., was held for ransom of $240,000. After payment, the kidnappers were apprehended and most of the money recovered. J. Paul Getty III was taken in 1973 and returned after a payment of more than $2 million. Patty Hearst's 1974 abduction by a radical revolutionary group involved a ransom request that money be distributed to the poor. She was captured 19 months later and spent some time in prison for participating in a bank robbery before being granted executive clemency by President Carter.[14]

For many reasons the 1970s saw a great increase in public concern about missing children. Adolescent runaways, some fleeing abuse or drawn by the youth culture of the campuses and cities, were acknowledged to be a social problem. Families whose children were missing feared for their welfare and worried that they were in the hands of kidnappers or other adults who would exploit or harm them. The surge in divorce rates that followed liberalization of many state divorce laws increased the number of children living with single parents, and parental abduction became another nightmare for those with primary custody. During the 1970s the popular press began to deal with abduction by parents, often with accounts of individual family stories.[15] Public concern about the safety of young people coalesced around what came to be called the "missing children's problem," and in that context abductions by parents received greater attention and societal response than they otherwise might have.[16]

The tragic case of Adam Walsh caught the attention of the public in 1981 when the six-year-old was taken from the Sears toy department in Hollywood, Florida, where he was playing two aisles away from his mother. A national search was undertaken but to no avail. Adam's head was found in a Florida waterway two weeks later.[17] Like the Lindbergh kidnapping 50 years earlier, the Adam Walsh case was one that galvanized policymakers to hold Congressional hearings and consider legislation.[18] One result of the concern generated by that case was the establishment in 1984 of the National Center for Missing and Exploited Children.[19]

Running parallel to the growing concern about missing children was greater willingness by many in society to recognize and deal with illegal acts involving members of families. Child abuse had become widely recognized as a medical and social problem in the 1960s, but law enforcement authorities and the criminal courts became much more interested in prosecution of abusers in the 1970s and 1980s. Those also were the decades when the women's movement focused concern on domestic violence and marital rape. Society was coming to recognize that acts that harm or violate the rights of family members could not be treated solely as private troubles. Growing awareness that family members can be violent, dangerous people probably also influenced public concern about children abducted by parents. No longer could it safely be assumed, as it had been in the 1930s, that abductions by parents always lacked the criminal intent inherent in kidnappings by strangers.

Among the best known recent cases of parental abduction is the Hilary Morgan case. Hilary was the product of the short-lived marriage between Eric Foretich, a dental surgeon, and Elizabeth Morgan, a physician. Morgan sent Hilary into hiding with

Morgan's parents rather than allow Foretich, who she believed was sexually abusing Hilary, to continue visiting her after their marriage ended. While charges of child abuse are not uncommon in custody disputes, the legal consequences to Morgan for hiding Hilary were highly unusual. She was placed in jail in Washington, D.C., for contempt of court in refusing to reveal the whereabouts of her daughter, until an act of Congress limiting jail time for contempt freed her nearly two years later. Hilary, in the meantime, had been spirited away by her grandparents to Canada, Great Britain, and Christchurch, New Zealand, where she was reported to be progressing well. At this writing, Hilary is still living in New Zealand with her grandparents and mother, who has won custody there. Foretich is no longer attempting to gain custody because, he says, "I made a decision it was best for Hilary to no longer be in the center of any protracted litigation. She deserves the right to be a little girl for a change so I have stepped aside." Foretich also says the court and other related costs have exacted an impossibly steep financial toll that makes continuing the battle unfeasible.[20]

Of the many roles children play within families, parental abduction highlights the most tragic. In some abductions children are taken because they have become indispensable to a parent's well-being; in others they are removed from danger by parental acts of courage. One study of 86 parents who were contemplating abducting their children (only a small percentage had serious plans) found that almost half were motivated by the perceived need to protect the child from physical, sexual, and emotional abuse.[21] In other cases of abduction they are abused as sexual objects, as targets for abuse, or as sources of power, money, or revenge. Children have frequently been used for adult purposes with their own needs being ignored. Broader issues concerning the needs and rights of children underpin our thinking about parental abduction as we explore the nature of the problem and its possible solutions.

THE CHANGING FAMILY AND PARENTAL ABDUCTION

Parental kidnapping results from breakdowns in family functioning and in the capacity of family members to deal with family disruption. If the family system were functioning, there would be no need for an abduction. If separating parents were able to effect a smooth transition to a mutually satisfactory single-parent arrangement that included resolution of key emotional, custodial, and financial issues, there would be no abduction. Although it falls at the extreme end of the continuum, abduction can be viewed from the perspective of family disruption. At the other extreme of that continuum, depending on the family situation, are amicably maintained joint custody or primary custody arrangements. In those healthier situations, parental interactions are based on the needs of the child rather than on either parent's need to exact an emotional toll from the other.

Divorce today occurs in a vastly different social and personal context than when Henry Schreiner was accused of abducting his own children nearly 125 years ago. While it is well known that the number of divorces has skyrocketed since the 1960s, the longer-term history of family stability in the United States is less familiar to most people. Gaining an understanding of those changes helps to place the current divorce scene in perspective. With few exceptions, most notably around the two world wars, the incidence of divorce has increased steadily. For example, in 1870 there were 1.5 divorces for every 1,000 marriages, and by 1950 that ratio had increased by almost sevenfold.[22] Although 1950 actually saw many fewer divorces than in the five years immediately after World War II,[23] the decrease was only a temporary lull. Between 1950 and 1980 there was an additional doubling of the number of divorces.[24]

Because the statistics tell only part of the story, it is important to consider the reasons for these changes. In 1870 many marriages were short-lived because of death from illness, accidents, or childbirth (these were the primary reasons parents raised children alone, not unwed parenthood or marital separation, as is the case today).[25]

As health care improved and marriages lasted longer in the 20th century, a number of other factors led to an increase in divorce. One of those was the establishment of legal aid for the poor.[26] Desertions at that time were considered the poor man's way to end the marriage. With legal aid the poor were able to divorce inexpensively or at no charge. They swelled the official statistics. Additional factors were spawned by World War II: After that war, people had an increased feeling of impermanence; the war afforded many who would otherwise not have traveled far a greater sense of life outside of their hometowns. In the years since the war, travel has become easier, reducing the feeling of being stuck in one place, and religion, once a cohesive force for many families and communities, has become less important. And throughout the century, reforms in divorce laws have made breaking up easier for those who considered it.

In the 1960s and 1970s declining birth rates and the women's movement further opened the door to divorce by promoting women's access to employment. Women became less constrained to remain in marriages for their own economic survival. In addition, people's expectations about their own happiness and an increased willingness to seek the fulfillment of their emotional needs provided further motivation to seek divorce. And with greater numbers of people divorcing, the stigma abated.[27] As a result, the number of households with children that were headed by both parents actually declined from 1970 to 1985, while those headed by single parents more than doubled.[28] It can be noted that the United States has not been alone in this phenomenon. Many western European countries have seen their divorce rates soar, in some cases sixfold, in the period from 1961 to 1981.[29]

Parental abduction has an obvious link to divorce. When parents are splitting up, decisions have to be made about the children. The greater the number of divorces, the greater the possibility that some former partners will be unhappy with the custody arrangement and will take such decisions into their own hands (in some cases, however, the abduction itself precipitates the divorce).

While no reliable estimates exist of the rate of increase in parental abduction, experts generally agree that it is on the rise.[30] The increase in divorce is the clearest reason for this, but others also need consideration. One is the growing number of fathers who gain custody and mothers who become noncustodial parents. Between 1980 and 1988 the number of single fathers raising children under age 18 increased by 70% to well over one million, while the number of families headed by single mothers increased by only 15%.[31] Why are fathers more often gaining custody? The reasons are, at least in part, intertwined with the reasons for the rise in divorce. For example, one result of the women's movement is the increased likelihood of gender-neutral court decisions regarding custody. Fathers seeking custody now have a greater chance to achieve it. Some changes also are apparent in men's behavior, as more fathers show an interest in parenting.[32]

How would this contribute to the likelihood of abduction? Fathers who are rebuffed in their attempts to win custody may feel a greater sense of deprivation than did their predecessors. They may attempt to right perceived wrongs through abduction. Similarly, the growth in the proportion of noncustodial mothers may result in a new population of parents unhappy with their custody arrangements. These mothers experience enormous personal and social pressure to conform to the societal norm of mothers raising their children, a pressure they feel to a greater extent than do noncustodial fathers.[33] One way of dealing with this pressure is through abduction.

While abductions take place within the context of our changing society and family structure, they also stem from the personal histories of the individuals involved. Many abducting parents sustained losses as children that seem to shape their behavior as adults. Some of the left-behind parents appear to be repeating in adulthood patterns of victimization or abandonment begun early in life. With marriages characterized by unhappiness, pain, anger, violence, and substance abuse, a few of these parents may be products of families that also struggled with substance abuse and violence. Establishing loving relationships may be quite difficult for them. Thus, underlying the reported reasons for abduction— such as unhappiness with custody, visitation, or child support arrangements; anger and a desire for revenge; or the belief that the child is being harmed[34]—are both the societal changes that provide a context for abduction and the personal histories of the parents involved.

The storm of social, familial, and individual forces that give rise to parental abduction have their ultimate impact on those at the center of the vortex; the children. The trauma they undergo through abduction and often through life on the run is difficult to comprehend and raises many questions. Whereas children of divorce are innocent victims of their parents' inability to sustain a loving relationship with each other,[35] children who are abducted carry an even heavier weight. How can they integrate such an event into their view of life? How can they come to trust one or both of their parents when they have been exposed to so much uncertainty and anger? Many abducted children suffer extreme reactions, ranging from sleep difficulties to fear of authority, school problems, and suicidal behavior. Yet many do survive emotionally intact. Their lives may never be totally back to normal, particularly after an extended abduction, but they do survive emotionally and, in some cases, grow from the experience. Many parents report their children are doing well. But we cannot forget that this is a trauma that places children at tremendous emotional and physical risk.

Is an abduction ever justified? A few abductors have compelling stories, retold in this book, that might make a reader believe it sometimes is. Some argue that when the law does not properly protect a child, a parent must take action. But this becomes an individual decision and one that can never be condoned on more than a case-by-case basis. Many parents abduct because they despair of having problems resolved to their satisfaction through legal means. The legal system must be the first resort in resolving disputes, and when it is clear the system is failing, it must be changed.

OTHER RESEARCH ON PARENTAL ABDUCTION

Beyond the many firsthand accounts of individual parents, little has been written about the experiences of those affected by parental kidnapping. However, there are a few professionals from a variety of disciplines who have written about or are doing research in the area. Criminologist Michael Agopian was one of the first to explore the phenomenon of parental abduction. Using a sample of 91 families known to the court system in Los Angeles County for child snatching in the 1970s, he described a predominantly white group in which the abductor was much more likely to be male than female.[36] One third of the children were between three and five years old when abducted, and children between six and eight and between nine and eleven each accounted for about a quarter of the children abducted. Single abductions were more common than those involving multiple children, and victims were equally likely to be male or female. Abductors tended to have previous criminal records. Less than half of the children were recovered.[37] After interviews with five children, Agopian hypothesized that those abducted for shorter periods of time were apt to experience less trauma than those missing for longer periods.[38]

Janvier, McCormick, and Donaldson more recently surveyed 65 parents who had sought help in locating their children from five missing children's organizations. International kidnappings accounted for 40% of the sample, with men more likely to go abroad and women more likely to be the perpetrators in domestic snatchings. The domestic kidnappings were resolved less often; children were recovered in only 8% of these situations, compared with 19% of the international abductions. The parents left behind generally believed law enforcement agencies were less interested in helping them than in helping parents whose children were taken by strangers. Attempts to recover the children proved expensive, particularly in international abductions, where more than half of the searching parents spent more than $10,000 and a handful spent in excess of $50,000.[39]

Sagatun and Barrett examined 43 parental abduction cases in one California county between 1983 and 1987 and found that fathers were more likely to abduct before custody had been established while mothers were more apt to abduct after it had been established. The length of the abductions ranged from four hours to 13 years, and revenge was a consistent theme in why the abductions occurred. Also cited as reasons for the abduction were the abductor's desire to be pursued, which was seen as a replay of the couple's courtship dance, and the serious emotional problems of one of the parents.[40]

Chris Hatcher at the University of California, San Francisco, and his colleagues currently are involved in longitudinal research concerning the impact of abduction on parents and children. Gathering data from five sites that assist searching parents throughout the country, the researchers are studying, among other issues, how to help children reunify with their families and how to reduce the trauma of the abduction on recovered children. They also have recently completed a three-year prospective study of 280 families from four sites throughout the United States.[41] The work is funded by the Office of Juvenile Justice and Delinquency Prevention.

Other research, using much smaller samples of affected families, provides anecdotal information concerning the effects of abduction on children and families as well as suggestions on how to ameliorate the impact of such an experience and on how to prevent future abductions.[42]

The most recent and thorough study of missing children, sponsored by the Justice Department and conducted by David Finkelhor and his colleagues, estimates that there are more than 350,000 cases of family abduction annually in the United States.[43] (Stranger abduction was found to be relatively rare by comparison, occurring only slightly more than 3,500 times in the year studied. Runaway children and thrownaway children, the other categories of missing children, total a larger number than the children abducted by parents.) This study defined family abduction on two levels, the broader one including situations where a family member takes or fails to return a child for at least one night in violation of a custody order or agreement. The narrower definition resembles the popular conception of abduction and includes concealing the whereabouts of the child to prevent contact by the other parent, transporting the child out of state, or intending to keep the child indefinitely or to affect custody.[44] Finkelhor and his colleagues conducted a national telephone survey of more than 10,000 homes. Through this approach, which reached the most representative sample to date, they located 142 children in 104 households who met their broad definition of abduction; a subset met their more narrow definition. In-depth telephone interviews with the parents revealed that the children were taken out of state in less than 13% of the cases, that force was used in less than one-fifth of the abductions, and that in circumstances where children were physically removed when taken (as opposed to being retained past the agreed-upon visitation period), they were most likely to be taken from their home. Situations corresponding to the popular image of children being snatched out of school were almost nonexistent. Physical and sexual abuse during the abduction was rare, affecting less than 6% of the children. Although this figure for sexual and physical abuse is, fortunately, low, a significant number of children were believed to have suffered some degree of mental harm from the abduction experience. From the reports of parents who were interviewed it was estimated that approximately one in six children had been "seriously" mentally harmed by the abduction experience and between one-quarter (using the broader definition) and one-third (using the narrower definition) had experienced a lesser degree of mental harm. Half of the abductions lasted less than a week, with many parents indicating that they knew where their child was during the abduction. Only a handful of the parents interviewed stated that the child was still missing.[45]

OUR DEFINITION OF PARENTAL ABDUCTION

In existing literature and policy statements, there is little uniformity in the use of terms to describe the phenomenon of parents taking their children in violation of another parent's rights to custody or access. In this book we use the terms *parental abduction, parental kidnapping,* and *child snatching* interchangeably.

Our study includes cases subsumed under Finkelhor and associates' broad definition, and most of them meet the additional criteria for the narrower definition. Our cases meet the first criterion of the narrower definition by virtue of the fact that a searching parent contacted a missing children's organization for help; they meet the second and third criteria because only a tiny proportion of the abductors and children remained in state and most of the abductors clearly intended to keep the children indefinitely.

Both the broadly and narrowly defined abduction cases in Finkelhor's study included instances of child snatchings that occurred before a custody order was issued.[46] Other studies of abduction have also documented such situations.[47] For example, the most extensive study of missing children to be done in Canada found that in parental abductions the absence of a custody order was more than three and a half times more common than the presence of a decision to award custody.[48] In approximately one-third of the abduction cases we studied, the child was removed by a parent who was not violating a custody decree: At the time of the abduction, the parents were married and living together or separated without a court having awarded custody. In most states these situations turn into abductions that satisfy a legal definition as soon as the left-behind parent secures a custody order in his or her favor. As other researchers have done, we included in our study abductions that do not violate a custody order because from the viewpoints of the people most involved these are abductions from the moment they occur.

AN OVERVIEW OF OUR STUDY

Information for this study was gained through two primary methods: questionnaire responses and in-depth personal and telephone interviews. In order to gain information from a sizable group of parents, we contacted 14 organizations throughout the United States and Canada whose sole purpose is to assist parents searching for missing children. The names of these organizations were listed in a publication disseminated by the National Center for Missing and Exploited Children.[49] The organizations approached were all private because many organizations connected to law enforcement agencies are restricted from participating in research or require that extensive barriers be crossed.

The organizations agreed to mail an eight-page, 95-item survey to parents who had requested assistance following a family or parental abduction. Our hope was to get responses from parents who had recovered their children as well as from those who were still searching. Depending on the size of the caseload of the organization (some had records that went back a number of years), the organizations were mailed between 15 and 700 postage-paid packets that contained the survey instrument, a letter explaining the survey, and a stamped return envelope. Starting in August 1989, each organization addressed and mailed the packets with its own return address to guarantee that potential respondents would remain anonymous even if packets were returned as undeliverable. Some organizations included letters of support with the mailings. A total of 2,666 packets were mailed, of which 266 were returned as undeliverable. Between August and January 1990, responses were received from 380 parents reporting abductions that had occurred in 45 states and six countries. The final sample was winnowed down to 371 parents or grandparents (in three cases), who reported on the abduction of 519 children. Nine respondents fell outside the parameters of the study and were excluded. The return rate from this approach is conservatively placed at between 15% and 27% and may be higher.[50]

In addition, parents were asked at the end of the survey if they wished to provide further information in an interview. Eighty-five percent agreed and provided us with their telephone numbers. More than half were successfully reached for in-depth telephone interviews by the authors or by research assistants. About three-quarters of this group were reached a second time two years after the initial survey so that follow-up information could be gathered. Other family members also interviewed in person or by telephone include abductors, children who had been abducted, grandparents, relatives of abductors or searching parents, and adults who had been abducted as children. Some of these sources were interviewed in depth while others permitted us brief glimpses into their lives, providing us with impressionistic material only.

It is important to note here that this sample has limitations that make generalizations to other parents whose children have been abducted problematic. First, this is a sample of parents who contacted missing children's organizations, something not all parents whose children are abducted do. For example, it is likely that parents who are wanted by the police, have a police record, or have battered their spouses or children are less inclined to provide the background information and documentation that missing children's organizations often require. Second, some parents who received the questionnaire and who had recovered their children may, in the interest of trying to put the experience behind them, have chosen to not participate. Third, parents who responded to the questionnaire believed that their participation in a survey would assist them in their situation.[51] Fourth, the questionnaire was eight pages long and required a willingness to commit time to complete it, as well as a certain facility with reading. Fifth, minority parents in particular may be underrepresented if they did not contact these self-help organizations for assistance to the same extent that white parents did. Minority individuals sometimes seek help less readily than others because of reluctance to share family problems with outsiders. In addition, the abductors we interviewed (not all of whose stories appear in the book but who all helped shape our thinking about therapeutic approaches) were also self-selected.

Perhaps as important as the aforementioned limitations to generalizing from the sample is the fact that in most cases presented in this book only one side of the story was known. Adults who experience the breakup of a relationship frequently paint a bright picture of their own behavior while coloring in the behavior of their ex-partner with less complimentary hues. The period leading up to and immediately following an abduction is apt to be a time when feelings run particularly high. Even months or years after recovery of a child, a parent's perception of past events or of the emotional state of the child may be skewed. The accounts presented by the parents in this book must be viewed through a lens that filters out or takes into account the deep hurt that many of them felt at the hands of the abductors.[52]

Despite these limitations, the study provides a comprehensive portrait of families experiencing abduction. It is restricted neither to people being criminally prosecuted[53] nor to those receiving treatment,[54] as earlier studies have been. Further, it is diverse in terms of the economic status of the respondents and the region of the United States from which they report and is composed overwhelmingly of families in which the abduction lasted a month or longer (98% of the sample), thus providing an in-depth look at abductions that extend over a period of time.

Description of the Sample

Although other studies report that a large preponderance of abductors were fathers,[55] almost half (45%) of parents left behind in our study were fathers. The parents left behind had, in general, more education than the abductors and were more apt to be employed and to be working in professional or managerial positions (see Appendix A for comparative data). The responding parents indicated that they were predominately white (92%), and two-thirds gave their income as less than $27,500 a year, making this a largely middle- to lower-middle-class group. Of those who identified a religious affiliation, about half were Protestant, with smaller proportions identifying themselves as Catholic, Jewish, or other religions. In most cases the abduction had occurred within the three years preceding our contact with the parent, and in two-thirds of the situations involved only one child (occasionally, as many as four children had been taken). Three-quarters of all children were six or less at the time of abduction, and the most common age for a snatched child was two. Abducted children were less likely to be female ($n = 231$) than male ($n = 272$).

The marriages of the parents tended to be characterized by

domestic violence. This is often a reflection of gender imbalance in a society where men have more economic power than women in addition to their greater physical strength. Compared with other research concerning reasons for divorce, parents in this study more often reported the presence of physical, emotional, and substance abuse.[56] The customary contact between the abductor and the child just before the snatching varied greatly and was, in part, a function of where the child was living. For example, in half (51%) of the cases the parent left behind had custody, in 29% the child lived with the abductor in either a joint custody arrangement or while the parents were still married, in 14% of the cases the abductor had custody, and in the remaining situations custody was with someone else. When the child did not live in the household with the abducting parent, the amount of contact between them varied widely. Weekly or twice-weekly visitation was more common than has been described in other research concerning noncustodial fathers and mothers.[57] Finally, as is discussed in detail in Chapter 3, 49% of the searching parents had located their children by the time they participated in the study. For the families who had recovered their children, abductions had lasted an average of more than one and a half years.[58] Abducted children still missing at the time of the survey had been gone for more than four years.[59]

A PREVIEW OF THIS BOOK

In the five chapters that focus on the families who have shared their stories with us, this book describes the experiences of a wide range of searching parents, abducting parents, and children. The next chapter details the experiences of parents whose children were abducted. Here we explore their own childhood, the early stages of their marriage, the nature of their relationship with the abductor, the end of their marriage, and the circumstances leading up to and including the abduction. Pain and anger over the abduction are seen at every turn.

Chapter 2 also introduces a typology of five patterns of abduction that provides a central and organizing theme for much that follows. Using this typology we show that the custody arrangement (whether custody was shared or whether the parent left behind or the abductor had primary custody) and the presence of violence in the marital relationship are two key factors in understanding the nature of parental abduction. Not only do these factors aid understanding of the complex nature of abductions, but they also can be used to guide the steps undertaken to prevent and resolve abductions.

In Chapter 3 we hear the voices of the abductors. A number of men and women from around the country agreed to be interviewed about their reasons for abducting and about their experiences since the abduction was resolved. Four are highlighted here. These stories return us to the question of whether an abduction is ever justified.

Chapter 4 tells the stories of parents and children who have been reunited. We report specific circumstances that differentiate parents who recover from those who do not. Parents describe the assistance they received from private investigators, missing children's organizations, the private dissemination of posters, and the efforts of police and the FBI. In addition, Ken Lewis, who has helped numerous families in the recovery process and has served as *guardian ad litem* to children in different state courts, writes of two of his experiences recovering children following abductions. The children's stories are told in Chapter 5. Drawn primarily from interviews with parents whose children were abducted as well as from the children themselves, some of whom are now adults, the chapter sketches a multifaceted picture of the impact that abduction has on children's lives.

Chapter 6 completes the findings presented from our study with an examination of international abductions. In approximately one-fifth of the circumstances we studied, children were known or believed to be taken outside the boundaries of the United States. Here we show some of the differences between domestic and international kidnappings, the relationship between cross-cultural marriage and international abduction, and the characteristics of those snatchings in which the children remained missing. The Hague Convention on International Abduction also is discussed.

In Chapter 7 we examine therapeutic interventions for parents and children. Strategies here are drawn from information gained from our own work, contact with the families in this study, and interviews with other professionals. Treating abduction as an extension of marital separation and divorce, as well as a separate trauma, we give professionals as well as parents information about how people work through abduction-related issues within the context of a therapeutic relationship.

After a discussion of the clinical issues involved in helping individual parents, we next consider how society can act to prevent and resolve parental abductions. Chapter 8 discusses what prevention means in a complex arena like this one, and it offers two overarching principles and seven specific recommendations designed to eliminate some of the motivations for parents to kidnap. Chapter 9 follows a similar pattern, proposing three guiding principles and nine recommendations for resolving abductions when they do occur. A central theme of the two chapters is that abductions are motivated by different factors and carried out under a range of circumstances. Responses to abductions must therefore vary in accord with these factors. The typology of abduction situations set forth in Chapter 2 is used to guide discussion; a brief summary and conclusion also are included.

The abduction of a child by a parent is an event that places a family at the crossroads of many disciplines: social work, law, public policy, mental health, law enforcement, education, and medicine. On a personal level, it not only disrupts the lives of family members who go through it, but it also touches a chord in most parents who have experienced a divorce or have had marital difficulties. Gaining an understanding of abductions, what they are and what they mean, can enable society to respond in ways that transcend emotion. This complex and painful type of family disruption cries out for a response that combines the fullest knowledge and insight with the best of our professional skills. We hope the next chapters lead in that direction.

CHAPTER 2

Parents Whose Children Are Abducted

This chapter describes mothers and fathers whose children have been abducted by the other parent. It is the voices of the parents who are left behind that we hear. They are the parent victims. In the next chapter the abductors speak. For now, we are learning about one side of these complex relationships. In order to understand the pain that these parents undergo, we first must consider that they are dealing not only with separation from their children but also with feelings that arise from a failed partnership. When a child is abducted by a parent, it usually is within the context of a divorce, a marital separation, or the breakup of a long-standing nonmarital relationship. A relationship is coming to an end or has ended, and one of the parents removes a child from contact with the other parent. It can occur before one of the parents knows the partnership has ended, as it is ending, or months or years later. With the dissolution of long-standing relationships can come feelings of failure, loss, anger, depression, guilt, and relief; a breakup involves many conflicted feelings as a person who once was loved becomes more and more distant with time. Whatever the feelings involved and the reasons for the breakup, the couple remain tied to each other by their mutual history.

That tie is made all the more binding when children are involved. Children represent for a parent not only his or her own past and hopes for the future but also the partner. When children are not present, there is little to keep a separating couple in contact with each other; but when children are present, untangling the emotional web is an unrelenting task.

Few relationships end without some degree of hurt; many contain a great deal of acrimony. Breakups leave open wounds into which the other parent can rub salt in a variety of ways. As each parent tries to resolve the loss involved in the breakup, the other can help or hinder that process. When a child is abducted, the resolution is made immeasurably more difficult because the ex-partner becomes a larger-than-life presence. Every time the parent feels the child's absence, he or she is reminded that the relationship with the other parent failed and remains unresolved. Abduction blocks all exits from the partnership and leaves no way to work on resolving it.

While the parent is struggling to cope with the unresolved partnership, he or she is dealing simultaneously with something more devastating: the loss of contact with the child. Even though most parents know it is the other parent who has snatched the child, many of them still fear for the child's safety. In many cases they ended the relationship and gained custody because of worries about the other parent's emotional state, drug abuse, or history of physical abuse. The abduction may be seen as a ploy to reconcile a marital separation, an attempt to win a better property settlement, or a last-ditch expression of anger. The more dangerous the abductor is perceived to be, the harder it is for the parent who is left behind.

But even when the abductor is believed to be well intentioned, the parent left behind loses in the child a key person, a loved one, a centerpiece in her or his life. The abduction is not a final statement, as a death would be, allowing formal grieving and then the beginning of a coping process. An abduction spurs the parent into action to search for the child. And if the child is not recovered, there may never be a time for grief.

The importance of a child to a parent's well-being cannot be overestimated. Studies show that parents suffer when separated from their children, whether because of illness, war, child placement, incarceration, divorce, or abduction.[1] Not having custody following a divorce has been linked to difficult psychological adjustment and to alcohol abuse.[2] Children give most parents a focus for their lives. When deprived of that focus—particularly after a breakup, when the need to feel connected is strongest—the parent suffers. This need for the child explains both how the parent whose child is taken feels and, in some cases, why the child was snatched. The abductor may act because of loss of contact or fear of such a loss.

The scant research currently available on parents whose children have been abducted has been gathered primarily from studies by Michael Agopian,[3] Rosemary Janvier and colleagues,[4] David Finkelhor and associates,[5] and Rex Forehand and colleagues.[6] In Agopian's work in Los Angeles County the most common age range of the parent left behind was between 27 and 31 years, with the mean age of the group being 33. Most were employed at the time of the abduction. Agopian writes eloquently of the contacts he has had with parents left behind: "The frustration and sorrow expressed by these parents was wrenching. They expressed disbelief at the confusion within the laws, the ease with which offenders circumvent authorities, the limitations of police agencies assisting them. . . . The pain and chaos that pervades the life of a parent who has lost a child was manifest."[7]

In Janvier and associates' study of 65 parents who had contacted five missing children's organizations for help with recovery, custody orders were not in place in approximately one-quarter of the cases. Prior threats of abduction had been made in almost half of the situations. Mothers and fathers reported similar effects of the abduction: From a checklist of items, both mothers and fathers described experiencing problems with sleep, anxiety, depression, sadness, despair, defeat, and helplessness.[8] In a post recovery study of 17 abduction cases, Forehand and colleagues noted that 9 of the 17 left-behind parents had legal custody at the time of abduction. According to a variety of standardized tests, some pathology was present in the left-behind parent group while the children were missing, though it never reached a severe level. Problem-focused attempts at coping, that is, taking some kind of action to resolve the problem, were more common among the parents than emotion-focused action, such as trying to take a more objective view of the situation or focusing on the positives. One conclusion was that the effects on the parents were not permanent.[9]

We now introduce two parents, Fred and Rita, whose stories we will follow through this chapter.

* * *

After a lengthy and costly custody battle for his son, Fred was optimistic. A week before the judge was to hand down his decision, which Fred was convinced would go in his favor, he received mail from his wife informing him that she was taking their son on a two-week vacation. That was in 1988. Fred has not seen either of them since.

* * *

Rita had already had sole legal custody for two years when her son was snatched. She and her ex-husband, both recovering drug addicts, had been separately working to put their lives back together again. She had entered a nursing program, and he was working steadily at a construction job. One week before her final exams, Rita asked her ex-husband to keep their three-year-old for a few days so she could study in peace. When Rita went to pick him up after the last exam, father and son had vanished. Since 1980 Rita has not heard a thing from them.

* * *

Once a child is abducted, most parents react by fighting vehemently for recovery. They contact the police and the FBI, hire private detectives, call missing children's organizations or the National Center for Missing and Exploited Children, and design fliers showing their child's picture to mail across the United States. These efforts, which are sometimes successful, help parents as they try to master a situation in which they have lost control. A few parents make only halfhearted attempts at recovery, saying they do not have the money or the energy to pursue their child. It is as if the loss of the child confirms their own feelings of low self-worth. Some have been so victimized by the abductor that chasing him or her seems out of the question. Regardless of the recovery attempts made by the parent, the abduction and loss of contact with the child are devastating blows.

In order to fill in the background in this portrait of parents who lose children through abduction, we start by sketching their early

life histories, looking for clues that might foretell later involvement in an abduction. We focus next on the nature of their
relationship with the abductor, the abduction itself, and its
aftermath. Even then the scene remains unclear. Are the parents
left behind somehow at fault? Are *they* victimizing the child
and/or the abductor, forcing that parent to leave to save the child
and himself or herself? Or are they victims, innocent of any
wrongdoing and suffering greatly at the hands of an illegal and
often violent act? In this and the succeeding chapters, we address
these questions by following the chronology of the family's
development.

This chapter also introduces important comparisons between
groups of parents. Differences are described as significant when
their magnitude reaches certain generally accepted levels based on
statistical tests. The figures that appear in many of the notes
throughout the book are based on cross tabulation, analysis of
variance, or correlation, depending on the types of data.[10]

PORTRAIT OF THE LEFT-BEHIND PARENT

Early Family History

With the discoveries of Freudian psychology over the last
century has come a curiosity about the link between early history
and later behavior and feelings. Most of us have an intrinsic
fascination with our own childhoods and family roots. Is there a
connection between parents whose children are abducted and
their early experiences? Of the parents we interviewed whose
children were abducted, slightly less than one-third spent some
time in single-parent homes while they were growing up, a higher
proportion than would be typical of children raised in the 1960s
and 1970s before the incidence of divorce boomed.[11] Although
spending part of childhood in a single-parent family may be a
better predictor of later divorce than of parental abduction, there
is a potential connection between being raised by one parent and
considering abduction as a viable option. It is interesting to note
that a significant percentage of the left-behind parents we interviewed who were raised in single-parent families lost virtually all
contact with their fathers for a number of years and some could
not remember ever seeing them. While it is not unheard of for

fathers to drop out of sight after a divorce, the high percentage of families where this occurred makes it worth mentioning. It is a piece of personal history that may help create a sense of impermanence in family relationships.

* * *

Fred's parents were divorced when he was an infant; he was raised by his mother and had no contact with his father until he entered college. Rita also had no contact with her father during her childhood. Following her parents' divorce, she lived with her mother's parents until her mother remarried when Rita was five. Returning to her mother and new stepfather's home, Rita felt like she had entered a combat zone. The constant fighting between the two adults spilled over into an increasingly strained relationship between Rita and her stepfather. Four years later that marriage ended. Her mother married for a third time when Rita was 13; this time Rita formed a very close bond with her new stepfather but fought constantly with his children from a previous marriage. When she was 17, about the same time her mother had a nervous breakdown, she left home. For Rita, escaping was the only logical course of action. While many youngsters follow this same course, others remain and attempt to work things out.

* * *

Almost none of the parents we interviewed had experienced abduction as children. Approximately one-quarter reported that alcohol or drugs were abused by one or both of their parents. In addition, almost one-fifth witnessed violence between their parents, with one in eight having been physically abused and one in twenty sexually abused when growing up. This is important to keep in mind because allegations of violence and abuse are not uncommon in many of the relationships these people developed in adulthood.

Most family histories were unremarkable except for the higher than usual rate of divorce. Estimates of domestic violence from the general period when these parents were growing up are harder to compare but do not appear to be unusually high.[12] Their early histories cannot be used as a basis for predicting that these parents later would be involved in relationships with abductors. For those whose parents divorced, and especially for those who lost contact with the father and may have been exposed to violence, it may be hypothesized that such early experiences set the stage for a lack of permanence in later relationships. A separation in early life may make a person more vulnerable to separations such as marital breakups and abductions. We wonder whether some of these parents have great dependency needs and seek out a degree of intimacy and reassurance that no one could provide or whether, at the opposite extreme, they avoid intimacy.

The Nature of the Relationship with the Abductor

How do people meet a spouse who eventually becomes an abductor? Were these parents rushing into marriage and exercising bad judgment? Was there any clue in the early stages of the relationship that an abduction was in the offing? With few exceptions, the beginning stages of these relationships do not appear different from the vast majority of others. The parents report their reasons for being attracted to their spouse in psychological terms—"I was looking for a caretaker, and he wanted to play that role"; "I was attracted to her because she was available and interested in me"; "I was lonely"—and in physical terms ("He was cute" or "She was sexy"). (Between one-fifth and one-quarter of the searching parents, as well as the abductors, had been married before, with about half of these parents having children from those unions.)

Although some parents were not especially smitten with their future spouses, many moved into marriage optimistically, feeling there was a great deal of love in the relationship. But there were a number of storm clouds on the horizon: In our in-depth telephone interviews, 46% admitted they knew about a substance abuse problem with the abductor during the courtship period. In at least one situation it was drugs that attracted the parents to each other. Almost one-third reported a premarital pregnancy that necessitated or speeded up a marriage, and slightly less than one-third described some premarital violence between the partners.[13]

Whatever love existed before the marriage, the bloom soon was gone. After the wedding (about one in seven parents never married the abductor) few relationships were described as being successful, even in the early stages. Conflict between spouses over racial and ethnic differences was reported in one-sixth of the relationships; religious and social class differences plagued almost one-quarter.

Some partners soon became aware of the spouse's violent side or of a drug or alcohol problem.

*   *   *

Fred met his ex-wife, Sarah, through a church-sponsored singles group. An avid bicyclist, he was teaching long-distance bicycling to a group that included her. With many outdoor activities in common, they quickly became attracted to each other. Fred was 29 and Sarah was 35; Each had been planning an independent trip to Europe to pursue bicycling. They decided to marry and make that trip as a honeymoon. Unlike many of the couples in this book, Fred and Sarah reported that their honeymoon and the early months of their marriage were happy. Their difficulties began when they shifted from being a couple to being parents. Sarah, feeling her biological clock ticking, wanted to have children immediately. She soon became pregnant and gave birth to a son, Timothy. Sarah quit her job in sales to devote her full attention to him. These rapid changes in his life were agreeable to Fred until he realized the depth of Sarah's need to be a parent. She became obsessed with Timothy to the point of resenting any time that Fred wanted to spend with him. The couple's communication began to deteriorate, and they started arguing all the time. Fred said he did not realize until after the abduction how obsessed Sarah was with motherhood and that she perceived his attempts to establish a normal relationship with his son as a threat to her own role of mother.

*   *   *

Rita met her husband while she was still living at home. She was working part-time as a waitress and was introduced to Bob by a mutual friend. Rita was attracted to Bob because he was friendly and charming. As tensions mounted in her own home and she made plans to move out, Bob's family offered to take her in. Nine months later Bob and Rita were married. They both worked during the early years of the marriage despite what became for Bob a burgeoning drug addiction. He began using heroin and would torment Rita, finally convincing her to start using drugs also. Still young and somewhat naive, Rita wanted to please Bob but was also frightened of him. When he was not abusing drugs, according to Rita, the communication between them was wonderful; at these times, the charming Bob who had first attracted her seemed to be back. Bob would occasionally seek help for his abuse, check into a drug abuse program, stay abstinent awhile, and then begin abusing again.

Rita's sporadic use was less serious but still a problem. Five years into the marriage their son, Hank, was born. Rita stopped working to stay home and care for him. With Hank's birth, their drug use waxed and waned; finally both entered a detox program.

*   *   *

While neither Fred nor Rita was involved in a marriage where physical violence existed, it is common for marriages that involve child snatching to be violent. More than half of the parents in our study were victims of violence, with a handful describing themselves as the sole perpetrator or claiming that both parents were violent. That incidence of marital violence is unusually high. Studies of the general population show that about a quarter of couples experience violence during marriage;[14] the incidence of violence among divorcing couples is somewhat higher but not as high as the rate in our sample.[15]

In a case that is typical of many others, the wife, Brigitte, described a long-standing pattern of being battered. The marriage, following a two-year courtship, involved beatings that began when the couple returned from their honeymoon. Brigitte recalled having ribs broken, being threatened with a knife, and being hit with a metal chair when she was pregnant. As is sometimes the case in spouse battering, Brigitte's husband was a heavy drinker. In other situations both parents are violent. One father, Richard, described being provoked by his wife: "She would frequently get angry at me and fight and throw stuff. I was pushed to the point where I had to fight back and then she would get hurt and I would be blamed."

As many of these relationships spiraled into unhappiness, violence, or substance abuse, some parents took steps to correct their problems. Approximately one-fifth of the parents reported going for marital counseling; others sought help for family-related problems or for anxiety, depression, and spouse abuse. A few were treated for alcohol or drug abuse. There were other stressors to the married lives of these parents: A significant minority experienced run-ins with the law. Fifteen percent reported that they had been accused of child abuse (usually by the other parent), and 15% said they had been arrested. The most common reason for arrest was driving while intoxicated.

As in many relationships that end in divorce, these marriages clearly were fraught with problems. Cultural, religious, and economic differences were present. Some couples were compelled to marry by a pregnancy. Most notably, these marriages seemed to be marred by violence and substance abuse, which often began during courtship and which made them pressure cookers ready to explode from the buildup of stress. This may be particularly true for the parents who had themselves grown up in single-parent families or been victims of childhood abuse. The breakup and abduction were the crowning blow.

THE END OF THE MARRIAGE

As the dissatisfaction mounted in these relationships, the marriages came to an end, occasionally with abduction as the last straw. Reasons that parents gave for the breakup vary greatly, with incompatibility being mentioned most frequently (by 31%). In these cases, the parents reported that they fell out of love with each other, grew apart, or found they were no longer happy together. The parents noting incompatibility blamed neither their spouse nor themselves for the breakup but, rather, accepted partial responsibility for the termination. The remainder of parents tended to blame the abductor for the breakup. Nearly a quarter of the parents said that the relationship ended because they were victims of physical and emotional abuse. Substance abuse, usually by the abductor, was cited by one in six parents, and the abductor's emotional problems or infidelity were cited slightly less often.

* * *

As Fred continued to fight with Sarah for time with their son, problems escalated. In the summer of 1987 Sarah made plans to go to a church-related camp with Timothy for one month. Fred objected strenuously, not wanting to be separated from his son for such a long period of time. Sarah resolved the conflict unilaterally by leaving for the camp. Fred was disconsolate with Timothy gone. Tensions mounted when valuable items started disappearing mysteriously from their house; Fred, presuming that Sarah was sneaking back to steal them, fought back by changing the locks. Sarah returned from camp and filed for separation when she could not get back into their home.

Thus began two years of legal wrangling, charges of sexual and physical abuse, psychological evaluations, and court appearances, involving a host of attorneys. First Sarah charged Fred with physically abusing her, in an attempt, Fred believed, to speed up the court process. Then Sarah and Fred were evaluated by court-appointed experts to determine who was most competent to have custody of Timothy. When Sarah was found to have numerous psychological problems, the court began to consider joint custody or giving sole custody to Fred. Then Sarah accused Fred of sexually abusing Timothy during his visitation with him, a charge that was thrown out pending further evaluation. Most likely, it was when Sarah began to feel the weight of the case sliding against her that she began considering abduction.

*   *   *

Rita's marriage, following a different pattern, also unraveled. The point of no return came for her when Bob again began using drugs again and "turned crazy." She and Hank moved out and headed to Florida to live with her father and stepmother (an abduction in Bob's eyes). She filed for divorce but Bob wouldn't let go. Having followed his wife and son to their new location, Bob began harassing her. He painted obscenities on her car and garage and sent threatening letters to her and her father. When the divorce was finalized, Rita was given full custody, Bob was granted visitation rights, and a relatively stable period in the family's life ensued.

*   *   *

Fred and Rita were both separated from their spouses and on the verge of divorce when their children were abducted. More than 80% of the parents we surveyed were separated or divorced at the time of the abduction; the rest were living together or still married when the abduction occurred. Primary legal custody was with the parent whose child was abducted in half of the situations, and it was shared in another third of the families (because of a joint custody decree or no custody order.) Primary legal custody belonged to the abductor in the remaining cases. Usually, if custody had been awarded to one parent, it was because that parent had been the primary caretaker during the marriage or because the other parent was perceived by the court to be unfit.

Visitation and Child Support

Once a marital breakup occurs, the family usually attempts to settle into a routine involving visitation and child support. In the typical situation among the families we studied, the parent whose child was abducted had custody initially. In most of the cases (70%) visitation took place at least every other week and the abductor was quite involved with the child. In the remaining 30% of the situations, visitation was rare. The geographic distance between a parent and child is frequently a deterrent to visitation. In our sample over half of the separated or divorced parents lived within 25 miles of the abductors, and visitation declined as the distance increased.

Child support, ranging from $5 to $300 per child per week, had been court ordered in nearly half of the custody arrangements, though it went unpaid more often than not. While these figures for child support are not vastly different from other divorced families,[16] our findings about visitation are. The literature suggests that the abducting parents in our study visited their children more frequently than is common in postdivorce families.[17] The level of involvement with their children suggests that for these abducting parents being with their children is of primary importance. This thought is pursued further in the next section.

THE ABDUCTION

Few parents were caught completely off guard by the abduction. In half of the families abduction had been threatened before it occurred. Sometimes the threat was made as part of a power play to get the custodial parent to return home. For example, a custodial parent might hear, "If you don't come back to me, I'm going to take the children and you'll never find us." In other situations, where the children were pawns in the divorce, one parent might say to the other, "If you try for custody of the children, you'll never see us again." Even in cases where an actual threat was not made, the parent worried about it; the abductor might have been seen as emotionally unstable, or there might have been a history of abduction in the abductor's past. Parents whose ex-spouses had close ties in another country were particularly worried (those situations are explored thoroughly in Chapter 6).

At the time of the abduction the child usually was already with the abductor, that is, during visitation or as part of the custody arrangement, as opposed to being snatched out of school, from the other parent, or from some other relative. Violence or force was used in 15% of the abductions. When violence was used, the abductor knocked out the other parent and then took the children or physically pulled the child away from the grasp of the other parent.

Most parents believed the abduction was motivated by revenge and anger. Many were convinced that it was not a desire to be with the child that drove the abductor but, rather, the chance to get back at them, usually for ending the relationship. The parents, some listing two answers, gave the following reasons on the survey for why they thought the abduction occurred: to hurt me (77%); anger over the breakup (23%); a desire to be with the child (16%); pressure from others (13%); dissatisfaction with visitation (13%); and the new marriage or relationship of the parent left behind (9%). Mentioned less frequently were the following reasons: to avoid paying child support; to reconcile a marriage; to protect the child; and to harm the child. While only one parent in six believed the abduction was due to a desire to be with the child and only one in eight believed it was due to dissatisfaction with visitation, most of the parents believed the abductor was using the children as pawns in a game of trying to hurt them. At the same time, only three parents believed the abduction was motivated by a wish to harm the child. Thus, from the perspective of the parent left behind, the children themselves are secondary in the minds of most abductors. It is interesting to consider this view of the abductor's motives in light of that parent's reported frequent visitation before the abduction.

Although the self-reported motives of the abductors are discussed in a later chapter, it is important to raise some of them now as a counterpoint. Interviews with personnel in missing children's organizations, government employees, people with connections to the underground networks that hide abductors, and the abductors themselves leave a different impression of why some abductions take place. These observers and participants in the child snatching scene believe that in many cases the abductor takes the child because child abuse is being committed by the custodial parent or because of the fear (or reality) of visitation being greatly restricted. In fact, suspicion and accusations against the searching parent concerning child abuse, sexual abuse, and domestic violence, an area probed in our telephone interviews, may play a significant role. Approximately one-quarter of the searching parents told us they had been accused of physically abusing the children and of violence against the abductor. Eighteen percent said they were accused of sexually abusing the abducted child. Almost no one admitted to any such action. In these complex relationships the truth may lie between the perspectives of the parents left behind and the abductors. Certainly, it is clear that abductions have taken place for a wealth of reasons, from the best-intentioned to the most selfish.

*   *   *

In Fred's situation the abduction followed from Sarah's intense desire to be with their child. Fred believed that the court was going to order joint custody to resolve their long-standing custody battle, which had begun as soon as Sarah returned to find herself locked out of the house, and that Sarah would not be able to tolerate sharing Timothy. Just before Fred was scheduled to have Timothy for the summer, he received a letter from Sarah saying that she was going to take their son on a two-week vacation first. While Fred was in the process of objecting to this, Sarah and Timothy vanished. The two-week vacation gambit may have bought Sarah a little bit of time before Fred began looking for her.

Fred is convinced that Sarah was assisted by an underground network, a loose coalition of "safe" houses, where parents on the run with their children can find safety and anonymity. He believes she had been planning the abduction for three months and that the end of Timothy's day care program and the summer vacation plans nicely coincided with her time schedule. Her sales job also was coming to an end, so it was a relatively easy time to make a transition.

*   *   *

Rita's husband, Bob, abducted Hank after Rita asked Bob to watch him for a few days while she studied for a nursing exam. When she went to pick Hank up after the exam, the house had been completely vacated. Rita immediately called her father-in-law, who gave her no information but hinted that he knew where her son and husband were. Months later, he told her that Bob had threatened to kill himself and Hank unless he helped them escape. Whereas

Sarah had been planning Timothy's abduction for months, this one appears to have been more spontaneous, springing from Bob's opportunity to have his son for a few days without any interference from Rita.

*   *   *

As we describe the context of parental abductions, three factors seem key in understanding the conditions under which abductions occur: (1) who has custody, (2) whether there has been a history of violence in the relationship, and (3) the gender of the abductor. These factors are important for different but interrelated reasons. Concerning the first factor, an abductor who violates a court order giving custody to the other parent commits an act that has clear and immediate legal implications and repercussions in all jurisdictions. Because a legal document has been violated, the potential for the left-behind parent to receive help from law enforcement agencies is increased. In addition, since the parent whose child is abducted has already gone through the courts to gain custody, there may be a greater sense that the abduction has exceeded certain prearranged boundaries.

The second factor, family violence, marks these relationships to an unusual degree; it was present in 54% of the couples in our sample, with the abductor reportedly the only violent partner 90% of the time. When one or both spouses have resorted to violence to resolve conflicts during the marriage, the qualitative nature of the marriage is different. One spouse may live in mortal fear of the other, and the chance to negotiate disputes peaceably is greatly diminished. Custody matters may have been resolved through a veil of threatened violence rather than rationally and with the best interests of the child at the heart of the decision making.

Finally, the gender of the abductor and of the parent left behind is a key variable in understanding the nature of the relationships and, later in this book, in explaining the reactions of law enforcement officials. (A section near the end of this chapter discusses some of the differences between male and female parents whose children have been abducted.)

These factors provide the springboard for later discussions of how abductions can be prevented and resolved. The different circumstances surrounding abductions that call for differential responses from law enforcement agencies and policymakers are examined further in the final part of the book.

A TYPOLOGY OF ABDUCTIONS: PUTTING THE PIECES TOGETHER

In getting to know parents whose children had been abducted, it became clear to us that custody and violence are key factors in understanding their experiences. We have grouped the circumstances surrounding abduction into broad patterns based on who had custody (the abductor, the other parent, or both) and whether or not the abductor had been violent in the marriage. Because of the small number of situations where a violent abducting parent had sole custody, those cases were omitted, leaving a total of five patterns in this typology of abduction.

In our groupings we have used a transactional view, one that considers what impact each parent's behavior has on the other parent. Analysis of the different patterns makes it apparent that parental abduction is not a single phenomenon. In the balance of this section we explore how the parents' situations differed with respect to the reasons for divorce, the perceived motives for abduction, and the circumstances surrounding it. Because gender is linked to societal patterns of both custody and violence, it emerges as a central factor for understanding the experiences of the parents. Analysis of the five patterns, along with the stories of parents who have lived them, helps us to understand the different contexts of parental abduction.

Pattern 1: Abduction by a Violent Visitor

In this group of abductions the parents who are left behind had sole custody of the children at the time of the abduction, and the marriages were marked by violence perpetrated by the abductor. Men are dramatically more likely to be the abducting parents in situations following this pattern.[18] Almost 40% of the abducting males fall into this category, compared with 10% of the abducting females. These situations take two common courses: (1) The woman leaves with the children following battering by the father (this often constitutes an abduction in the father's eyes) and gets custody from the court; the father then tracks them down and abducts the children. (2) A violent marriage ends in divorce and the mother gets custody of the children; some months or even years later the father snatches the children. These abductors' motives are ascribed by the left-behind parent disproportionately to hurting the other parent,[19] expressing anger at the breakup,[20] and forcing a reconciliation.[21] Abductions following this pattern may have their roots in childhood and in a marriage where violence has been a way of life. These marriages are more likely than in other cases to have ended because of violence,[22] substance abuse,[23] and mistreatment of the children.[24] Threats about abduction are more likely to have been made,[25] and abductions are more likely to involve force than in other cases.[26] Twenty-six percent of the abductions we studied follow this violent visitor pattern; it constitutes the largest group in the typology of five patterns of abduction.

Case History

One example of this scenario is provided by Eileen, whose marriage ended because she couldn't tolerate her husband Rob's abusiveness and alcoholism any more. She took the three children with her and had them call their father to let him know they were all right. She obtained a divorce and custody decree. Rob visited them once the next year in their new home, but he was drunk at the time. A year later Eileen and the children moved again. During discussions with her Rob assured Eileen that he would never abduct the children, whom he had always been permitted to visit, though they lived a thousand miles apart.

When Eileen and Rob's oldest daughter, who was seven at the time, went to visit a friend near their old home not far from where Rob was living, Rob heard about it and abducted the child. She was brainwashed into thinking that her mother did not want her anymore and had sent her father to take her. Mother and daughter had no contact for two years. Finally, following a psychiatric hospitalization of the child when she was ten, Rob returned her to Eileen. Eileen believes that the abduction took place purely to get back at her for leaving. The daughter still is troubled by psychological problems but is doing better now.

Pattern 2: Abduction by a Nonviolent Visitor

In the second pattern the parent who is left behind had sole custody and was not a victim of domestic violence. These abductions, which at 18% of the sample constitute the second largest category, are quite different from the first group. This group includes only 14% of the abducting fathers and a quarter of the abducting mothers, making it disproportionately female.[27] In this situation more than in others the abductors are perceived by the other parent to be motivated by a desire to be with the children[28] or by a fear of loss of visitation,[29] often because it is being blocked by the custodial parent or because that parent is going to move away. The abductors are seeking more contact with their children.

The childhoods of these abducting parents seem more typical than those of the abductors in the previous group, since they tend not to be marked by abuse. The reasons the parents left behind give for the divorce center more often than in other patterns on the abductor's pathological behavior[30] and on incompatibility in the marriage.[31] As discussed earlier, incompatibility is cited in marriages where each partner accepts some responsibility for the breakup. This suggests that the marriage and the breakup were not acrimonious. Spouse abuse[32] and child maltreatment[33] are less likely to be mentioned as reasons for the breakup. Many of the respondents in this group were taken by surprise by the abduction because it was less likely to have been threatened before it occurred.[34] Force was less often used to achieve it:[35] There was less need for force to be used because abductions were more likely to take place during prearranged visitation times.[36]

Case History

An example of this pattern of the nonviolent abductor with visitation rights seeking greater or sole contact with children is provided by the case of Harry and Amy. The couple married in the middle 1970s, and a boy and girl were born soon afterward. Harry says the marriage was never marked by especially good communication. For reasons Harry does not understand, Amy began sleeping in a spare bedroom and their sexual relationship ended after the birth of their second child. Following a vacation that Amy took with the two children but without Harry (he couldn't take off time from work), she announced that she wanted a divorce and had never loved him. The process was surprisingly amicable, with Amy agreeing that Harry would get custody.

After the divorce became final, Amy remained in the house; the couple kept their decision secret while they saved up money to move into two separate apartments. Three months after the divorce Harry went to visit some friends in a different state. Upon his return he found the house empty of everything but his personal belongings. Harry says abduction was the furthest thing from his mind because Amy had voluntarily given up custody and had never threatened abduction. The children were five and six at the time.

Attempts to recover the children were made but were not successful. Even though Harry had a better relationship with Amy's mother than she did, his in-laws would not help him find them. He commented with resignation, "I guess blood is thicker than water." Twelve years later Harry did locate his children but learned they did not want to see him. They had been told there had been no contact over the years with their father because he sexually abused them, a charge Harry vehemently denies.

Pattern 3: Abduction by a Nonviolent Shared Custodian

The third abduction pattern is similar to the previous pattern in that violence on the part of the abductor does not characterize the marital relationship. Here, though, custody was shared prior to the abduction either because the parents were still married or because of a joint custody decree. Violence may have been perpetrated by the parent left behind but not admitted by those in our study. It is interesting to note that of the very few cases where the parents in our study admit to being the only violent party, 67% of them fall into this group.

While this group is the third largest in our sample, comprising 15% of the cases, it may be much more common among the general population of abductions, since this pattern fits the news stories and the reports from those who help abductors. Typically, these parents who take their children and flee fear pursuit by an angry spouse who has been committing a crime like child abuse or battering. The parent left behind may not perceive these actions as illegal or necessarily harmful to the fleeing parent or child. In our sample this group is dramatically more likely to be composed of female abductors, accounting for 27% of the women and only 6% of the men.[37] These may be cases where the wife leaves with the children soon after the marriage has ended. She may be under pressure from others to hold on to her children, or she may be on the run from what she perceives as an abusive situation. She may have sought legal help and found it ineffective in protecting her. The reasons for divorce for this group are less likely to involve spouse abuse[38] or infidelity by the abductor[39] and more likely to be connected to the abduction itself.[40]

As in the previous pattern, motivations for the abduction are more likely to involve dissatisfaction with visitation[41] and are less likely to involve a desire to hurt the parent left behind[42] or to avoid paying child support.[43] Finally, the abductions are less apt to follow a threat[44] or to involve force.[45] They usually occur (and do so more often than in other patterns) while the child is with the abductor.[46]

Although our information about motivations is incomplete because it was provided by the parent left behind, this pattern may include many situations where that parent is perceived as having perpetrated some wrong that has compelled the abductor to act. As in the nonviolent visitor pattern, abuse of some kind may be present. These abductions usually occur as the marriage is breaking apart.

Case History

An example of such an abduction is presented by Henry. He met his ex-wife on the job, but she left soon afterward to open her own counseling practice. They began to socialize with the clients that she was seeing in treatment, something Henry believed was professionally unethical. Their marriage broke up after six years, when their son and daughter were four and five, and a custody battle followed. Even though joint custody was awarded, each parent continued to fight for sole custody. Henry's ex-wife alleged that he had sexually abused their daughter; with the help of her new husband she eventually abducted both children. They were on the run for a year before being apprehended. In this situation, three scenarios are possible: Henry's ex-wife may have believed correctly that he abused the child; she may have incorrectly believed, on the basis of misleading information, that he abused the child; or she may have fabricated the abuse allegation. If she believed there had been abuse, an abduction may have been justified in her eyes.

Pattern 4: Abduction by a Violent Shared Custodian

There is also a pattern of abductions in which the parents share custody and the abductor has been violent. This group, 11% of our sample, includes a slightly higher proportion of the male abductors (13%) than of the female abductors (8%).[47] The relationships and the reasons for breaking up are more likely than in other patterns to include spouse abuse.[48] Battles over money are also more common than usual.[49] In keeping with the pattern of violence in the marriage, the abduction is also more apt than in other groups to involve force.[50] In this group more than any other the parent left behind may believe that the abductor will harm the child and that the child's welfare is generally endangered by the abduction. The impression here is that the abductor fears a loss of contact with the child or is losing control of other aspects of his or her life. In the latter situation, taking the child is one way to gain some control and to be with the one person who, perhaps, gives unconditional love.

Case History

Julia gave birth to a daughter out of wedlock and lived with the father, Manny, for three years without marrying before asking him to leave. Their relationship had been a physically abusive one and also had involved drug abuse. They had been involved with each other since they were both very young, and it was difficult for Julia to think of herself as self-supporting. Asking Manny to leave was Julia's first step toward taking care of herself. Three years later, with the help of some schooling, a job, and some counseling, Julia met and married her husband. Manny, who had been in close contact with their daughter, Jenny, over the years, had joint custody and had been paying child support until the last year. When he learned that Julia had remarried and that Jenny was calling someone else Daddy, he became very upset. At the same time, he was served with papers for back child support. Julia believes these two events triggered the abduction.

On the day of the abduction, Manny arrived at Julia's house with his mother and asked to take Jenny for a walk. Julia was a little suspicious and followed them outside only to see Manny grab Jenny and push her into his van. His mother ran away. Julia ran down the street after them and was able to get inside the van, where a fight broke out. Manny stopped the van and screamed at her, "This is all your fault! You belong to me. You are not a normal woman. When you have a child with someone, you are supposed to stay with him!" They stopped fighting and he began driving, telling her that she was forcing him to do this to protect his daughter. At an intersection Manny jumped out of the van with Jenny and began running.

That was five years ago, when Jenny was four. Julia has not seen or heard from them since. Her hope is that Manny will be arrested one day because of his involvement with drugs and that Jenny will be returned to her.

Type 5: Abduction by a Sole Custodian

In this group, which constitutes 12% of our sample, custody at the time of the abduction is not with the future parent left behind but with the nonviolent abductor. This group of abductors includes a disproportionate number of the sample's females (17% vs. 4% of the males),[51] perhaps because mothers are more apt to be given custody than fathers. In our sample the abductors usually were very involved with the children prior to the custody decision, which may account for why they obtained custody. The divorce is more likely to involve incompatibility[52] and less likely to be the result of spouse abuse than in other cases.[53] The abduction is seen as being more likely to have occurred as a result of pressure from others[54] and the remarriage of the parent who is left behind.[55] Anger[56] and the desire to hurt[57] are less likely to be cited as reasons for the abduction. Overall, the marital relationship between the parent and the abductor is less acrimonious than in the other patterns. The abductors believe that the child is theirs and that it is fitting to move with the child wherever they wanted to. For example, one divorced mother had gained custody by mutual agreement and a year after the breakup wanted to relocate to California. When her husband and the court said no, she abducted the child.

Some of these abductions take place because the abductor believes the other parent is abusing the child sexually or physically, as in the Hilary Morgan case. In our sample, of the very small number of parents left behind who admitted using violence, 33% (all of those not falling into the nonviolent shared custodian pattern) fall into this category. In some cases, the abductor's behavior is difficult to understand or reflects an emotionally troubled state of mind.

Case History

The pattern just described is illustrated by Barry and Kay, who split up after he kicked her out of the house. She took the baby and went to live with his mother. Barry's mother permitted this arrangement because she was worried about the baby and wanted to keep an eye on him. After a series of irresponsible acts (wrecking Barry's mother's car and having a series of men in the home overnight), Kay moved into her own apartment. A visitation battle followed, with Barry wanting to initiate spending time with his son. He won the right to visit but only after successfully defending himself against false charges of abuse toward Kay and the baby. Despite his winning visitation, Kay would often come up with excuses so that father and son couldn't see each other.

After about a year of this pattern, Barry was scheduled to have visitation for an extended weekend and was told by Kay to keep the toddler for a few months and to wait for her and her new husband to contact them. Barry became suspicious and began pursuing a custody decree. When Kay returned she took the toddler and vanished. Barry learned that she had been charged with cocaine distribution, that her mortgage was being foreclosed, and that she was under investigation by the department of social services concerning care of her new husband's children. He heard nothing from Kay for months, until he was offered custody in exchange for $5,000. Because extortion is a federal offense, he was able to involve the FBI, who finally helped him locate his son.

Summary of the Typology

These groupings are not all inclusive and cannot account for every circumstance leading up to an abduction. As with the nonviolent shared custodian group, we may have underrepresented those situations where the parent felt compelled to abduct. Men who batter their wives or abuse their children may be less likely to seek assistance from the police or from missing children's organizations that men who are innocent of such charges. If so, they would not show up in our sample, and if they did, they would be unlikely to disclose their abuse histories. Also underrepresented may be situations where the parent left behind believes that police and other potentially helpful organizations will not assist them. These might include parents involved in criminal activities or those who perceive such help providers to be biased against them or not interested because of their race or gender.

What we are presenting in our typology is information on the vast range of circumstances within which abductions occur. These are exceedingly complex events that, like a deep pool of water, look slightly different depending upon the angle; each time one stares into the water something new is seen. The five patterns of abduction and their major characteristics are shown in Table 1.

SINCE THE ABDUCTION

Once the child is gone, pain sets in. It is an emptiness that leaves parents wandering around the house and believing they see images of their children. It is hearing the name *Daddy* or *Mommy* in a store and thinking it is the missing child calling. It is sitting alone in the child's room, which one keeps just the way it was before the abduction. It is staying in touch with the child's friends so that they will be interested in seeing the child when he or she returns. And, finally, the pain is the thousand little things that remind a parent of a child—a favorite TV show, a song, a book, a favorite color.

The pain from the loss is not something parents passively

Table 1. Five Patterns of Parental Abduction of Children

Characteristics	Violent visitor (28%)	Nonviolent visitor (18%)	Nonviolent shared custodian (15%)	Violent shared custodian (11%)	Custodian (12%)
Custody status	searching parent	searching parent	shared	shared	abductor
Abductor violent	yes	no	no	yes	no
Abductor gender	83% male 17% female	43% male 57% female	21% male 79% female	68% male 32% female	24% male 76% female
Typical reasons for breakup	violence; substance abuse	incompatibility; abductor's problems	abduction	spouse abuse	incompatibility
Typical reasons for abductions	to hurt searching parent	desire to be with child	unhappy with visits	fears loss of contact/control	pressure from others
Use of force in abduction likely	yes	no	no trend	yes	no

Note. Characteristics are based on responses from searching parents. Not every case could be classified successfully and a sixth pattern, violent custodians, was excluded from the analysis because their numbers were too small.

accept. Many spring into action and fervently try to recover the child. From our study we learned that the vast majority contact the police within the week of the abduction, and most report the abduction within 24 hours. They do not stop there. They also contact a variety of public and private agencies and organizations for assistance. Almost all call missing children's organizations (remember that this sample was drawn from these organizations) and attorneys. The FBI, social service agencies (contacted to learn if the child has been placed in foster care), private investigators, and self-help groups, (i.e., those not officially associated with a missing children's organization) also are utilized in the search.

When there is no word from the abductor or child (nearly two-thirds of subjects in our sample who had not recovered their children had had no communication with the abductors), the parents' worst fears begin to take over, namely, that they will never see their children again or that some harm has been done to them. For parents, these fears are excruciating. Almost all the parents in our study described themselves as having been emotionally close to the children who were abducted. For most, recovery of the children became an obsession, one way to begin to cope with their loss. They sent out flyers, contacted missing children's organizations in different states, called the police in different jurisdictions, sought media exposure, and interviewed relatives and friends of the abductors. (The successful culmination of this process is discussed further in Chapter 4.)

A number of parents become increasingly involved in religion as a way of coping with the loss. They rely on faith to give some meaning to their pain. Others find solace in drugs. As time goes on and they still have not seen or heard from their children, some parents become superstitious, believing that any little thing they do will somehow result in getting their child back. Some parents join lobbying groups or engage in other self-help activities to fight for parents' rights, and many (like those who participated in this study) take part in every survey they can in the belief that if they help someone, another person may someday help them and make it possible for their child to be returned.

It is not necessarily magical thinking that leads to this kind of behavior. It is often a belief in networking, which is fueled by the stories of other parents who miraculously recovered their children; that is, parents believe that if they do the groundwork, they will be more likely to recover their child while also holding out the hope that through chance a break will come their way.

The manner in which children are abducted and recovered takes many forms. One mother (Ava, whom we describe in detail later in this book) who was on the run with her children from her abusive husband had moved 500 miles away and had started a new life. She was working in a department store when her ex-husband's brother happened to walk in while he was on vacation. He reported her whereabouts to his brother, who abducted the children a few weeks later. Ava recovered the children years later when a friend notified her that one of her children was in a foster home.

These stories keep parents' hopes alive. At the same time, as the months and years go by, there is the need for parents who have not recovered their children to get on with their lives. How long can one stay obsessed with recovering one's child when it is taking an incredible toll? Physical and mental health suffer. People lose time at work, change jobs, or move. They spend thousands of dollars hiring private investigators, following up tips of sightings, and sending out flyers. The pressures on these parents to recover are enormous. Their self-concepts can suffer as they take on the persona of people whose children were abducted and relinquish the role of parents raising children. Moreover, society may not be sympathetic to them. If it is a man whose child was abducted, people may believe he was physically or sexually abusing the child and that his wife was forced to abduct for the child's protection. A man may also be perceived as a wife batterer. If it is a woman whose child was abducted, she may be viewed as an unfit mother or one who allowed herself to be victimized by her husband.

In our study nearly all of the parents whose children were abducted said they experienced feelings of loss as a result of their children being gone. Three-quarters said they suffered from lack of sleep and nightmares, with an equal number experiencing feelings of rage at their situation. Anger is a quite common and often healthy reaction to a situation where a parent has been hurt or feels he or she has no control. It can be a driving force behind attempts to recover. Parents also experience loneliness and fearfulness, loss of appetite, severe depression, and feelings of guilt. These reactions are common also among people suffering from posttraumatic stress disorder. That is, victims of this disorder are not only those who have been exposed to a traumatic situation (e.g., being beaten, raped, or tortured) but also those whose children or other loved ones have been kidnapped or exposed to some other extreme circumstance.[58]

The guilt that parents feel seems to be from having been involved with a partner who would abduct and from not having taken steps to prevent the abduction. Parents question their own judgment, particularly when they have been involved with a batterer or substance abuser; in many ways, they blame themselves for having submitted their children to this type of life. If they had warnings about the abduction and did not protect their children successfully, they are likely to feel even more guilty about the ordeal.

One quarter of the parents in our study reported physical health problems as a result of the abduction, and another quarter had to move out of their homes. Interestingly enough, one in five parents experienced feelings of relief; these parents were more likely to have been in violent relationships[59] and to be fearful of the abductor.[60] Our impression is that they had been in a very stressful situation and were waiting for the other shoe to drop; they were never sure what was going to happen next with their family and may have had conflictual relationships with their children. Feeling relief in these situations was part of an ambivalent reaction: it was always accompanied by other feelings, like guilt and anger. No parent reported feeling only relief.

Finally, one in six left-behind parents in our study had to change jobs. This happened in some instances because parents wanted to spend time pursuing the abductor and could not in their current position. Other times it was accompanied by a move to another state to be closer to where the child was reported to be or to spend time with the child in cases where recovery resulted in the abductor retaining custody and visitation being established.

The parents we studied usually did not suffer the pain of loss alone. Slightly more than half sought assistance from a mental health professional or a physician after the abduction. Depression was the most common reason for seeking help, but parents were also motivated by anxiety, family-related problems, marital problems, spouse abuse, and substance abuse. The parents also had help and support from friends, family, and others who suffered along with them. Lawyers, neighbors, clergy, and missing children's networks provided additional support, though to a lesser degree. Not everyone was perceived as helpful. Law enforcement agencies, for example, did not fare extremely well when parents rated their sources of support. The local police were perceived as being supportive in half the cases and the FBI in only one-third. In-laws rarely were perceived by the parents as supportive.

In one situation a mother, Susan, reported that her 16-year-old daughter was abducted by her father, who sexually molested and then threatened to kill her if she revealed what happened. While Susan was searching for them, they moved from state to state. After three months, the daughter's older brother found them and Susan herself picked her daughter up. Susan described the police as unhelpful during the search; the FBI refused to become involved. While the daughter was missing and since the recovery, Susan has been in treatment for being suicidal. She feels a tremendous amount of guilt and has found little support from anyone; her parents are both dead. "The horror, the aftermath of this kind of trauma, go on and on, maybe forever," she tearfully told us.

Muriel has been searching for her son for 12 years. He was one year old when he was taken. Muriel and her husband had been fighting for months, and each had given up on the relationship at different times. Finally, he struck first. Muriel knows her son is all right because her ex-husband's brother sends her photographs every few years. But still she searches. Friends and relatives have been supportive yet offer little to her in the way of concrete assistance. She has had to search alone and feels extremely limited in what she can afford to do in her attempts to find her son. Counseling has helped her, as has a local support group. "I often need to shut out the world and the people in it. I get quiet and moody. I am not sure how I cope," she said. "The anger and helplessness are always with me."

Judy is a grandmother who is raising her 10-year-old grand-daughter. Judy's daughter, Erica, has a history of problems with alcohol, anxiety, and depression, as does Erica's ex-husband. Erica and her husband lived with Judy for a few years before their marriage broke up. During that time, Judy forged a strong relationship with her granddaughter. One year after the marriage ended, Erica's husband abducted his daughter (Judy believes his motive was revenge). Extended police surveillance resulted in the little girl's location and recovery, but during the time she was missing, Erica vanished. The stress of the abduction was too much for her. Judy became the guardian of the child. Even though Erica has been back in the picture on an intermittent basis, Judy remains the mainstay in her granddaughter's life. As she told us, "My granddaughter seems to be functioning well now (four years after the recovery) though not as well as before the abduction. She is still somewhat fearful and suspicious of strange cars. Erica is not doing well."

These parents (and grandparents)—even those who have received support from others—suffer greatly. Whether they have recovered their children or not, their family has been scarred, often irreparably. As time goes on, the wounds may heal but the pain remains.

DIFFERENCES BETWEEN MEN'S AND WOMEN'S EXPERIENCES

It is important to note the different situations of men and women who are left behind following an abduction. In our study their profiles differ as a function of role expectations and family violence, with women being more likely to be physically victimized. One difference concerns the preabduction custody status. Mothers whose children were abducted were more likely to have sole custody than were fathers.[61] This reflects the general tendency for mothers to retain custody following a divorce in the United States, but it may also be an outgrowth of the high incidence of violence, substance abuse, and legal problems among male abductors. Women in this study also had fewer resources to bring to bear in trying to recover their children. They had less education,[62] were more apt to be unemployed or employed in lower-status jobs,[63] and were earning significantly less money than men whose children were abducted.[64] Other common gender-linked discrepancies appear in the patterns of family violence. Women were much more likely than were men to be the victims of violence perpetrated by the abductor.[65] Women also were more apt to cite violence as a reason for the breakup than were men.[66] Finally, male abductors more frequently used force to carry out the abduction than did females.[67]

The reasons for the abduction also showed some interesting patterns based on gender. Women were more likely than men to believe that the abduction took place to hurt them or because of anger at them, while men more often cited visitation problems or pressure from third parties as reasons a mother abducted the children.[68] These gender-based patterns reinforce the popular perception that men abduct out of revenge while women abduct because of a desire to be with their children. While this perception is supported by the data in this study, we have also found many exceptions in the behavior of both men and women. It also may be that when their children are abducted, women have difficulty understanding the depth of the attachment of fathers to children. Thus, they ascribe to the male abductors other motives, ones that are more consistent with the societal perception that men typically are not invested in childrearing.

The participants' characteristics and experiences (including those linked to gender) shape the course and pattern of each abduction. If it is a father who is abducting, he is much more apt to have a history of using force to accomplish his goals, a finding that is consistent with what is known about gender and family violence. And, as is discussed in Chapter 4, men may have a harder time recovering their children.

COMPARISON WITH OTHER STUDIES OF PARENTS LEFT BEHIND

The five patterns of abduction and the differences between the experiences of male and female parents are themes that run through the remainder of this book. One reason that we were able to differentiate among abduction patterns and gender-based experiences is that we asked more questions of a larger number of parents than participated in previous studies. However, it is interesting to note that what we have learned is consistent in many ways with prior research.

For example, Janvier and her colleagues, who also surveyed parents in contact with missing children's organizations, found that the data on marital status at the time of abduction were very similar to what our parents reported: the figures for our study and theirs show 43% versus 40% divorced, 27% versus 38% separated, and 13% versus 12% never married to the abductor.[69] Only in the proportion still married did the two differ substantially, with 17% in our study and 9% in theirs. The gender breakdown of parents left behind (55% female) and of abducted children (about 55% male) were almost identical in the two studies.

Prior threats of abduction had been made in slightly less than half the situations in each study, and both note similar reactions to the abduction by the left-behind parents, including depression, anxiety, loss of sleep, and despair. The two groups of parents also rated sources of help in a very similar fashion; low scores for the FBI, moderate ratings for local police and the courts, and higher ratings for family members, attorneys, and missing children's organizations.[70]

When the parents we dealt with are compared to Agopian's 1970s sample, more differences emerge. In terms of race, Agopian's group of Los Angeles parents was 69% white, in contrast to our national sample of parents left behind, which was 92% white.[71] Agopian's study also included a larger proportion of female parents left behind (71%) than did our study (55%) or the one headed by Janvier (55%). However, the ages of the parents left behind were similar, with mean ages of 32 and 33 years for our study and Agopian's. In both samples, more than half of the abductions began when the child was visiting or living with the abducting parent.[72]

CONCLUSION

In summing up the experiences of parents left behind in abductions, we return to the stories of Fred and Rita, whose children remain missing.

*   *   *

Fred has suffered greatly in the abduction of his son, Timothy, by his nonviolent wife, with whom he shared custody. He has experienced a vast array of feelings and has sought help for depression. He still loses sleep, does not have an appetite, and feels guilty. Following the abduction, he gained sole legal custody of Timothy and reports that there are arrest warrants out for Sarah. He feels the police were "as helpful as they could be in locating Timothy." He believes that Sarah and Timothy may have left the country, although he has no evidence to support his feeling that his wife may have returned to one of the countries they visited, ironically enough, on their honeymoon. He believes at least two of his in-laws may know his son's whereabouts, but they have refused to cooperate. Three years after the abduction (at the time of this writing) Fred has not seen or heard from wife or child. Fred has tried to go on with his life, having recently married a woman who brought a seven-year-old stepson into his life. Being surrounded by supportive family and friends has helped him, but he hasn't forgotten Timothy. He maintains contact with a number of missing children's organizations in the hope that recovery may still happen.

*   *   *

Rita heard nothing from her emotionally abusive, noncustodial ex-husband or son for nine months; then Bob began harassing her with telephone threats, saying she would never see Hank again. Rita believes that her in-laws know where Bob and Hank are but refuse to help her. She maintained contact with her ex-father-in-law over the years in an attempt to find Bob but eventually lost track of him. According to Rita, the police were of no help and the FBI, at that time, was not getting involved in abduction resolution unless there was clear evidence that the abductor had crossed state lines. When the abduction occurred more than 10 years ago, bond was set at $5,000. Bond amounts have increased since then, but Rita cannot get the $5,000 bond raised. Thus, if Bob were ever arrested, he would be able to make bond easily and go on the run again.

Rita has made various videotapes for publicity and has joined self-help groups involved in recovery actions. She is exploring having computer-enhanced aging pictures done of Hank. Rita knows the abduction took place only to hurt her and for revenge. While therapy has helped her deal with her feelings and prepare for the possibility of her son's return, she knows realistically that after 12 years she and Hank would be complete strangers to each other. Yet she still goes through periods of activity in which she looks desperately for Hank for six months; then she stops because the search is too painful.

*   *   *

Fred, Rita, and the hundreds of thousands of other parents who have not recovered their abducted children are continuing to struggle. According to many of these parents, abductions occur to hurt them. They are victims. In a marriage to an unpredictable and perhaps violent spouse, the child snatching merely continues the pattern. For all of these parents, a giant hole has been opened up in their lives. Some are more successful than others in filling it, yet it is still always present. Few give up hope completely, but many wonder if they will ever see their child again or if they will recognize each other if there is a reunion. Until then, for parents whose child is missing, life is a matter of searching and waiting while simultaneously trying to find some happiness. For those who have recovered their children, life consists of trying to integrate the experience, to find some meaning, and then to live for today.

CHAPTER 3

Parents Who Abduct Their Children

What motivates parents to abduct a child? Is it something rational people might do, or are these only crazed parents seeking control in a life where control is slipping away? We know from the previous chapter that abductors are seen by the parents left behind primarily as wanting revenge or acting out of anger, but the wish for increased contact with the child can also be a motivating force. One popular perception of abductors is the one elicited by the Elizabeth Morgan case. Some observers believe that in this situation, and others like it, a parent snatches the child or arranges a snatching to protect the child from harm at the hands of the other parent. (Because Elizabeth Morgan had custody, this may not have been an abduction in a criminal sense in many jurisdictions, but it does fit the definition we use here.) Custodial or noncustodial parents who go into hiding to protect the child usually are viewed sympathetically, as acting out of deep concern and being willing to give up everything in order to save the child.

Seen either through the eyes of the parent left behind or through the lens provided by the popular press, the abductor appears two-dimensional, like a sketch or a painting without the perspective provided by shading and color. However, the stories told by

56

abductors we interviewed often paint a different and more complex picture: we hear of actions motivated by abuse of the child, emotional distancing from the spouse, and frustrating legal experiences. This chapter focuses on the left-behind parents' impressions of the abductors and on the in-depth stories of four abductors who share their reasons for abducting their children and an account of what life was like on the run. They give a retrospective view of their experiences as abductors (one abduction lasted for 12 years). It is important to note that none of the abductors we interviewed was in violation of a court order at the time of the interview. It is also important to note that the parents described here were willing to be interviewed. What we have, then, is a collection of accounts by people whose actions may sound justifiable to the reader, in contrast to abductors who take their children for selfish or malevolent reasons and who might well refuse to be interviewed.

Other researchers have provided some information about abductors that can be compared to ours. In Agopian's research,[1] the abductors were most apt to be between the ages of 27 and 36, to be employed (70%), and to have a criminal record. Agopian argues that in an abduction, either parent can find justification for his or her behavior. Often the social context, including the expected roles for mothers and fathers in the United States, affects abduction, as well as the custody battle that frequently precedes it. Agopian offers some scenarios where abduction may be justifiable. In the description of one case, the abductor, a father, is driven to snatch his son from a drug-abusing mother who has been neglecting the child and having sexual intercourse with two men in the child's presence. Agopian also argues that mothers may feel societal pressure to abduct because of the widely held expectation that children should be raised by their mothers.

In another study the majority of the respondents described the abductors as having emotional problems and as growing up in dysfunctional families. The abductors were seen by the other parents as being revengeful, controlling, impulsive, and unpredictable.[2] The abductors also were described as being abusive to the parent left behind in a majority of the cases and abusive to the children in as much as one-quarter of the cases and as abusing substances in almost one-third of the cases.[3]

Before we hear the voices of the abductors, the parents left behind who participated in our study provide their impressions of the abductors. This background information helps to set the stage for learning why a parent abducts.

WHO ARE THE ABDUCTORS?

According to the parents left behind, the abductors (55% of whom were male) tended to be slightly older by a few years. The abductors were about twice as often nonwhite (16% vs. 7%) and foreign-born (13% vs. 6%) as the parents left behind. Reports of the abductors' childhoods also differ from the reports provided by the parents left behind about their own childhoods. Approximately half of the abductors were raised in a home with a substance-abusing parent, one-third were described as having been physically abused and one-fifth sexually abused, and one-third having witnessed violence between the adults in the home. By comparison, many fewer of the parents left behind had these experiences. The abductors also were less apt than left-behind parents to have finished any education after high school (40% had some post–high school education), were less likely to be professionals, and were twice as likely to be unemployed at the time of the abduction, with almost half of them holding no job. Thus, the backgrounds of the abductors and the parents left behind were reported to be markedly different, with the abductors clearly exposed to more dysfunctional family behavior. In addition, as adults with less likelihood of having a job or being a professional, they had less to lose vocationally by leaving their surroundings. Clearly, a parent who is employed, particularly in an occupation where it is necessary to establish oneself to be successful, risks more by picking up and leaving. Of the four abductors we describe here in depth, none was anticipating long-term successful employment when the abduction took place.

As mentioned in Chapter 2, visitation had been fairly frequent between the abductors in our study and the child who was subsequently snatched. In two-thirds of those situations where the parents were living apart, the abductors were visiting at least every other week. However, one in four abductors hardly ever visited. The distance that separated their homes was a factor because slightly more than one in ten lived more than 1,000 miles away.

The frequency of visitation does indicate that these parents had been actively involved with their children in the majority of situations.[4] It should be noted that the parents in our study may even have underreported visitation contact, as left-behind parents have been known to do from other studies when describing the other parent's involvement.[5] This suggests that a common perception of abductions—that is, that they occur without much desire on the part of the abductor to have more contact with the children—may not be accurate.

By the parent victims' descriptions in our study, the abductors were relatively consistent forces in their children's lives. About half of the abductors were violent toward the parent left behind during the marriage, almost half threatened that an abduction was going to occur, and one in seven used force to carry it out. These relationships were obviously acrimonious ones in which the threat of harm loomed in the background or was a constant presence.

The abductors generally were characterized as being unhappy and in questionable mental health. In only a few cases (6%) was the abductor described as being in good spirits before the abduction. In two-thirds of the situations the abductor's mood was described as "mixed," and in the remaining 29% it was seen by the other parent as being predominantly sad. In contrast, the parent victim described himself or herself as happy in 40% of the preabduction situations and sad in only 19%.

A number of abductors had received treatment from a mental health professional or a physician before the abduction. A quarter were treated for depression, with slightly smaller proportions having been seen for marital problems, family problems, or anxiety. About one in seven had been treated for substance abuse, and approximately the same number had been hospitalized in a psychiatric facility. Many were apparently treated for more than one condition. In total, only one-third of the abductors were reported to have sought help for mental health problems. Additional problems also faced this group: Three out of ten abductors had been accused of child abuse (compared with half that proportion of parent victims), and about a quarter had spent some time in jail (though it was rare for abductors who were located to spend any appreciable amount of time in jail for the abduction.)

Clearly, this was a troubled group of parents. In addition to those with identified legal, mental health, or family problems, many others may have been troubled but chose not to seek help. Thus, the specter of child abuse, family violence, and behavior aberrant enough to lead to incarceration overshadows many of these situations.

Child Abuse in Abduction

While 15% of the parents left behind said they had been accused of child abuse and 30% of those same parents said the abductor had been accused of abuse, the incidence of abuse allegations made to authorities in abductions may be much higher. According to missing children's organizations and legal authorities, accusations of abuse are rampant on both sides. Such allegations can be a motivation for others to assist searching parents. Abductors who are apprehended by authorities will almost invariably say that physical or psychological abuse was the motivating factor behind their drastic actions. In three of the four cases presented later in this chapter, allegations of abuse are made. While physical and sexual abuse provide clear-cut motivations for abduction in some parents' minds, the effect of emotional abuse is less clear. Emotional abuse and neglect are among the most difficult types of child maltreatment to define.[6] This legal and professional ambiguity allows parents to label any less than optimal experience of their children as emotional abuse by the other parent, that is, experiences such as being separated from one parent, hearing bad things about a parent, or being raised incorrectly.

Involvement with the Children

The abductor's behavior also can be understood by looking at his or her involvement with the children while still living in the home, that is, during the period of time that preceded the visitation patterns just described. During the period just before the abductor ceased living with the family (here we are only speaking about situations where the abductor was a noncustodial parent), according to the parents left behind, almost half were described by the left-behind parent as involved or very involved with the physical care of the children, with a similar number involved with the children in recreation. It was also reported that 40% were involved in supervision, 40% in discipline, and a quarter in school activities and studies. However, the abductors' level of involvement with the children just before moving out of the house varied by gender. Female abductors were described by left-behind parents as having been significantly more involved in the physical care,[7] supervision,[8] and school activities[9] of their children than male abductors. Male and female abductors were described as being about equally involved in discipline and recreation.

Not only were the abductors involved with their children in a variety of activities but almost two-thirds were also described as maintaining a close emotional relationship with the child when still living at home. The remaining third were seen as being distant. In addition, female abductors were described as closer to their children during this period than male abductors.[10] A general pattern of uninvolvement before the breakup was related to infrequent visitation after the separation, particularly for male abductors.[11]

USING THE TYPOLOGY OF ABDUCTIONS

The five abduction patterns introduced in Chapter 2 provide additional insight into the behavior of abducting parents. Here we consider further those violent visitors, nonviolent visitors, violent shared custodians, nonviolent shared custodians, and sole custodian parents.

The Violent Visitor

In these situations the child is taken from a parent having sole custody by an abducting parent with a history of domestic violence. In our study these abductions, following a marriage characterized by spouse and often substance abuse and where the parent left behind had custody, were the ones where the abductor was viewed the most negatively. The parent left behind, most often a woman, described the abductor as being less close emotionally with the abducted child prior to the abduction than in other patterns.[12] In addition, his or her involvement with the children in various areas, including physical care,[13] recreation,[14] school activities,[15] and supervision[16] was reported as low when compared with abductors in the other situations. There was also a somewhat greater tendency for the abductors to have been accused of child abuse.[17]

The Nonviolent Visitor

Here the parent left behind had custody and was not a victim of violence. The abductor, who was often female, was seen as seeking more contact with the child. Consistent with that portrayal, the abductor was described as being marginally closer with the children before the abduction than parents in other groups.[18] Having ready access to the children, these abductors were more likely than others to abduct during visitation,[19] and not to use force.[20]

The Violent Shared Custodian

In this group the abductor and the other parent share custody and the abductor has been violent, as in the first pattern described. Here the left-behind parent reported the abductor as being either very involved or very uninvolved in physical care[21] and supervision[22] as compared with the other abduction situations. The level of involvement tends to be gender linked, with women reported to have greater involvement with their children.

The Nonviolent Shared Custodian and the Sole Custodian

Within the nonviolent shared custodian group, the abductor, usually a female, was seen as being significantly closer to the children[23] and more involved in a range of activities with them while still living in the home. This pattern of involvement is similar to the sole custodial abductions, where the nonviolent abductor who had custody, also usually a female, also was very involved with the children in their activities before the abduction.

Comparing the Patterns

Examining the role of abductors in the children's lives prior to the abduction further develops the patterns described in Chapter 2. For example, in violent visitor abductions, the parents left behind consistently described patterns of behavior that suggest the abductors acted more out of their own needs than out of concern for the needs of the children. Had the abductors been very involved with the children they abducted, a different impression might have been gained. But here abductors were seen as more distant than in other families and were depicted as wanting the children not for the children's benefit but for their own.

In the violent shared custodian situation the picture is less clear-cut. Some of the parents described the abductor as having been quite involved with the children before the abduction while others describe a distant relationship. In the first situation we see parents who fought with each other but who also showed a great deal of concern and connection with their children. Fearing loss of that contact and having a primary interest in their children, they acted first. This is contrasted with the latter situation, where the abduction was designed to gain revenge against the other parent and use the children as pawns.

The other patterns show a greater level of closeness and involvement of the abductor with the children. In many ways, they reflect a higher degree of concern on the abductor's part for the children and the impact that the abduction may have on them.

In sum, the typical description of the abductor provided by the parent left behind is that he or she was slightly more likely to be violent in the marriage than not, was apt to be unemployed, and was likely to have received treatment for mental health problems. Generally, the abductor was not seen as being a particularly happy person. He or she was seen to have a close relationship with the children, but not as close as that of the parent left behind, and to have been visiting at least every other week in most instances. Women abductors were seen to be more involved with their children before the breakup of the relationship than men. All told, this information presents a multifaceted picture of the abductor. On the one hand, abductors appear to be unhappy and usually violent, and they act out of a desire for revenge. On the other hand, there is a desire for a close relationship and a history of having been close with the child and of having visited frequently.

To further our understanding, we interviewed a number of abductors to get their stories. We believe this information offers another side to what we have reported about parental abduction up to this point. As mentioned earlier, all of these cases had been resolved at the time of the interviews, and in some cases the children had been returned to the other parent. In one case the situation was resolved and the child still lived with the abductor, while in another the child was over 18 and no longer in the care of either parent. The abductors' stories follow.

The Case of Cathy:

TRYING TO UNDO THE PAST

After a headline in a local newspaper reading "Mother's Year-long Flight with Son and Daughter Ends," this article follows:

Two small children are back in their father's care after a yearlong search, and their mother faces charges of interstate flight and transporting the children across state lines in violation of a court order. Sarah, 7, and Richard [not their real names], 6, were met at their father's home Friday evening by over 50 people when their father, Michael Smythe, and other family members brought them home to Florida.

"They were really happy that everybody cared that much," Smythe said. "There were little signs, all along the road from about three miles from the house, saying things like 'We missed you,' and 'Welcome home.'"

Cathy Smythe was caught and the children recovered in Pennsylvania en route to New York, evidence suggests. Cathy Smythe, who failed to bring the children back from a two-week vacation a year ago was almost caught early last week in West Virginia, where, apparently, she had been living and working for a year.

Police Chief Jones of Allentown, PA, said that at about 3:45 A.M. Thursday an officer patrolling a truck stop saw a car parked in an area primarily used for 18-wheelers. It was missing the license plate, and a woman and two children were sleeping in it. He called in the vehicle identification number, and the car came back as one that might be used by a wanted person. The officer brought the woman, the children, and the impounded vehicle to the station. "She was traveling very lightly," Jones said, "just maps, a few clothes, and some food for the children—and appeared to have left in a hurry."

"Initially, she provided some false information as to her identity," Jones said. "Once she realized what the situation was, she became very cooperative and was very concerned about the welfare of the children and what would happen to them next."

The children went home that night with Judy Harris, the county secretary. "They're very mature for their ages," Harris said. "They're good children, well mannered. I was very impressed. You wouldn't have thought they were going through anything. They seemed to be real glad to see their father when he arrived. I think they'll be alright."

Mr. Smythe said he found the children to be rather tired and worn but otherwise physically well. "Emotionally, they seem all right so far," he said. "I honestly don't think everything is great, but on the surface they seem alright." Smythe said he anticipates a period of adjustment.[24]

What the public learns about abductions often is encapsulated only in newspaper articles like this one, but there is another side to these stories. Cathy Smythe, an attractive woman in her late twenties, articulately described her life, from her childhood, her courtship, and her marriage to Michael to how she came to be the focus of a newspaper account about abduction. When interviewed, she presented as a person who had a survivor's tough exterior. Yet all her features softened when she talked about her children. It was almost as if a metamorphosis had occurred, so astonishingly different did she look. She cried occasionally and was eager to show pictures of them. But by the end of the interview the retransformation was complete, and the survivor was sitting in her chair once again.

Cathy was born in Florida, the youngest of three children. Her parents divorced when she was 10, after many years of fighting. Her experiences surrounding her parents' breakup had a profound influence on Cathy's own decision to abduct her children 17 years later. Cathy's father had sexually abused all of the females in the house, forcing Cathy's mother to run away with the children. He found them and brought them back home but subsequently kicked Cathy's mother out of the house. He told her that if she ever tried to see her children again, he would have her arrested for kidnapping. As Cathy tells it, "My mother was naive. She did not have much education and didn't know what her rights were. She tried to contact us but he stopped it, even to the point of not giving us gifts she sent us. He told us that she wasn't coming around anymore because she didn't love us." The pain of being cut off from her mother for years was instrumental in the formation of Cathy's personality.

As the children grew older, the two oldest eventually moved out of the father's home, finding life elsewhere more comfortable than living with their father and the woman he married. Cathy was kicked out of the home when she was 16, after her father discovered she had been corresponding secretly with her mother, whom she had not seen in six years. Cathy then hitchhiked to Georgia, moved in with her mother, and attempted to reconstruct the mother–daughter relationship she had missed for so many years. Three months later, seeking stability not only in her relationship with her mother but in her life as a young adult she met and started dating Michael, whom she would later marry.

What most attracted Cathy to Michael was what she most missed growing up: a warm family. She loved his brothers and sisters and the fun family outings they always seemed to be having. Their courtship was anything but idyllic, though. The most memorable incident by far occurred around a breach of trust, a recurring theme in Cathy's life: Michael had gone to Cathy's house to take a shower because the water had been temporarily turned off where he was living. While Cathy was working, he came across her diary and read it. He was shocked by revelations she made about her sexual activity prior to their relationship. Michael had been sexually inexperienced when they began dating and was not totally secure with his own sexuality. A huge fight followed when he confronted her at her job about what she had written. Cathy, afraid of his anger, ran home. "At the time I was no longer the party girl I had been," Cathy said. "His reaction made me feel like a tramp, very cheap. When I got home I tried to commit suicide by taking an overdose of pills. My friend came over and found me and rushed me to the hospital. When I look back on it, I know I was being overly dramatic. I left a suicide note next to a picture of him. I wanted to get revenge."

Cathy refused to see Michael after the diary incident. Michael's father, whom Cathy admired, intervened and convinced Cathy to give Michael a second chance. Four months later they were married.

The marriage did not start out on the best foot, but the tensions that characterized Cathy and Michael's relationship were easily masked by familial distractions. The couple moved into a trailer 50 yards from Michael's family. Cathy describes that period:

> At first, living next to them was great. I was still an impressionable teenager and liked living next to the "Brady bunch." After a year, though, the fighting between Michael and me began. He was very jealous and wanted me to be a country bumpkin, devoted to him. He wanted me to not talk back to him or see my friends or anything. He wanted me to stay home with his family, and I wanted to go out. I was suffocating.

Despite a deteriorating marriage, Cathy became pregnant and gave birth in the next few years to a daughter, Sarah, and a son, Richard. Having children did not improve the marriage and only entwined the couple's lives even more with Michael's family, who would cook for them and expect them to spend every free moment at their home. Cathy felt increasingly trapped, living in a small trailer in the woods with no means of transportation. When Sarah was five and Richard was three, Cathy and the children moved out.

Cathy went to a lawyer, had papers drawn up concerning the property settlement and custody, and presented them to Michael, who said he would sign them. One night when the children were visiting at Michael's parents' house, he came over with a minister and told Cathy he was not going to sign the papers and that he was going to keep custody. She returned the threat by saying she was going to take the children.

A court battle followed. Cathy's past history of premarital sexual promiscuity was brought up against her, as were her suicide attempt, her smoking marijuana in high school, her lack of full-time employment, and her threat to abduct. The minister's testimony supported Michael's claims, and he was granted primary physical custody of the children, although legal custody was joint.

A year later, in 1988, Cathy and Michael returned to court because the arrangement was not working out. "Both my children were having a very difficult time with going back and forth," Cathy said. "Michael ended up getting sole custody of the children, and there was no reason for that to have happened. I wanted to appeal the decision. My attorney told me to forget it. He told me, 'You're a beautiful, smart young lady. Go back to college, find a rich man, and get married.' He thought I should just forget my kids and have some more."

Cathy hired a new lawyer. They returned to court and won on the grounds that she had improved her situation through her employment. Joint custody was restored. But Michael immediately put in a new motion on the grounds that he had just remarried and could provide a better home life. Michael's marriage was a complete shock to everyone, and Cathy believes he remarried only to get custody. Michael was awarded sole custody, with Cathy being granted liberal visitation rights and the obligation to pay child support. Cathy was furious and did not know where to turn.

Six months later Cathy was again subpoenaed. Michael wanted to reduce her visitation rights, claiming she was not a good influence on the children. This time, due to a change of attorneys on Cathy's part and some confusion in scheduling the court date, Cathy and her attorney missed the hearing. Without her present, the court decided to cut her visitation schedule in half.

Cathy was beside herself. She immediately called her children and was confronted by Sarah and Richard's asking why she had missed the court date. They wondered if it was because she did not want to see them anymore. Then they said that their father had told them that she did not love them anymore. Cathy's story continues in her own words:

> I talked with them and tried to explain the situation. But it was hard. That's when I decided I had to abduct them. I could have lived with seeing them every other weekend. But when I heard that they were being told I didn't love them, it was like déjà vu. That is what had happened to my mother. Very slowly, Michael was trying to work me out of their lives. He was telling them and the courts lies, and I could see where this was all going. Each time he went into court, he would accuse me of neglecting the kids when they visited. One time my daughter burned her hand a little bit while cooking toast at my house. That was used against me—that she was cooking without being supervised. I would let the children play outside, and

they would get the normal bruises and bumps that children get. He would always keep them inside watching TV. Well, their bruises and scrapes would be used against me in court. I couldn't stand the way he was raising them. I knew, finally, I couldn't subject myself and my kids to what I had gone through without a mom!

Cathy made plans to take the children on their summer vacation and never come back.

I told a few people what I was going to do. I got blank birth certificates from West Virginia and changed my name. I reversed some numbers in my social security number, so I had a new one. I got a new driver's license in Maryland with my new ID and rented a storage shed in Pennsylvania. I got a friend to rent a truck and told her I needed it to help a friend move out. I drove the truck to my house in the middle of the night and loaded everything I could into the truck and put it into storage in Pennsylvania. I bought a used car in my new name, hid that at a friend's house, and got insurance for it in my new name.

The following weekend when I got the kids for the two weeks visitation, I picked them up in my old car, sold that at a junk yard and went and got the car I had just bought. Then we went camping around the north for a few weeks before we settled in West Virginia.

When they enrolled in school in the fall, the children, then six and five, were not given new names because Cathy thought that would be too confusing. Cathy, worrying that there was a national tracing system for missing children, told school personnel that she was running away from an abusive husband and did not want to be found. Life settled down for them, and Cathy began working as a teacher's aide. One of her biggest struggles was relaxing about being on the run. She decided that she would not worry about being caught. Living in fear of every siren would make life miserable for her and her children, she concluded.

According to Cathy, Richard only asked to see his father once. When she asked him why he wanted to see his father, Richard said he wanted to show his friend some of his toys that were at his father's house. "They just did not ask about seeing their father," Cathy said. "We've talked about him. I would overhear one of them telling a friend about something they had done with their father, like going fishing. I had told them that their dad was a good man, that it was just that we did not like each other."

Cathy was ambivalent when asked if she thought the abduction was harmful to the children:

> I had the choice of leaving them where they were and being slowly wiped out of their lives and having them think I was a bad person. I did not like how they were being raised. Or I could take them with me and have them live a stable life where they would get to know me and where they would be told their father was a good person, because I would not put him down. I wanted them to have a life that was full of love and not full of hatred, which is what they would have gotten with him. Maybe that's not the best way to look at it, but that is how I saw it.

In order to maintain their new life, Cathy had been very careful about who knew her history. Her family had always known where she was living and had even visited her at various times. Cathy believes that it was a cousin who told of her whereabouts, someone with whom she had never had a good relationship. When the FBI began investigating different branches of Cathy's family, the cousin became frightened and turned them in. Cathy and the children had a year together before they were found.

The night the authorities arrived at her doorstep, the children had been left with a sitter and Cathy had gone out. An arrest warrant made out to both her aliases and her real name was left on the door and greeted her when she returned. "I freaked when I saw it," Cathy said. "I grabbed the kids and drove through the night to get a head start. Five days later they caught me."

Cathy described her dealings with the authorities:

> The police were supernice to me when they found me and tried to make it as easy as possible. The kids became hysterical. They did not want me to go, and they did not want to go back to their daddy. The police cheered them up by having them ride in their car and turning on the siren and so on. They let me spend the day playing with them. Then I saw the judge and we talked about extradition and he talked to the kids. I was then put in jail for a week before I got extradited to Florida. [see the newspaper account at the beginning of this case history for further details].

When Cathy arrived in Florida, bond was set at $200,000. It was later lowered, and she was released under the conditions that she receive therapy and not return to Florida unless she had a hearing. She was initially allowed only two phone calls to the children a week. Subsequent court hearings and a psychological evaluation ordered by the court have resulted in her being permitted supervised visitation for a few hours once a month.

Upon her return to West Virginia, Cathy learned that she had been fired from her job (for lying about her work history) and that she had lost her apartment because of missed rent payments. She moved in with friends and slowly got her life back together again. Today, one year later, she is working in sales.

Cathy recently has been asked to begin paying child support as well as restitution for back child support. She has been court-ordered to see a psychiatrist if she wants to maintain visitation rights. She lives for her visits with the children, brief as they are. She never believed when she abducted the children that she would have such a restrictive visitation schedule if she were caught: "I thought I would have supervised visitation for six months and then be able to see them unsupervised. When I see them now it is in a small room at the courthouse and there is not anything to do and I think they are starting to get real bored." The children appear to be adjusting adequately, Cathy said, and they still ask about seeing her more and living with her, especially when she describes the house in the mountains where she lives.

Knowing the outcome, is Cathy sorry she abducted her children? No.

I spent 13 great months with my children without the stress of their being pulled in different directions. Before that I was seeing them only one day every other weekend. Those 13 months were the best in my life. They did not know they were on the run. There was a lot of loving there. I am not considering it again. I have been through enough.

The message the abduction gave the children is the one she most wanted them to hear: that she cared for them enough to risk everything. The cycle begun in her own childhood has been broken.

This case history follows the pattern of the nonviolent noncustodial visitor abductor who is seeking more contact with the children. Custody resided with Cathy's husband, and she was clearly upset with the notion that her children were being turned against her and that her visitation with them was being blocked. The abduction took place during visitation, and force was not used. As the newspaper column that begins this case study attests, the children were well taken care of, though the potential for emotional problems in the future still exists. The great concern and care shown the children is consistent with what we know about abductions by a non-violent visitor. The children's needs and feelings were given high priority, as illustrated by Cathy's decision not to resist arrest. Looking back on the abduction, Cathy explains the rationale for her behavior: "I spent time with them, and I gave them something they would not have had otherwise."

The Case of Nick:

WHEN ONE PARENT IS ALLOWING ABUSE

Nick, a 40-year-old engineer living outside of Atlanta, snatched two of his three children in violation of a court order and was in hiding for four months before being picked up by the police. For Nick the abduction was the culmination of many months of frustration with the courts and of years of frustration with his wife's behavior. In this situation, though, a form of sexual abuse appears to have been the final straw in Nick's deciding to abduct.

During the interview Nick was reticent about providing information. He was initially reluctant to be interviewed, and follow-up contacts with him over the next six months found him to be even more closemouthed. He spoke in a soft voice and taped our discussions. His behavior was perhaps a reflection of his learned distrust of legal and mental health professionals. It also suggests that, by being circumspect, he may have tried to present himself in an unrealistically favorable light.

The middle of three children, Nick was the product of an intact marriage. His mother was an alcoholic, a problem that later resurfaced in Nick's own life. After high school, Nick went to trade school to become an airplane engineer. When he was 22 he met his future wife, Betty, at a dance and married her after a four-month courtship. Their first son, Jerry, was born seven months later. "I never was really attracted to her and obviously we shouldn't have gotten married, despite the pregnancy," Nick admitted. He was in the armed forces in California at the time of the birth and returned to visit only sporadically over the next year. Betty moved in with her parents until Nick completed his service.

The next four years were the best years of the marriage. Nick was working full-time at a job he enjoyed, and Betty stayed home to care for Jerry. But with the birth of their second child, a daughter, things turned sour. "Betty moved out of the bedroom and began sleeping on the couch. I don't know why. I suspect she was fooling around on me." Five years later, despite the growing tension in the home and the sleeping arrangements, a third child, a son, was born.

By this time Nick had completely given up any hope of staying married to Betty. "She didn't grow during the marriage. She didn't clean house. She became a recluse and gained a lot of weight, refusing to put any energy into anything. I began going out with the kids and leaving her at home." Counseling did not help, since Betty refused to go more than one time. Finally, Betty, who must have been feeling as unhappy as Nick, filed for divorce, and Nick moved to his parents' house.

Within a few weeks Betty began visiting Nick and trying to persuade him to move back into the house. He discerned that she really was more interested in someone who could take care of the children than in a husband. Because of Nick's desire to be with the children, he agreed to move back home but only if Betty would move out. Betty stopped the divorce proceedings so Nick could legally return. But, Nick says, he did not move in (nor did Betty move out); he would only stay in the house long enough to put the children to bed before returning to his parents' house.

During this period Nick's employment was the only stabilizing factor in his life. He was very ambivalent about his relationship with Betty, on the one hand wanting to work things out through counseling so that he could be with the children but also, on the other hand, fearing that nothing would save the relationship. Under the stress, he began abusing alcohol.

Nick and Betty continued their on-again, off-again relationship, with Betty wanting him back home and Nick wanting them in counseling as a prerequisite to his returning. One problem for

Nick was that Betty was totally unpredictable. In one instance, Nick returned from a camping trip with Jerry, their oldest son, only to be confronted by the police; Betty had charged him with assault. Nick continued:

> I began to argue with them but they told me to leave to avoid a hassle. She blew up and threatened me. She was holding all the cards at that point. I didn't know what to do. Legally, she had me over a barrel. There was more going on at that time, too. My oldest son had sexually molested my daughter, and Betty hadn't done anything to stop it. In addition, when she would nurse the two-year-old, she would masturbate with his leg.

Following the assault charge, Nick called the children's school the next day, because of his concerns about his children's well-being only to learn that they were absent. "I went to the house to see them and we got into another fight. My youngest son came running out and jumped into my arms and I talked my daughter (then 7) into coming with me, too. Jerry refused to come out of the house. That's when I went on the run."

For four months Nick and the two children moved from town to town in Tennessee. He had quit his job, but he knew he was going to be laid off in a few weeks, anyway. He told his daughter they were on the run because her mother was not protecting her from her brother. "She never asked about her at all after that. Betty had been playing keep away with me from my children and I could see it was only going to get worse. I had to take them to protect them."

Nick was apprehended six years ago when he was stopped for speeding. The police ran a computer check on him and learned the children were to be picked up. He was arrested on the spot since the assault charge from Betty was still pending. The children were taken with Nick to a police station, where they were returned to Betty. "The kids were real upset by the whole thing—seeing me in cuffs and in jail. They didn't want to go back to their mother." Nick was released on bond and has never been prosecuted.

Since his arrest, Nick has pressed for increased visitation rights through the courts. He has not been successful. Following court-ordered evaluations, his visitation frequency has been increased only slightly. And arranging court-approved visitation has been a struggle for him. All visits with the younger children are to be supervised, and the courts have been dragging their feet, Nick feels, in setting up these visits. According to Nick, visitation is to be supervised because of the false charges of child abuse that Betty brought against him. Two years ago Jerry, the child who was not abducted, requested to have more contact with Nick. By the time Jerry turned 16, one year later, father and son had established a strong enough relationship that Jerry asked to move in with him. That kind of shift in living arrangements often drives a wedge into other relationships. Jerry has had little contact with his mother and two siblings since he moved in with his father. He doesn't even know their phone number, and Betty has not tried to contact him, according to Nick: "The younger two, who I haven't seen for a year now, are living a reclusive life with her. They are getting kind of loony. She turned over custody of Jerry because of problems he was having. He was on drugs and was suicidal. He's clean now and doing much better."

Nick has not been problem free himself. He has battled alcoholism and has been known to exhibit quite an explosive temper. Nick is glad he has custody of Jerry but is bitter about his lack of contact with his other two children. To him, everyone is retarding the process of setting up his supervised visitation schedule. In the interim, Nick worries about his children's mental health. Recently, he saw them at their school's open house but they were not allowed to speak with him. It was his first sighting of them in a year.

Nick, like most abductors, believes that snatching his children was justified by the circumstances. He seems convinced that the children were experiencing various forms of abuse owing to the environment that Betty was providing for them, but he himself is being denied fuller access to his children because of charges of assault and sexual abuse. Finally, he sees the courts as being irresponsible in their dispositions concerning his family. Unlike the other abductions described in this chapter, this one was almost completely spontaneous and was unassisted by any friends or relatives, a reflection perhaps of Nick's impulsive nature.

From his ex-wife's perspective, and from our analysis of patterns of abduction, Nick's behavior places him in the category of the violent visitor; he did not have custody at the time of the abduction, and there was a history of alleged domestic violence. Betty essentially ended the marriage by moving out of the bedroom and then asking Nick to leave; substance abuse was present, and force was used in the abduction, which did not occur during visitation. Although Nick describes himself as quite involved with the children prior to the abduction, from Betty's perspective his participation in their lives seems less substantial. From our experience, cases of this sort sometimes involve child physical or sexual abuse perpetrated by both parents.

Nick's arrest was typical of what happens when an abductor is apprehended: Approximately two-thirds are arrested, two in five are convicted of kidnapping, and one in five spends at least some time in jail. Usually, the length of time in jail is short. For Nick it was overnight and for Cathy, in the previous case study, it was two weeks (though for her, her current visitation schedule may seem like a prison term).

The Case of Dan:

THE 12-YEAR ABDUCTION

The most long-term abduction we encountered involved a situation where a daughter was snatched by her father when she was six years old and had no contact with her mother until she turned 18 and was about to graduate from high school. Interviews were conducted with all three family members when the daughter, Ruth, turned 22 and graduated from college. The parents, Dan and Sandy, provide their sides of the abduction situation here while their daughter Ruth's version appears in Chapter 5, which deals with the child's experience of abduction. Through interviews with Dan's parents and his sister, we also have information about the involvement of other family members, all of whom helped in various ways.

Dan, now 50, was the product of a two-parent Pennsylvania-based family. He describes his childhood as being normal, with no alcohol or physical abuse. Dan finished college with a business degree at the age of 25, after having served two years in the Navy. It was at that time that he met Sandy, who at 21 was just finishing college while working as an executive secretary. They dated for two years but were on rocky terms when they discovered Sandy was pregnant. "Even though we knew we were two different people, we got married. Actually, I really liked the woman. Aside from being very intelligent, she was very good-looking!" recalls Dan.

Dan describes himself in the early days of the relationship as being "vituperative. I would shout at her. She would be quiet and go off on her own. She would not use logic to decide things but, rather, would rely on emotion. I wasn't physically abusive, but there was shouting." Dan's relationship with Sandy's parents was also rocky. Her father was on disability and was trying to get by, according to Dan, by doing as little as possible. "Her father was a good man. There was just nothing that he and I had in common," Dan says. Dan perceived himself as an entrepreneur "looking to climb new mountains."

From the start the marriage was shaky. "I could see that she would have been happier marrying someone with a nine-to-five job and a vine-covered cottage, not someone like me who was always pushing for more and was gone from home a lot trying to make deals. Not that either was right or wrong. That's just how we were," says Dan. Within five years the couple had drifted completely apart and, according to Dan, Sandy ended the marriage because she became involved with another man. "I don't hold that against her. I don't see her in a negative light because of that, as she is still with the same guy. I saw it coming and it was for the better that we broke up. I tried the best I could for my daughter's sake to keep it together and, until this day, I still have an emotional attachment to her."

Dan had not participated much in Ruth's upbringing when she was a baby but became very involved with her when she started in preschool at the age of three. Despite his involvement, Dan believed he had no chance to win custody. He was right: Ruth started living with Sandy, and Dan began visiting on weekends. As Dan explains it:

Back then (in 1974) men in Illinois had no say in the matter, and if the woman told you to jump, you would do it. I first wanted joint custody, but she told me essentially, "You need to get a job and pay support, you bum." They want to knock the man to the ground and take away his dignity and make it look like it was all his fault. Men had a hard time getting custody then. She got Ruth and the house, and I was out in my own apartment.

Dan had just been fired from his job as a salesman. "It was pretty hard trying to make a big sale when your whole life was coming apart on you. Some men could do it, but I was one of those emotional wimps who couldn't hang in there."

Over the next year Dan finally got fed up with trying to get custody and resolve financial matters in the courts. He was still visiting Ruth but wanted to be a bigger part of her life. After the last court decision, when he was still unsuccessful in gaining custody, he asked Ruth if she wanted to go on a trip with him. The six-year-old girl, clearly not grasping the ramifications of her answer, said yes, and they went into hiding. Dan had been planning the abduction for some time and believed his actions would give him the extended contact with his daughter that the courts had refused.

Dan said he also was motivated to abduct by his daughter's behavior. Ruth would be in a great mood when he picked her up for their weekend visit, but her behavior would deteriorate over the next two days. At one point when Dan was dropping Ruth off at Sandy's house, Ruth screamed that she wanted to stay with Dan. "That was it," Dan said.

Sandy started cutting me off from her. I couldn't talk to her on the phone any more and the number was changed. Sandy would complain I was turning her daughter against her. She finally calmed down after that and realized it wasn't me, and we went on a regular schedule again. But it was really hard when your daughter asks why you haven't called her.

Dan describes in detail the preabduction planning he did:

I had made intricate plans. I enjoyed smoking pot, and I spent many hours thinking it out through every possible angle as I was drinking a bottle of wine. I went to the library and got every book I could find on the topic. I made sure I had every string cut off, so when I left that was it. I went to all kinds of trouble to spread false rumors. My parents lived in northern Montana and I wanted to give the impression I lived in the south of Montana rather than where I was really living, so I would write to Sandy, through my parents, that I was going *up* to see them in a few days. I wanted to let her know that Ruth was okay. With the false information I sent her they spent all their time looking for me in Montana and never got even close.

I got a new name, a new social security number, a new driver's license, new bank account, and I lied like hell to get credit. I had a friend who owned a big business and was able to establish credit through him. It was relatively easy. I did it out of a motivation to be with my daughter and not have her choose a life in the vine-covered cottage. She was a sharp girl and I wanted her to be a mover and shaker like her dad and not settle for less, like I feel would have happened if she had been raised by her mother. We were very, very close. I had seen children cut off from their fathers by a divorce and didn't want that to happen.

Dan and Ruth camped for the first week to make sure Ruth really wanted to stay with him. Just before they crossed the state line, Dan told her that she was about to go to a new state and wouldn't see her mother for a while. He wanted to make sure she was up to the move. Ruth pulled out a piece of paper with her mother's phone number on it and give it to Dan, saying that her mother had given that to her in case she was ever taken anywhere. She told her father, "Here's the paper. Don't worry about it." Their 12 years in hiding began.

Dan chose a western state where he thought the opportunities were abundant. He opened up a business based on one he knew from home and now, at the time of the interview 18 years later, feels quite successful. Dan's philosophy is that the trick to being a single parent is to have enough time to be with your child. Being self-employed allowed him that opportunity.

Dan said that if emotional or school-related problems had arisen over Ruth's living with him, he would have returned her to Sandy and "faced the music" for the abduction. Initially in our interviews, Dan believed that Ruth was not too upset about not seeing her mother. "I did not talk to her about it when she was young. She asked about it a bit as she got older. It came up once or twice and I steered her away from it and everything was all right. I always begged the question. I said her mother lived a long way away and we'd have to look into the idea of visits." When Ruth turned 18 and finally did see Sandy, she guessed that she had been abducted. At a later point in the interviews, when pressed further, Dan admitted that Ruth probably did want to see her mother and was "frustrated by the situation. It might have been an emotional strain on her in that respect. But I never told her her mother was dead."

Dan was defensive about his raising of Ruth. It was the day she was accepted at a topflight Ivy League school that he finally called Sandy and told her about the acceptance. In revealing their whereabouts and inviting her to Ruth's high school graduation, Dan maintained a posture that attempted to justify his taking his daughter with him all those years. He told Sandy on the telephone, "I just got this news about your daughter and you've been so worried about her and here she turned out okay." It took Sandy three weeks to come out and visit Ruth, according to Dan, a sufficiently long interim to make him wonder how much she really cared for Ruth. It confirmed for Dan some of the doubts about the passive nature of Sandy's lifestyle. "I know if it had been me, I would have chartered a flight out to see her," he said.

Dan was asked whether he thought Ruth resented not seeing her mother during her childhood. His response? "We talked about it. No, not really. Ruth saw how much conflict there was between us since we've been in contact again and is kind of glad she did not have to put up with that when she was growing up. But I bet she missed her mother a lot more than I realized at the time. Christmas time was not much fun." Dan went on to say that he always tried to raise Ruth to stick up for herself:

> I guess I was a feminist way back before I knew what that meant. I wanted her to get ahead and sometimes I may have motivated her a little harshly. I remember when she was about 11 and she wouldn't clean up her room, I told her she could go live in the car. The police came by after a few hours and she came back in but she was real angry about that. What do you do when a child doesn't want to clean up her room and is saying, "Make me"? Sometimes you have to back it up with actions.

Dan saw some action in his business life also. At one point during a law suit with an ex-partner, the man tried to blackmail him about having abducted Ruth. The lawyer for the partner asked Dan if he thought his ex-wife would like to know his whereabouts. Dan called their bluff and won the suit.

Socially, Dan has a quiet life. While he wants to date, he has not met anyone who he thinks respects children the way he does.

Why should Dan talk to us? Our impression was that he needed to justify why he abducted Ruth. Dan told us that he wanted to show the world that parents who abduct do not live as hermits and that he was quite successful. When he finally saw Sandy again after 12 years of hiding from her, he seemed pleased with being able to show her that he was not "some kind of bum." It is very important to Dan to prove that he has been a successful parent.

Sandy's side of the story is factually quite similar to Dan's. In her account, though, we hear the pain of 12 years of being separated from her daughter. Sandy first was drawn to Dan because "he was attractive, I did not know many people in college, and I was young and impressionable." Her story of their early relationship and other details matches Dan's. His picture of himself as a go-getter is slightly different from Sandy's impression, though. She saw Dan as moving from job to job a great deal and not being a consistent breadwinner, not unlike the "bum" that Dan thought he was in her eyes.

What caused Sandy to seek a divorce was her dissatisfaction with the marriage and with Dan: "He was going through a lot of job changes and was content to stay home. He was a chauvinist. He increased his own self-respect by belittling others. There were a lot of problems." Sandy said that because Ruth was only four, it was hard to explain the breakup to her. Using simple language, Ruth was told that her parents were unhappy together and that it would be better for everyone if they split up.

Battles over custody and property settlement followed. Dan attempted within the first year to get custody and a greater share of the proceeds from the sale of the house. During that period Sandy encouraged contact between father and daughter but the relationship between Dan and Sandy was becoming increasingly acrimonious because of the custody battle. The abduction came, Sandy believes, as a result of Dan's inability to get custody.

Sandy suspected an abduction was about to occur, and her worst fears were confirmed when after Dan and Ruth had been gone for a few weeks during a scheduled six-week vacation, a friend told her he had seen an advertisement that Dan had placed for a traveling companion. Sandy immediately called the place Dan and Ruth were supposed to be visiting and learned that they had never planned to be there. The six weeks had turned out to be a perfect time for Dan to get a head start on disappearing. The frustration Dan had been feeling now became Sandy's:

> After they had been missing a few weeks I was aware of his intentions but could not interest the authorities in doing anything because he had a legal right to see her at the time. He did communicate with me immediately, saying that they were fine, so I did not worry about her being harmed. He was good about that. None of his family knew of his whereabouts, or at least they wouldn't tell me where he was. I was aware he was very unhappy and that he felt I was trying to keep Ruth from him.

When asked further about this period, some of the details were hard for Sandy to recall. The pain of that period resulted in her blocking out the memories, she said. Attempts to recover Ruth began with Sandy going to the police department and then into court to get a legal document indicating that custody had been violated. The final legal step was getting a district attorney to issue a warrant. This took months owing to the authorities' lack of interest in this type of case, Sandy said. Other attempts she made to recover could, in Sandy's words, "fill a book." Nothing worked.

As time went on, Sandy was faced with the frustration, loss, and guilt that almost always haunt searching parents.

> After ten years of searching, I realized I had to do something else with my life. I had been sending packages to his parents and sisters to relay to him. He would call and tell me how wonderfully they were doing, and I would have to sit and listen to him go on and on in the hopes of there being some clue as to their whereabouts. I had to block out the pain of all those years but I kept pursuing it legally by writing legislators, legal people in different states, and every organization I could think of that deals with abduction, as well as every organization that he would have belonged to. I sent private detectives to his parents' house on holidays, hoping they would show up. You do that for a certain number of years and then you have to stop and get on with your life. I honestly don't know what else I could have done but there is always the guilt that you could do more.

Whereas Dan described the abduction as ending because Ruth was accepted in college, Sandy offers a different perspective, one that recognizes the lobbying Ruth herself was doing:

> He began calling me in February and saying that (I'll never forget it) maybe I should keep a bag packed in the corner of my office and someday soon I might get a call from him telling me where they lived and that I'd have to leave at the drop of the hat. The impression I got was that she was putting pressure on him to see me. Finally, when she got into college, the call came.

Sandy called Ruth immediately. "We both babbled on and on. We didn't know what to say. I said to her to just talk, that I needed to hear her voice. It's a very cherished conversation." Sandy did not fly out to see Ruth the next day. "I had to arrange things at work, but more importantly, I had to adjust psychologically to Ruth's being located." Their initial meeting took place in the airport. "She asked if she could bring friends to the gate to be with her, and I said bring anything you need to make it easier. It was exhilarating, exciting, scary, and everything when we first saw each other. I still had the picture of her as being six. So it was hard getting used to her."

A summer visit followed, as did the slow, often painful process of getting to know each other after 12 years. One key aspect of their new relationship that needed attention was the anger that Sandy and Ruth held for each other; each was angry with the other for not trying to find her.

This, and similar themes, inform their continuing relationship. Sandy explains:

> We had to meet as strangers with a very intimate connection. She was very defensive of her father, which I had a hard time dealing with. She saw him as a white knight who had swept her away, and she may still not quite understand what the abduction did to me. So we had to work through that. I took the approach that the last thing I wanted to do was alienate her by bad-mouthing him. I was grateful that she loved him but saw him as a stumbling block in our relationship. After everything that has happened, I think it is amazing that Ruth and I get along as well as we do. We're very close.

Sandy married soon after her divorce from Dan and is quite content with her husband of 15 years; he has been a consistent source of support in her life. Sandy avoids contact with Dan, saying, "It is only because of Ruth that I don't call him and rant and rave at him. He has caused her such problems. I'm sure he will not admit that. But I don't think there is any reason to tell him. For her sake, I have maintained a distance from him. I have made this clear to her."

To gain other perspectives on Dan's and Sandy's situation and to highlight the importance of gaining a family perspective on the impact of an abduction, we interviewed Dan's parents and sister. Dan's parents, in particular, were an important link between Dan and Sandy, relaying packages and messages.

"I don't think he could have done anything else. He was right about what he did," Dan's mother responded to a question concerning her son's abduction. Dan's father chimed in; "I saw when my son took her (Ruth) back to the mother after visitation with him. She wouldn't let him go. He had to force her into the house. It broke his heart and her heart (to separate)."

Both of Dan's parents, who were the conduits between Sandy and Dan for so many years, feel the abduction was justified because Ruth was so attached to Dan. During those years they visited Dan and Ruth, sometimes for two to three months, and found their granddaughter to be a happy, well-adjusted child who had everything she needed. "I do believe, though, that she missed something by not being raised by her mother," Dan's father, (who was also raised by his father—and his aunt—following his mother's death when he was young) admits. "It is a little lapse she will have. She did talk about wanting to see her mother occasionally."

At the beginning of the abduction, Dan's parents were on several occasions visited by the police, who wanted to know Dan's whereabouts. The response was always that they only saw Dan when he picked up the mail. This was another attempt to throw the police and private detectives off guard with the impression that Dan lived nearby. Sandy's parents also called them. "They screamed at us for helping to keep her in hiding," Dan's father said. "They told us what a terrible thing we had done."

Did Dan's parents ever lose any sleep over what had happened and how they had assisted their son? "No. We didn't know he was going to do it, but we never tried to talk him into sending her back. I think if he hadn't taken her, he would have ended up in the gutter. He would have been a bum. He needed her, and that's why I helped him. He did it because he couldn't stand to see her cry," Dan's father said.

Dan's sister, Helen, felt more conflicted about the abduction than did his parents. "I was caught in the middle. When he first took Ruth, Sandy would call me and ask if I knew where they were and, if so, how could I as a mother not help her to get her daughter back? But I didn't know for two years where they were." Helen was involved in the abduction only in that she would receive gifts from Sandy to be given to Ruth. Helen then would forward them to Dan's parents, who sent them to Ruth. She was not interviewed by the police, which was a surprise to her. If they had inquired about Dan's location, she is not sure what she would have told them, once she knew where they lived:

"I never tried to talk Dan into returning Ruth. But I was assured, even though I didn't see her for 12 years, that she was doing well where she was. She was a daddy's girl so I didn't try to stop it. He did it for her and not for himself." (Ruth gives her perspective in Chapter 5.)

Sandy and Dan's is one of the more unusual stories we have heard because of the length of time of the abduction and the access we have been permitted to all of the family members. The elements of the stories of each member are essentially the same, though the perceptions are quite different. Dan believes he provided Ruth a better life than she would have had with Sandy. He feels vindicated by Ruth's acceptance to and graduation from a top-notch university. While admitting to some difficulties that may have arisen during Ruth's teen years, he points out that he cannot know which of them she would have experienced anyway or if they are that different from the experiences of other children of divorce. Sandy is naturally more focused on the loss in her own life, while also keeping an eye on potential difficulties that may arise for Ruth because of being kept in the dark about her mother for 12 years.

It was the anger of a father who wanted more contact with his daughter and believed the courts were unfair that spawned the abduction initially; the pain that Dan perceived Ruth to be in and the importance she played in giving his own life meaning were also contributing factors. And it is anger that remains nearly a generation later for at least some, if not all, of the family members. For the three of them, as the years of keeping family matters repressed begin to bubble up, new feelings and revelations are slowly emerging. Some are difficult for all three of them to examine. Many issues within the family are treated very gently, as if to not upset a carefully balanced applecart. The two women, to some extent, are victims of Dan and are starting to experience anew the anger that comes with being victimized.

The reasons for this abduction seem difficult to grasp and set it apart from the other abductions described in this chapter. Ruth was not in imminent danger; she was not being abused. Yet Dan subverted the court decision bearing on custody and took matters into his own hands. Dan feels guilt about this and tries to rationalize it. Unlike the other abductors, though, Dan maintained frequent contact with Sandy to let her know Ruth was progressing well. Of all the abductors, he had by far the best opinion of his ex-spouse. Perhaps, too, he kept Sandy abreast of Ruth's progress to assuage his own guilt for having abducted her.

This abduction is not completely typical of any one pattern. While Dan might believe himself to have been seeking greater contact with his daughter, there also are aspects here of other patterns. The abductor is male and some verbal abuse may have preceded the abduction, although there had been no other physical violence in the marriage that would have put it clearly into the violent visitor category. In addition, Dan feared a loss of control over his life and loss of contact with Ruth. He gained her unconditional love through the abduction. In 1974, when sole or joint custody were extremely rare for men, Dan had liberal visitation and was being encouraged to visit, as close a situation to shared custody as may have been reasonably possible in many jurisdictions at that time. Nonviolent shared custodians who abduct often are very involved with their children before the abduction, as was the case with Dan.

Dan also was atypical as an abductor in that he maintained contact with Sandy over the years. Two-thirds of the searching parents said they had no communication from the abductor, the remaining third said the abductor wrote or phoned them, and only a few had the children call or write.

The Case of Connie:

WHEN THE ABDUCTING PARENT LEAVES THE COUNTRY WITH THE CHILD

What compels an American-born U.S. citizen to leave the country with her son? In Chapter 6 we discuss international abduction in greater depth. The story of Connie provided here offers insight into the motivations of one woman who lived in two foreign countries in an attempt to escape her ex-husband.

Connie was born and raised in California, one of three children in a well-to-do family. Her father, a lawyer, died when she was nine, leaving the family very well-off financially. Her mother never worked outside of the home and remained single for the remainder of her life. Connie married a lawyer when she was just out of college. Three years later he was killed in a car accident, leaving her even more financially secure than had her inheritance from her father.

As with many love relationships, what attracted Connie to her second husband, Rob, is not readily apparent. She may have been seeking companionship or someone to take care of. Whatever it was, objectively it was not a good match. The couple met at a dance and became engaged six months later. Connie was older than Rob by ten years and had finished a master's program in business. He was a college student. He came from an alcoholic and abusive family, a fact he hid from her along with his marijuana use, a habit he picked up while serving in Vietnam. Admits Connie: "I realized the night I married him that I had made a mistake, and it was confirmed on the honeymoon by the way he treated me and everybody else. We weren't married very long, and he became abusive. There were arguments from the start. I became pregnant immediately, which complicated matters."

Connie hoped that things would improve with the birth of their son, Rick, and with a move from California to Oregon to get away from Rob's family. Nothing helped, and Connie moved out during a particularly abusive period. Rick was one year old at the time. Following Rob's pleading, Connie and Rick moved back in after Rob vowed he would go for counseling. He soon reneged on his promise to seek help and was asked to move out again. During a Christmas holiday the couple tried another reconciliation, perhaps because both were feeling the loneliness of the season. The attempt failed.

A messy divorce followed, with Rob seeking custody and a sizable portion of the assets that Connie had brought into the marriage from her first husband's and her father's estates. Connie won custody and was able to retain most of her inheritance; Rob was awarded regular visitation rights.

Visitation problems emerged almost immediately. Connie reports that Rick developed allergies and was often sick, causing frequent cancellations of Rick's time with Rob. Rescheduling was difficult owing to Rob's work demands. After a number of cancellations, Rob dragged Connie back into court on a violation of the visitation agreement. While this most recent battle raged, Rick's allergies were being exacerbated by the foliage in Oregon. Connie, upon consultation with an allergist, made a decision to move to Texas. She reasoned that this decision would not only be beneficial to Rick's health but would also prevent her from being so easily harassed by Rob:

> He would call me at all hours of the day and night and then hang up. When they were together, Ricky was not given the proper food for his allergies. So I got permission to move, but I was also found in contempt of court. I decided to let the contempt charge go because I got what I wanted, which was sole custody. Six months after we moved, Ricky [then five] was free of allergies.
>
> His father would call [to Texas], but Ricky did not want to speak with him. I had to *make* Ricky talk to his father. Ricky was sent for visitation in the spring and summer as part of the agreement.

Rob, despite the distance, continued his court battles, only now the venue had changed to Texas. Every six months he fought Connie for joint custody, more visitation, or more property. He was making good on a threat that he would find some way to break her financially. Connie could never understand how he could afford to sue her so often; she even hired a private investigator to explore the matter, but it was to no avail. Connie watched her financial resources slowly being stripped away as she fought increasingly expensive court battles.

In 1988 Rob again dragged Connie into court, an event that coincided with the death of Connie's mother:

> When this last battle began and with both my parents dead, I felt kind of free to leave the country. I decided I would see what the outcome would be of the court case. My son was getting very paranoid about seeing his father and going through more litigation. I began selling things that we did not need in anticipation of moving away. My plan was to leave at the end of the summer vacation when Ricky came back from visiting Rob. I would use that time to plan where we should go. But in March, Ricky said that Rob had been sexually abusing him. That was the breaking point, and as soon as school was out in June we left.

Before they left (in a scene reminiscent of the one described by Dan in which he asked his young daughter to leave with him), Connie asked Rick if he wanted to leave with her. Rick readily agreed and seemed happy he would never have to see his father again.

Their first international stop was Hong Kong, where Connie changed their names. That process was surprisingly easy. A lawyer helped them petition for new ones. They were then issued new passports, which eased their way into Australia, where they lived for a year. "We chose Australia because we needed an English-speaking place and because of my son's allergies," Connie said. Rick enrolled in the first grade. Life was stable again, and Rick seemed quite happy. Then the first stumbling block to their new life arose: They applied for residency and were denied. They appealed. They were denied again, so they had to leave. Connie recalls her dilemma:

> I did not know where to go at that point because I knew it took a year to get residency in most countries and that most countries would only give me a six-month visa. I couldn't go back to the U.S.

and apply for a visa easily because we had changed our names. So I went to the Philippines. I enrolled Rick in school, and I could work there because I was a U.S. citizen (Connie had been unable to work in Australia).

This was our best time together. Rick was very good about keeping our being in hiding a secret. He was almost paranoid about it and would hush me up from talking about it, being worried that we would be found. It showed to me how much he did not want to return to the mainland and his father.

Their life in the Philippines did not last, though. One year later came the knock on the door that Connie had feared; mother and son were taken into custody. Of the arrest Connie says, "I never knew for sure how I was found. Some people say I was traced through the passport but other information I have indicates that a private detective I had hired to help me file my taxes and handle all mail in Texas may have turned me in. I would write to him and receive mail from him. He must have been going for a reward at some point."

Ricky was placed in a foster home, and Connie went to jail in the Philippines. She posted bail and was advised by her lawyer to return on her own recognizance to Texas to face charges there. Rick did not do well being separated from his mother. Connie recalls: "He screamed hysterically before they put him in a foster home that he wanted to be with his mother. There was no way we could escape from the island so it was silly of them not to give him back to me until he was sent back to the States. It would have made for an easier adjustment for us both."

Rob arrived in the Philippines three days later and picked up Rick. Rob had gained custody through a court order while Connie was out of the country. She had not been represented at the hearing and claimed that Rob told a number of lies in order to get custody. Upon her release from police custody, she returned to the States, surrendered herself to the authorities, and went through criminal proceedings. She was fined $2,500 and put on probation.

Since being back in the United States, Connie has only had short supervised visitation with Rick on holidays. Attempts to extend her visitation rights have been unsuccessful. She talks to Rick every week on the phone and is allowed to write him twice a week. Connie describes his present circumstances and analyzes the past:

Recently he has problems understanding why I can't see him. He wants me to come for open house at his school. He wants to see me on my birthday. Luckily, I think he is out of the woods in terms of being in danger of being sexually abused because he can run away now or lock doors. But his allergies are returning.

The question I am asked the most is would I do it over again? The answer is yes, but I would do it differently. I would not trust anyone who could turn me in. I do believe that if we had gotten residency in Australia, we would have been safe. They signed the Hague Convention while we were there, but I doubt they would have extradited us.

For Connie, the abduction seemed the only logical way out of a situation where she was being bled to death financially, where her son's well-being was at stake because of his allergies, and where he was being sexually abused. Our impression is that Connie had already decided to abduct on the basis of the first two issues. Finding out about the abuse motivated her to abduct sooner rather than later, but, most likely, the abuse alone would have been sufficient reason for her to act.

Connie's story involves a typical custodial abduction: Violence and sexual abuse were being perpetrated by the parent left behind; the mother had custody at the time of the abduction and was the more involved parent; the abductor believed it was appropriate to abduct for the child's own protection.

THE WEEKEND ABDUCTOR

While almost all the abductions we discuss in this book lasted for at least a month, giving them considerable potential for wreaking havoc on the family, weekend or brief abductions are much more common, according to a national survey[25] and other sources. Police in Baltimore County, Maryland, as well as missing children's organizations, have helped us to piece together the following profile of the typical weekend abduction: The parent left behind often knows where the abductor is.[26] These abductions tend to occur when a marriage is beginning to break up or a number of years after the divorce, rather than immediately after the breakup.[27] In Baltimore County the abductor is as likely to be female as male, reflecting the growing trend in Maryland toward fathers winning or obtaining sole or joint custody (in states that have traditional ideas about mothers retaining custody, the abductors may be more likely to be male).[28]

The parents who abduct for the weekend tend to be acting spontaneously, having made few or no plans for where to go or what to do with the child. The abduction often occurs during visitation and may be precipitated by a particular event: For example, one parent may learn about the other parent's dating and be sufficiently incensed by that to refuse to return the child; a child may cry about not wanting to return to the other parent and ask to stay with the abductor; or a parent may hear about misconduct on the part of the other parent, such as partying, drug or alcohol abuse, physical abuse, or neglect.

Usually with these abductions there has been some frustration with the legal system, but not as long a history of problems as with the preplanned and longer-term abductions. Once the child has been snatched, the abductor may keep the child at home or go with the child to a friend's or relative's house. They may occasionally leave the state. Many of these abductors are gainfully employed in jobs they cannot afford to jeopardize. Ultimately, they may have more faith and trust in the legal process than do those abductors who disappear. It is this faith and trust, as well as their ability to assess accurately the consequences of their actions, that cause these weekend abductors to return the child. Once they are located, and that is often within a short period of time, a visit or a phone call from the police is usually enough to convince them to return their child. The more upset or frustrated the abductor is, the more difficult he or she will be in negotiations. In Baltimore County, for example, the problem usually is resolved without the abductor being arrested. Police encourage parents to negotiate about possible changes in visitation rights or custody, issues often behind the snatching, or to take the disputed issues back to court.

A typical weekend abduction in Maryland might involve one parent trying to get back at the other parent for a perceived past injustice by refusing to return the child after a visit. The left-behind parent calls the police and informs them that an abduction has taken place, whereupon attempts are made to locate the missing parent and child. When the abductor is located, he or she is advised of the law and has a 48-hour period in which to return the child (laws differ by state). That 48-hour period begins when the parent is informed by the authorities of the need to return the child or when court papers drawn up at the time of the custody agreement say it begins. In other words, if a custody agreement specifies return of the child at 6:00 P.M., that is when the 48-hour period begins.

If that early intervention does not end the abduction, lawyers for both parties often will get involved and negotiate an end to the custody dispute within one to two weeks. Usually, criminal charges are not brought against the abductor in Maryland, and it is extremely rare for these brief abductions to be committed or resolved through violence.[29]

The weekend abduction, while more common than the longer-term one, takes less of a toll on the family members. Astute and sensitive handling of these cases by local police can lead to their quick resolution, which reduces their impact on the family as well as on the court system.

ABDUCTIONS TO WOMEN'S SHELTERS

When a parent seeks help because of domestic violence, a first step often is to call a crisis hotline or counseling center for information. Women, the most frequent victims in domestic violence situations,[30] often are told about the availability of women's centers and shelters in their communities. Virtually unknown less than 20 years ago, the shelter movement now offers aid to women in almost all U.S. cities and in many smaller towns. Centers or shelters typically offer information, referrals, crisis counseling, and support groups; many have short-term residential facilities. All or nearly all of these also accept the young children a mother might bring with her as she seeks help.

Many of those who stay in shelters for a while return home, despite the abuse. Others remain in their communities and use counseling and other services to help them try to alter or leave their abusive relationships. Still others go into long-term hiding from the violent partner, and some of these become abducting parents.[31] Frequently, domestic violence and child abuse occur within the same family,[32] and even when they have not been harmed physically, children suffer emotionally from violence in their homes.[33]

A typical case of a parental abduction that begins at a women's shelter might feature a woman who fled from her husband several times in the past. Previously, she may have left to stay with relatives, may have received counseling help for herself, may have tried to involve her husband in couples counseling, and may even have tried to obtain legal assistance with a protection order and marital separation. Her husband was always able to resist change and to convince her to return. Their three children (perhaps a teenage boy and a younger son and daughter) have been through a great deal, and the mother is concerned about what her daughter and youngest son are learning about family life. The oldest son may already be starting to copy the way his father treats his mother and his siblings. After two beatings in one week, the mother flees to a women's shelter with the two younger children. She is unable to bring her oldest son because she does not trust him not to call his father and because the shelter does not accept adolescent boys. After the latest violent episode, she decides that she must go on the run with her children if she is going to escape her marriage. When she leaves the shelter, her first destination is the home of a friend who lives in another state.

The woman who flees to a shelter may see no other options or may feel that she has exhausted them. Although her actions may arouse the sympathy of many, they constitute a parental abduction under some state laws; if her husband gets a custody order in his favor, any jurisdiction would consider her actions an abduction. One of the risks for a mother who flees a violent spouse is that if she is found, the father may snatch the children back, often in an effort to force her return to the marriage. In Chapters 8 and 9 we address the special problems of preventing and resolving parental abductions when family violence is part of the problem.

ABDUCTIONS INVOLVING UNDERGROUND SAFE-HOUSES

Some people on the parental abduction scene are convinced that the legal and social service systems offer little or no hope of a safe and fair resolution to some family problems. Some of these people become involved in helping abducting parents hide while they are on the run through what is variously called an underground railroad, a network of safe-houses, or just "the underground." In our study, almost one-quarter of the searching parents suspected or were certain that the underground had assisted the abductor. This underground is not one network but many, and while some of the people involved, (such as Faye Yager, who is considered the founder of the underground) have gained fame or notoriety,[34] others try to remain as invisible as possible. The cause taken up most vigorously by underground advocates is that of women and children fleeing alleged abuse, particularly sexual abuse of children.[35] According to Pennington, writing from her perspective as an attorney:

> Typically when women go underground, they do so after months or years of litigation, in cases involving allegations of child sexual abuse by fathers. Mothers usually resort to hiding only after the courts have failed to believe their claims of sexual abuse. . . . Women go into hiding by themselves, with help from friends or family or with the help of an organized network.[36]

We have also been told that other networks help fathers who believe they could never get a fair custody hearing by working through the legal system.

There are perhaps a handful of loosely organized networks of safe-houses that help parents in such situations. An individualized network may spring into action for a particular parent and child and may later hide another or even a few more families known to those connected with the first case. Some situations of children concealed from searching parents have gained notoriety through press coverage of their disappearance and of the legal consequences suffered by those who have hidden them.[37]

What motivates people to break the law and risk serious consequences for their own lives on behalf not of loved ones but of people who are strangers to them? The rescuers often act out of a strong identification with the experiences of those they see as victimized: Many who help feel that they also have suffered injustice at the hands of the civil court system that hears child custody matters; others identify with different aspects of the fleeing parent's experience, such as the battering or sexual abuse; and some tend to believe that one gender, the one they help, is always disadvantaged in child custody disputes, that the system is inherently biased. Some are galvanized first by what they see as an extreme miscarriage of justice in a particular situation, and they stay involved to help others whose situations may or may not be similar. Those who seem to seek publicity and visibility are outnumbered by others who guard their privacy.

Whatever motivates them, the people who become involved in hiding abducting parents believe that they are acting righteously. As the names given to this movement suggest, they feel they are as justified as those who helped fleeing slaves on the underground railroad or those who help the undocumented people in the sanctuary movement. Although some participants in the underground for abducting parents justify their actions as civil disobedience,[38] other members of society condemn their motivations and actions.[39] Law enforcement and court personnel view their actions as contributing to disrespect for the law, and those who aid abductors can be prosecuted.

One of the abductions we learned about firsthand (i.e., from someone who had helped a fleeing mother) involved a young Mississippi girl named Chrissy, whose story has been widely reported in the press as follows:[40] A divorce in 1984 resulted in custody of two-year-old Chrissy being given to her mother, with visitation rights being granted to her father. Suspicions and allegations of sexual abuse by the father surfaced, and the mother was held in contempt of court when she resisted visitation. Later, when even more substantial time with Chrissy was granted to the father by the court, the mother, after failing to get medical evaluations of the child admitted as evidence of the sexual abuse, fled the state with her young daughter. Chrissy's mother, still in hiding, then died suddenly, perhaps of an aneurysm. A court in another state ordered Chrissy, in hiding with friends of the mother, returned to Mississippi, and there the original judge placed Chrissy with her father, where she remains today.

What is remarkable about this story, which is well known among those who sympathize with abductors fleeing abuse, is that a federal court recently ordered a new custody hearing under a different judge, ruling that the previous process surrounding custody had violated Chrissy's constitutional rights. This unusual outcome arose from a finding by the federal court that the custody proceedings were "woefully short of those basic features which mark an adequate adjudicatory proceeding."[41] If upheld after a possible appeal, this case will extend the protection of children's rights in custody hearings.

Religious Abductions

When a parent abducts, he or she usually is acting individually or with the support of one or two friends or family members. Abductions have also been known to occur among religious subcultures in the United States, such as Mormons, Hassidic Jews, and the Amish. In these cases, there is some sense of a community supporting the actions. What may precipitate the abduction is the granting of custody of a child by the court to one member of the community who wishes to leave the group and start a new life. In order to preserve the child as part of the community and to maintain the child's cultural upbringing, members of the community may work together to abduct and hide the child from the custodial parent and the authorities. The incidence of this type of abduction is difficult to document.

Satanic Cults and Abduction

In interviewing people for this book, we learned about a possible connection between parental abduction and satanic cults, where, it is feared, children are involved in ritualized abuse, group sex, and even human sacrifice. References to allegations that ritual abuse occurs in the context of parental abduction also have appeared in the popular press, for example, in stories about participants in the underground railroad.[42] Suspicions about a link between abduction and cults surface on both sides of the issue: Some who help abductors allege that the parents are fleeing bizarre forms of child maltreatment whereas some who aid searching parents suspect that underground networks of safe houses are linked to cults and endanger the children they purport to help.

It is difficult to evaluate these claims, and our own research turned up no allegations by searching or abducting parents concerning satanic cults. The belief that they exist and pose a threat to abducted children may have several deeply buried roots: First, belief in satanism may be the ultimate way to give form and a name to the unknown dangers that some people fear threaten vulnerable children. Second, since an aura of righteousness adheres to anyone contending with evil, allegations about suspicious cults may win sympathy and help. Finally, "cult" may be a convenient label for unpopular or poorly understood lifestyles. For example, we have heard satanism linked to communes, Eastern religious philosophies, Cuban drug traffickers, and lesbians. Despite rumors connecting satanism with child abduction, a recent column in a news journal in Texas, where concern about these issues seems to run especially high, concluded with the following statement: "Claims that organized devil worshippers are kidnapping or buying babies for sacrifice have not been substantiated by any law enforcement agency . . . in the U.S. or anywhere else."[43] Law enforcement officers charged with investigating ritual abuse and sacrifice, as well as others interested in the matter, have come to similar conclusions.[44] Most charges of cult involvement in parental abduction appear to be a new chapter in the cultural mythology that grows out of fear for the safety of children. However, the suspicions persist.

CONCLUSIONS

The four abductors highlighted in this chapter are not unusual people one could pick out of a crowd immediately, but they became desperate people. Even though separation and divorce have become quite common, their experiences place them on the extreme end of the divorce continuum. Sorting out motivations in an abduction is a difficult and complex task; consistent with what we described in Chapter 2, no single profile of the abductor exists. Parents who abduct are motivated by a range of reasons, some seemingly noble and others clearly egocentric, such as when the child is being used as a pawn in a marital dispute. Rarely is a child snatching carried out with a clear intent to harm the child.

The abductors we have profiled each had unique reasons for their actions. Nick and Connie, a noncustodial and a custodial parent who abducted, respectively, were motivated by years of frustration with the court system and by reports of sexual abuse. Nick, Cathy, and Dan were upset by the way their children were being raised, by the messages the children were being given about life. Nick believed his children were being raised as recluses; Cathy felt her children were being poisoned against her; and Dan was convinced that Ruth would be raised to deal passively, rather than actively, with life's demands. Nick and Cathy believed a form of emotional abuse was occurring. Only Cathy appears to have been motivated by an unresolved loss: that of her mother. When she felt her children being pulled into the same emotional vortex that drained her of her own mother's love and attention, she acted.

Life on the run for these four parents lasted from four months to 12 years. For Cathy, Dan, and Connie, who were in hiding for over a year, social life came to a near halt. For Cathy and Connie, not socializing was a matter of self-protection whereas for Dan it may have been a means of justifying his own actions; that is, by setting high standards for the parenting abilities of the women he might date, Dan reinforced his self-image as a parent with high standards. Because of the brief nature of Nick's abduction and his guardedness, it was more difficult to draw a profile of him.

The work histories of the four parents varied. For Cathy and Dan, both of whom stayed in the United States, new careers began. Connie was blocked from employment by lack of a work visa until she was able to start working in the Philippines. Cathy worked out of economic necessity, and Connie worked as a way to fill her day and provide some extra income. Especially for Dan, work became a way of defining success on the run and shedding the label of bum; whether this is a male trait or something attributable to Dan's poor work history prior to the abduction is hard to tell.

The men in our case histories differed from the women in their history of violence and substance abuse. While this makes them typical of the male abductors described in some other studies, they seem at the same time, more driven by a desire to be with their children than is true of the abducting fathers described elsewhere. As mentioned in Chapter 2, men often are perceived to be motivated to abduct for their own selfish reasons, rather than out of a desire to be with their children; men are not generally viewed in society as being caretakers. Dan, at least, challenges that assumption.

All the parents in our case histories felt their relationships with their children blossomed during the abduction. For most, this was a period where the abductors emerged fully into the role of parent, giving their children literally everything they had. What better way to show that they would love and protect their children than to focus their total existence on them?

Since Connie, Cathy, and Nick's children were recovered, they have had much less contact with them than before they abducted.

Connie lost sole custody, and both she and Cathy have only limited, supervised visitation. Nick has custody now of the one child he did not abduct. In Dan's case, Ruth has grown up and moved on with her life. Despite their current losses, the parents do not regret having abducted. The time with their children was valuable. Not to have acted in the face of what they perceived were wrongdoings would have wreaked a different kind of havoc on their lives.

It is this last point that is so crucial to understanding the behavior of some of the abductors. What does a parent do when, correctly or incorrectly, she or he perceives some wrong—in some cases, harm—being inflicted upon the child? This is the question that haunted these parents before they acted illegally. It is also a question that haunted over half of the 86 parents in one study who were *contemplating* abduction because they believed their child was at risk.[45]

These parents did act illegally and their children may have suffered for it. However, the abducting parents who told us willingly of their experiences were usually able to see themselves in a favorable light, and they may in fact have been motivated differently from abductors who are more reticent. Some abductors do commit additional crimes when their children are abducted; some do abuse them physically, emotionally, and sexually. The harm inflicted on the children by some abductors is well documented in the next chapter. As compelling as the individual stories of abductors may be, they have, through their actions, placed themselves above the law, posing a complex challenge to society as it attempts to respond to parental abduction of children.

CHAPTER 4

How Parents
Recover Their
Children

This chapter considers the parent who recovers and describes how recovery happens. We discuss how certain types of abductions are more likely to end in recovery than others. The gender of the searching parent may be one factor in how likely a parent is to recover.

The vast majority of abductions in the United States are short-term, resolved within a week. Only 10% last a month or more, according to one national survey.[1] Short-term, or "weekend," abductions take a toll on families, but it is usually not as severe as the toll associated with long-term abductions. In our research 45% of the cases were resolved by the time the parent completed the questionnaire and another 25% recovered their children by the time we spoke with them, usually within the next 15 months. At the time of the initial survey, the average length of time recovered children were missing was 1.6 years while the length of time of the unresolved abductions was 4.1 years.

Whereas the pain and sense of loss experienced by a parent whose child is abducted are excruciating, the feelings of a parent whose child has been recovered are more complex. He or she has

101

struggled with the loss and has gone on to experience, in most cases, joy at recovery. We have heard wonderful tales of parent and child running through airports to hug each other, tearful reunions in the back of police stations, phone calls where parent and child who have not spoken to each other in years babble for hours, and large neighborhood and family parties that receive local media coverage. But recovery does not always bring joy. Sometimes, it brings added pain or new frustration. If the recovery comes after a relatively long abduction, other problems usually present themselves. The child may not remember the parent left behind (as in Ava's situation, a case we introduce in this chapter and continue in Chapter 5) or may want to remain with the abductor. The child may return in a troubled state and need therapy. The parent, after recovery, may live for years with the threat of another abduction. Depending upon the age of the child, there may be anger on the recovering parent's part (like that described by Sandy in Chapter 3 when she wonders why her daughter, Ruth, did not contact her). Occasionally, recovery is only temporary: If the child was missing for a long period, he or she may choose to return to the abductor (in one situation the court supported this outcome, angering the parent sufficiently that he threatened to harm the judge who made the decision).

Regardless of the difficulties the parent and child encounter in reestablishing their relationship, the parent who recovers becomes a beacon of hope for other left-behind parents. Stories of their recoveries are circulated at missing children's organizations or by police authorities involved in abduction work. Searching parents call them for advice. Some parents who have recovered stay in touch with different organizations, participate in studies like ours, and look for ways to help other searching parents. They say that staying involved lets them return in some measure the aid they received when searching. Not all parents who recover want this kind of attention. Some withdraw from helping others because continuing to work in the area is too painful.

WHO RECOVERS

For many parents, recovering their child appears to be a miraculous twist of good luck. Some mystical event, perhaps a dream or a vision, gives them the impetus to contact someone they had not reached before in their recovery efforts, and that new contact proves successful. For other parents it is their continuing pressure on legal authorities that helps uncover a new lead. And for still others it is their own conscientious efforts to locate the child that pay off. It is important to state that many parents pursue all the appropriate avenues in their attempts to recover and never succeed whereas others recover with much less work. Among our sample, there was no relationship between the number of sources contacted for help and success in recovery. Parents should not feel they have failed if they have not recovered. In many situations outcome clearly is beyond their control.

Research has found that parents suffer from the abduction in terms of the level of stress they experience. While stress diminishes upon recovery, the parent generally does not return quickly to the preabduction level of functioning.[2] Attempts to recover can be quite frustrating. Janvier and her colleagues report that many agencies set up to assist in recovery, particularly the FBI, were perceived by searching parents as unhelpful.[3] But this frustration, as well as stress at being separated from the child and concern about the child's well-being, are not the only issues the parent confronts. There is also the financial burden. Janvier reports that the average cost of recovery attempts was more than $25,000 for international abductions and over $8,000 for domestic abductions.[4] More often than not, the money was spent in vain; in Janvier's study parents who recover were in the minority. The same study cited five problems that hinder attempts to recover: "lack of clues to the child's whereabouts; lack of money to conduct a private search; low priority assigned parental kidnappings by law enforcement; lack of search efforts by police agencies; and inconsistencies in state laws."[5]

One searching father we interviewed, Glenn, ran into a few of these impediments in his attempts to locate his four-year-old abducted daughter. His situation also exemplifies the burden placed on searching parents to integrate their attempts to recover with the rest of their lifestyle. Glenn began dating, and then married a prostitute of Dutch nationality, who had moved to St. Louis. Their marriage was stormy from the start, with Glenn admitting to being both the perpetrator and victim of domestic violence. When his wife ran off with their daughter, Glenn had no idea where she had gone. He says that in the first few weeks they were gone he searched for them literally all of the time. The police were not particularly interested in helping him, but because he worked for a credit union he had numerous contacts that enabled him to gain access to information that would normally be difficult to obtain. He became obsessed with tracking down every computer lead he could follow. Despite becoming an expert on the laws concerning abduction, he ran up an enormous legal bill—over $100,000.

Glenn finally traced his daughter and wife to Amsterdam and arranged privately to have his daughter abducted and whisked back to the United States. His wife caught wind of the plot at the last minute, changed her daily routine, and vanished. The Dutch authorities were not interested in helping an American, and Glenn was back to square one.

As is true of many searching parents, attempts to recover had completely taken over Glenn's life. He missed his daughter terribly. Moreover, he was still reeling from the loss of his marriage, and his work was suffering. By the time his daughter had been missing for nine months, Glenn decided he had to change something. How much longer could he gear his total existence to searching before it destroyed him? he wondered. However, the thought of abandoning a full-time search made him feel terribly guilty. If he thought his daughter was in some danger, how could he not continue to turn over every stone in an attempt to find her? Yet he needed to find some normalcy for himself. Glenn vowed to spend one hour every day involved in helping himself or other parents recover. Involvement included attending a support group for parents left behind, teaching others about the search process, or continuing efforts on his own behalf. Since he made that vow, Glenn has found a little more peace, though he is far from being a happy person. His major efforts at recovery now involve periodic checks with all of the legal and personal contacts he thinks may help him eventually locate his child in the Netherlands.

In our study of parents who had sought help from missing children's organizations, almost all (93%) also had contacted the police for assistance in recovering their missing children. Other common sources of help were lawyers (81%), the FBI (62%), social service agencies (56%), and private investigators (51%). The typical searching parent contacted at least five different resources and spent about $10,000. Usually, attempts to get help in locating the missing child were swift; 71% of the parents contacted authorities within 24 hours after the child was missing. Another

15% contacted authorities within the week. Parents who did not seek help immediately most likely did not know the child was missing; this is often the case when abductions begin during periods of extended visitation.

Perhaps the most intriguing finding concerning who recovers has to do with gender. We first found that women are more apt to recover than men,[6] a situation due partly to more women than men in our sample having sole legal custody at the time of the abduction. Parents having sole custody were more apt to recover than those without it.[7] This is understandable since these parents can obtain assistance in their search from law enforcement and missing children's organizations more readily than those sharing custody during marriage or after divorce or those having only visitation rights.

What was most intriguing, though, was the finding that of the parents left behind, women with sole custody at the time of the abduction were more apt to recover their children than men with sole custody.[8] With the caveat that our sample is not representative of all parents involved in abductions, this finding leads to the formulation of some interesting hypotheses about the recovery process. One possible explanation for why custodial mothers are more apt to recover their child is that authorities, friends, relatives, child search organizations, and interested parties may work harder to assist searching women than searching men in that they may feel they are supporting the role of women in a society that views children as being the primary responsibility of their mothers.[9] The father may have to plead his case more strenuously than would a mother to convince those in a position to help that he deserves to have contact with his children. While both police and missing children's organizations deny that they assist mothers more than fathers, there was the perception among some of the men we interviewed that some of those organizations that are dominated by women work harder for mothers than for fathers.

A second explanation is linked to the first: women may pursue custody harder than men in part because of the societal pressure just described. Although mothers and fathers both may feel great loss at being separated from their children, society's pressures are brought to bear more on women than on men without custody. Earlier work by one of us (G.G.) found that noncustodial mothers received more negative criticism from others than did noncustodial fathers,[10] another reflection of the cultural reality that our society views mothers as the primary caregiver for children. It also may be that the underground (see Chapter 3) makes abducting women harder to locate than abducting men; women have an extra resource that most men on the run do not have.[11]

Another cultural reality that affects women and men in the search process also may help explain the higher rates of recovery for women: Male abductors have histories of much higher levels of violence in the marriage than do female abductors (discussed in Chapter 3). Consequently, searching mothers are much more likely than fathers to fear for the safety of their abducted children. In general, fathers may be less concerned about the welfare of their children; searching fathers are more apt to believe that the abducting parent has acted out of a desire to be with the children than are searching mothers, who are more apt to see the abduction as aimed at hurting the children. These feelings may motivate women to redouble their search efforts. They probably also influence those in a position to help. People working in the field may have a heightened index of suspicion about both abducting fathers and searching fathers because of the high incidence of spouse abuse and child sexual abuse perpetrated by men. This brush tars those fathers who have not been abusive.

Despite the cultural realities and forces that impact differently on searching fathers and mothers, not all mothers receive blanket support for their attempts to reunite with their children. One mother described her experience when she went to the police for help: "They looked at me like, what kind of a mother was I that the father would have to kidnap the child away from me. I found them to be very negative to me because I was a woman." Interviews with advocates for women also confirm our impressions that many mothers feel disempowered in the search process, particularly if the father has greater financial resources.

In addition to gender, the amount of emotional support searching parents receive from different people is also related to recovery. Parents who recovered found neighbors, clergy, lawyers, child find organizations, social services, local police, and the FBI to be more supportive of them than did parents who had not recovered.[12] It is unclear whether the support of such groups and individuals is a catalyst in spurring the parent on to recover. It is also unclear if the lawyers, FBI, and local police are viewed as being more supportive in retrospect after the recovery. Parents who have not recovered naturally may feel that those people who were supposed to help them were less supportive.

Other variables associated with a greater likelihood of recovery are related to the characteristics of the abductor or the relationship between abductor and searching parent. For example, recovery in our sample was somewhat more likely if the abductor had not completed any schooling past high school.[13] One possible explanation for this is that people with less education may have fewer job opportunities open to them when they go on the run. They also may have less money to draw on to sustain themselves than abductors with more education. Recovery in our sample also occurred more often if the abductor had been violent in the marriage and if he or she had been treated for an alcohol problem.[14] In these situations the potential for violence may spur the authorities to work harder toward location and recovery, and there may already be a police record, making it easier to mobilize intervention. Family violence also may be associated with the more impetuous abductors, who are less likely to have planned the abduction. Finally, abductors charged with child abuse may be less interested in the well-being of the child at the time of the abduction and more interested in getting revenge or using the child for another purpose. Thus, the overall picture when there is recovery is of an abductor who is less well educated, has been violent, has an alcohol problem, and is less likely to be committed to caring for the child. Drawing on our typology of five abduction patterns, it is abductions by violent visitors that are most apt to end in recovery.[15] Custodial abductions result in recovery less frequently than do other patterns.[16] This may be because that pattern does not fit the legal definition of abduction in most states and involving authorities in the search is therefore much more difficult.

In our study, some interesting facets of the life of the parent left behind were unrelated to recovery. For example, having a higher income was not linked to recovering a child; it may be that the obvious advantages that money can buy in mounting a search may be offset by the advantages of a wealthy abductor in continuing to hide. In addition, the age of the child was unrelated to recovery; younger children were no more apt to be recovered than older children.

Also of interest were findings concerning the sources of help contacted to resolve the abduction. The parents who recovered their children were not significantly different from those who did not recover in the assistance they sought. Specifically, of the 190 parents (out of 371) who contacted a private detective for help with recovery, 49% had recovered and 51% had not. Similar breakdowns appeared for those who contacted the FBI, social service agencies, and police; those who contacted a lawyer had a slightly increased chance of recovery.[17] This is not to say that parents were not helped by contacting others; they definitely were. Rather, the data show that no one source of help provides a reliable predictor of whether a child will be recovered.

Finally, and this speaks further to the life of the searching parent, those who sought mental health–related services before the abduction were no less likely to have recovered their child than those who did not. No consistent relationship was found between recovery and whether a searching parent had a history of treatment for depression, anxiety, alcoholism, spouse abuse, and so on.

In summarizing who recovers children and who does not, we can establish key characteristics in the relationship between the parent left behind and the abductor. Parents who have sole legal custody at the time of the abduction are more apt to recover, as are women in general. If the marital relationship has been a violent one or if the abductor is not highly educated or has had a history of alcohol or child abuse, recovery is more likely. For the parent left behind, his or her mental state before the abduction, as indicated by whether counseling help was sought for a particular problem, is not related to recovery whereas receiving assistance in the search from a variety of people is related only to a very limited extent.

In the previous chapters we established five patterns of abduction based on custody status and history of violence. In this chapter we see that custody, violence, and gender continue to be meaningful factors when considering who recovers. We learned here that parents with custody, particularly women, tend to recover and that violent abductors tend to be less successful; therefore, violent visitor abductions are less often successful. The custodial abductions, where the parent who snatches has custody and is most often female, are the ones where recovery is least likely. Here, the parent left behind is noncustodial and likely to be male, characteristics that are not highly associated with recovery.

In the nonviolent visitor abduction, the parent left behind, usually a male, has custody and there has been no violence, a combination of factors that makes a prediction of recovery problematic.[17] In abductions where custody is shared and no violence has been reported, the abductors are overwhelmingly female (and, we suspect, violence by the parents left behind may be underreported); in this pattern there is a tendency for the child not to be recovered.[18] Finally, the violent shared custody abductions are exactly evenly divided between those who recover and those who do not. In these abductions, the abductor is slightly more apt to be male and to have been violent, qualities linked to recovery. Yet he was also sharing custody at the time of the abduction, a fact that, as we discussed, makes legal authorities in some jurisdictions less apt to pursue him.

The Case of Ava:

A BATTERED WOMAN WHO TOOK, LOST, AND THEN RECOVERED HER CHILDREN

The following story illustrates many of the complexities involved in abduction and recovery. It involves first what we would characterize as a nonviolent shared custodial abduction by a woman who was being battered but was not violent herself. This abduction was followed by an abduction by her violent husband, who still shared custody with her. Four years passed before the woman recovered her children, who no longer remembered her and had been told she was dead.

"I live in constant fear that he will find us and snatch the kids again. He is a violent man who is capable of anything." Ava leans toward us as she speaks. Her voice is soft. The children have left the room to play, and she does not want them to hear her discussing their father, her ex-husband. Ava is in her early thirties, of medium height with long dark hair. Now living in a condominium community of modest houses 75 miles from San Francisco, she slowly unfolds her life story for us, as if she were unveiling an ancient treasure. Her life has been anything but happy. But, finally, within the last few weeks she has begun to find happiness, though it is tinged with fear of the danger that she feels awaits her when her ex-husband is released from prison. Ava is obsessed with the idea that he will try to find her. It is spring and his release is 18 months away. Such terror typifies many of the women we interviewed. They are convinced that the fathers of their children will ignore any existing court orders and abduct, harass, or do physical harm to their children, friends, and family. Without specific evidence of such a threat, the legal authorities can do little to reassure.

Ava was raised in Ann Arbor, Michigan, the youngest of four in a working-class family. Though it sounds like a cliché, Ava believes she was the child whose birth was supposed to save her parents' marriage. As is often the case when parents pin such hopes on a child, the plan did not work. Two years later, the marriage ended. Her father's infidelity was the last straw for Ava's mother, who felt she had put up with a mountain of injustices. This act of infidelity would come back to haunt Ava's own life. A pattern was begun where women in the family were abused either psychologically or physically by the men they loved.

When her father moved out, Ava and her three siblings remained in the home with their mother, for whom the strain of the breakup and the unrelenting pressures of raising four children alone was too much. "My mom snapped and they had to put her away in a hospital for a while," Ava recounted. "We all went to live with my father until my mother was better. When she came out of the home, my sister and I went back with her while my brothers stayed with my father."

Despite this emotional upheaval, the next few years were relatively placid ones for Ava. Living near the campus of the University of Michigan in the early 1970s was exciting, especially for an impressionable adolescent. Drugs were freely available in her junior high school, and Ava and her friends experimented with them. Ava's home life took a turn for the worse when her mother remarried. Ava's father had died a year before in a car accident, and her need for a father figure was great. But her stepfather turned out to be an alcoholic who physically and sexually abused Ava and her 18-year-old sister. The sister immediately moved out, leaving 12-year-old Ava with little protection. Her mother, still weakened by her earlier emotional breakdown, was unequal to the task of standing between her new husband and her daughter. Ava's only hope of survival was to leave. When she was 14, she packed her bag and moved in with her sister. Her mother made no attempt to stop her.

Life in the two rooms they shared in a big rooming house near the campus was every teenager's fantasy and every parent's nightmare. Drug use and casual sex were the norm, and the sisters moved from one party to the next. When she was 15, Ava dropped out of high school and, lying about her age, started working for an insurance company. "I had to support myself. My sister was working also, but she needed her money. I found I really liked working and was very good at helping to run the office." Over the next few years her career shot ahead, and she became office manager. She and her sister moved out of the party atmosphere in their rooming house and into an apartment.

When she was 17, Ava met Ralph. He was five years older than she, a salesman with a steady position and very good-looking. He treated her in a way that no other man had—with respect.

> He did not push me to have sex with him. I had not dated much, but when I did I seemed to attract aggressive guys. He was different. He told me very clearly he would be there to take care of me in case anything happened. We wouldn't see each other for a few months but he would always call to make sure I was okay. Up to that point I had been totally on my own.
>
> The stresses were really getting to me, paying the rent, making car payments, and so on. I would take a glass of wine to make the stress go away. Then I would drink more and more. He came back around again, and we started to date more seriously. It was clear he was offering me a sense of family, which I had not had for a long time, and that he was going to take care of me in a way that my parents could not. I knew I didn't love him, though.

The attraction Ava felt for Ralph could have been predicted. She had seen her mother abused by two men, and she felt alienated from her family. Ralph offered a strong shoulder and the chance to have a healthy relationship with a man. To some, having security is more important than being head over heels in love. For Ava, the spark was never there, but Ralph made her feel safe.

When she was 19, Ava and Ralph drove to Reno on the spur of the moment and were married there: "Basically I woke up and found I was married. I had too much to drink the night before. I made a vow to stay married to him and make things work out. I knew I had made one mistake by marrying him and did not want to make a second mistake by getting a divorce as my mother had done."

When they drove back to Ann Arbor after three days of honeymooning, Ava and Ralph settled into the routine of happily married newlyweds—but only for two months. Ava immediately became pregnant. For her, pregnancy was like having gasoline poured on a smoldering fire; it created a fierce destructive flame where none had existed, and as it burned, it began to eat away at everything in its path.

> Ralph and I began fighting constantly. He would scream at me for every little thing I would do. It was awful. He was like a different person. I had seen my father act this way with my mom and thought it was just him. Now I saw it could be the same with other men. At first I thought maybe I'm not doing something right. Maybe if I scrub the walls harder or vacuum better, things will work out. I blamed myself. Then, I prayed he would change. Of course, he didn't. He began going out at night, and when I was six months pregnant he was unfaithful. I found out from a friend. Then I prayed that having a baby would change things.

But when Ava went into the hospital to give birth, Ralph went on a three-day drinking binge, barely getting home at the time she and their new son, David, arrived from the hospital.

The first year of Ava and Ralph's marriage was a template of the years that were to follow. A cycle was established. Ava would attempt to please Ralph and would find herself severely physically and psychologically victimized. She would then build up her hopes that Ralph would change. First, she believed that her improved cleaning would change him; then it was the birth of David. Yet each promise or prayer for change invariably was followed by a painful disappointment. With her hands full, Ava turned to her mother for help for the first time in years. "I didn't know what to do with Ralph drinking and a new baby. But when I called my mom, all she could say was, 'That's just the way men are.' I knew I was going to have to go it alone then." It was also about that time that Ralph began taking speed, an amphetamine that affects the user's personality, giving him a great deal of energy but producing terrible lows when it wears off.

When Ralph was not using speed, Ava would talk to him about getting help and straightening out his life. He invariably would have periods of remorse during which he would return to work and promise that things would get better between them. Ava admits:

> I felt sorry for him. I did not want to leave him because of that. Also I just wanted things to be normal. I had not had a normal life, and I still hoped that I could have one with him. There was, and still is, a part of him that wants to get better and can be good. But something in him just snapped between my pregnancy and his getting into drugs. He became very possessive of me. He did not want me to go out with any of my friends. We moved into a deserted area in the woods. He wanted me to stay home and get pregnant again while he went out.

A daughter, Susan, was born a year later. Her birth did not change the rapidly disintegrating marital relationship, as Ava had prayed David's birth would. In fact, raising two children restricted Ava even more, and Ralph continued to insist that she stay home. His drug abuse resumed despite promises to the contrary, and he began to abuse her physically and psychologically. A large man, it was easy for Ralph to intimidate and hurt Ava. Being screamed at to stay home, not allowed to see any of her friends, occasionally being beaten, Ava felt she was living out her worst nightmare. Although the children were never directly abused by Ralph, they would get hurt every so often if they got in the way of his violence toward Ava. For example, Ralph once threw a television at Ava and it nicked David.

The fervent vow Ava made three years earlier in Reno to make the marriage work could no longer be kept. Why did it take so long for her to decide to leave? One reason was the magical thinking that something would change in Ralph, that he would go back to the way he was when they were courting. Another reason had to do with her wish to give her children two parents and a more stable home life than she had had. Finally, Ava had been scared to leave a situation where there was food on the table and a roof over her head.

When Ralph left on his next sales trip, Ava picked up the

children and ran for her mother's. "I just decided, and maybe it was with the help of God, that I had to get out of there if I was going to survive as a person and be someone for my children."

Ralph found them immediately and forced all three of them home in the middle of the night. In Ava's own words:

> These guys [abusive husbands] always seem to know where you are. He hired a friend to drive while he wrapped us up in a blanket, brought us back to the house and started to beat me for three days. He broke my jaw with a broomstick and I had a gash in my head. I must have passed out because I don't know what happened to the kids. Then he tied me up and locked me in a closet. I was able to finally escape and hobbled over to a neighbor's house. They saw how bloody I was, and I was begging them to call the police when he drove up. He put me back in the house and the neighbors never did call anyone. He was worried, though, after that. It was like the cat was out of the bag and he didn't beat me as much for a while. He told me if I called the police he would kill me. That's when I made plans to escape again.
>
> This time I left the state. I went to a shelter in Chicago, and that is when things started to turn around for me. I learned an incredible amount there. I learned that I had a spirit and a joy in me that he could not take away no matter how much he beat me. These guys can wipe you out if you don't keep your spirit. I was just so terrified of him. I knew I had to get out into the world to find out I was okay, and the shelter helped me with that. I got a job as a saleslady in a department store and began taking care of myself for the first time in years. I was doing fine until he found me.

How Ava was discovered six months later is one of those stories of bad luck that seemed to characterize her early life: Ralph's brother, shopping in the department store, recognized her. Ralph arrived three days later, begging for a reconciliation. He again promised to change, that things would be different if she would come home. This time—and it was a major turning point for her—she held firm. Ava told him she wanted a divorce. What she got was much more:

> I told him I was not trying to take away his kids but that I did want the marriage to end. He agreed as long as he could visit them.

David's birthday was coming up the next week, so I agreed that he could see him for the day. We arranged for a pickup in a parking lot because I still did not want him to know where we lived. When I arrived with both kids in the car, he punched me out and stole them.

Ava was shocked. She knew Ralph loved them in his own way, but she had never considered the possibility that he would just take the children. He had never changed a diaper and had never shown any great interest in the children. Ava later learned that some people abduct because when threatened with the loss of their family, they grasp for control of the only people who give them unconditional love: young children who idolize their parents. For Ralph, the ultimate rejection was hearing that Ava no longer wanted to be married to him. Despite all their battles, he had managed to delude himself, perhaps with the aid of drugs, into believing that she would return. Now he had to get back some vestige of love from someone; the children seemed to be his surest source.

Ralph left the state with David and Susan and went to a small town in Wisconsin. Ava immediately called the police, but because she did not have a custody order, Ralph was not breaking any law. Although he had struck first that time, he had as much right to the children as she did. She was stuck. She did not know where they were and could not get any help in recovering them.

It was at this time that she began to date the man who would become her second husband. Carl was a high school teacher whom Ava had met through a friend. "He was the kind of guy who seemed to attract kids in trouble," Ava said.

He was always taking care of people who were coming to him with their problems. I didn't even tell him at first that I had children and that they had been kidnapped. It wasn't until we had been dating for six weeks that I finally told him. He was great about it. He hugged me and told me everything would be okay. He was not scared off by Ralph. That really deepened things between us. It was the first time I had found a man I could trust.

Four months after the abduction, Ava located the children. A cousin of Ralph's broke a promise she made to him and revealed they were in Wisconsin. Knowing that much, Ava became obsessed with getting them back. She and Carl made plans to kidnap them. Once the children were in her possession, she intended to get custody papers drawn up that would make it illegal for Ralph to take them.

With the cooperation of the sitter in Wisconsin who was taking care of the children during the day, Ava and Carl snatched the children while Ralph was working. They drove through the night and returned to Carl's apartment, where they set up house together. Carl and the children hit it off immediately. But this honeymoon period was short-lived; a woman with whom Ralph had had an affair while he was still married to Ava let him know their whereabouts. Ralph drove back from Wisconsin and kidnapped the children again. Then he "stalked" Ava with a gun for two weeks, threatening to kill her. She was terrified.

> I tried to talk to him. I said he could have joint custody if he would bring them back to me. I couldn't believe that he would keep them. I was sure that being a man he would find it impossible to raise two young children and that he would turn them back over to me. This went on for months. I had no idea where he was living, and I was not seeing the children. Then he stopped communicating with me. I began calling every missing children's organization in the area. It was still no help. Finally, I was just going crazy. To keep me sane, Carl sent me out to the west coast to be with some old friends of his who could help get me settled.

When Ava arrived in California, her life was a mess. She had no job and had begun drinking heavily to numb the pain of being away from her children. Luckily, she was able to find work quickly:

> I went back into retail where I was supervising a sales force. This time all these young girls were coming to me for help. But I went through a bad period of drinking. I cried and hid all the time when I wasn't forcing myself out to go to work. I just couldn't stand the pain of not having my babies, and I had to drink to take it away. Finally, I realized I was not doing myself or anyone any good. When I came to that realization, I was able to then turn my life over to God and trust that He would take care of my babies until they came back to me. I prayed that I would at least have them back by the

time they were 16 so I could undo some of the damage that I thought was being done. Trusting in God helped me put some order into my life.

A few months later Carl moved out west to join her, and they were married; a divorce from Ralph had been granted on grounds of desertion. Ava immediately wanted to have another baby and became pregnant within the first few months of the marriage. A daughter was born close to their first anniversary. However, having one child was not enough to ease the pain of not seeing Susan and David. Ava still cried herself to sleep at night, worrying about them and praying that they would be taken care of. As the months added up to years, she began to wonder if they would know her if they saw her. She would sometimes hallucinate that she saw them running away from her on the street or imagine that she caught a glimpse of them in a passing car. She stayed in contact with the police and missing children's organizations but ultimately believed that God was watching over them. Then one night, something broke:

> I was staying up and crying about how much I missed them and this little voice came to me and said, "Call Mary." She had been a friend in Chicago. So I called her in the middle of the night, worrying I was going to wake her up. She said, "I can't believe you called. I just heard where your children are. They are in a foster home!" It was at night so I had to wait until the morning to call the home.
>
> At first they wouldn't tell me anything. What had happened was Ralph was in jail and the children had been placed in these different foster homes. So I flew east. The foster care workers were shocked to see me. They and the children had been told first that I was dead and then that I was a prostitute and drug user. Then here I was looking like a normal mother. While there was a battle going on between the foster care people and me as to who the children belonged to, Ralph was released from jail and snatched David from the foster home. The workers hadn't known who to believe, but when he snatched David right out of the foster home, they knew. I was then able to get a court order to return custody to me, which set the stage for my getting them back. I had to go through a home study first, though [a process where a social worker and other

professionals evaluate a family to ensure that they are suitable to assume custody]. When I passed that test, the way was clear for me to get them.

Unfortunately, the story was not over. Susan was given to Ava, but David was still on the run with Ralph. Ava was ecstatic to be reunited with one of her children. As she describes it, seeing Susan again after four years was an incredible experience: "It was just like in the movies. We ran and hugged each other and were crying and everything. Carl was there and he was crying, too." Even though Susan did not remember Ava, it only took a few days before she began feeling comfortable with her. Her experiences in foster homes and with her father had been so unhappy that the relationship that Ava offered her easily washed away any hesitations she had about living with her mother.

It would be another six months before Ava would regain custody of David. After Ralph abducted him from the foster home, he drove to Canada. Life on the run was exciting to the young boy. He was trained not to trust the police and to avoid telling anyone his real name. There were also traumatic periods during which he was exposed to his father's drug taking, to pornographic movies, and to sexual abuse at the hands of a female sitter. Ralph and David finally were tracked down and caught after a high-speed car chase that ended with their car crashing into a barrier and David going through the windshield.

Ralph went to prison for five years on kidnapping, drug, and theft charges. David was placed in yet another foster home, and Ava was still unable to locate him. Reuniting mother and son was not easy because Ralph had changed David's name. In addition, the foster care system is often overburdened, making reunification a slow process. It was not surprising that Ava's continued efforts to find David were thwarted.

Consistent with Ava's improving fortunes, something lucky happened: Ralph, still in prison, had a change of heart. He was in contact with David in the foster home and learned that David was having severe emotional problems stemming from his sexual abuse and from his life on the run. Ralph contacted his brother about the situation, and his brother got in touch with Ava. Then it was only a matter of days before mother and son were reunited.

The reunion of Ava and her children and their life since then are discussed in the next chapter, where we describe the impact of abduction on children. From our presentation of her case we see a woman's need to escape from a violent relationship. We also see one possible result of her leaving with the children: the husband strikes back. The motives for each partner's actions depend upon the perspective with which each views the situation. Ralph might have rationalized while he was on the run that taking his children was the only way to protect himself and them from another abduction by Ava. This would have been a clear denial of his battering behavior and the effect such abuse had on Ava and the children. From a legal standpoint, too, the picture is complex. Criminal law in each state determines whether an abduction prior to a custody decree is a criminal offense. Because there was no court order in effect while the children were being snatched back and forth, neither parent committed abduction in a legal sense. Until Ava finally obtained custody, Ralph could take comfort in his legal right to have his children with him. Although Ava's attempt to protect herself and her children escalated into a cycle of child snatches, the unfortunate fact is that women in her position sometimes have little recourse but to leave with the children.

Recovery for Ava was due to a combination of factors. Susan's return was the result of her hearing the little voice that came to her in the middle of the night advising her to call Mary. To Ava this was a miracle born of her faith in God. David's return was more a matter of Ralph's change of heart and Ava's perseverance. For Ava the fear of another abduction is overwhelming. Her only hope is to get a court order that will block visitation and prevent Ralph from having access to his children. Yet to do even that—and Ava is unsure how successful she will be—Ralph will have to learn her general whereabouts. In the meantime, she enjoys every second with her children. She also tries to prepare them to contact her if they are abducted again.

GETTING THE CHILDREN BACK HOME

With Ava's story as a backdrop, we can look at other parents' experiences in their attempts to locate and recover their children. In the majority of cases, the police and FBI are involved in some, if not all, stages of the search. Often, the searching parent locates the child or has an approximate idea of the child's location and then convinces the police to search further or make an arrest. Occasionally, it is the police or FBI, with little assistance from the parent, that locates the child. Other circumstances also can lead to recovery: The searching parent may hire a private investigator, the abductor may turn the child in, or the searching parent may put pressure on a relative or friend of the abductor's to reveal the child's whereabouts. No matter the process, recovery first means locating the child and then arranging to bring the child back.

Location and recovery are either the result of a logical progression or a single event. As a logical progression, the parent left behind moves from one step to the next. The police are often the first ones contacted, followed by a lawyer, the FBI, social services, and a private investigator; friends and relatives who might know the whereabouts of the abductor also are approached. Many parents make attempts to interest missing children's organizations in including their children on mailings. As each new contact is made, the odds of locating and then recovering the child increase. Sometimes it is this cumulative process, a pattern that is frequently observed, that leads to the recovery, as some of the brief cases we describe in this chapter illustrate.

Recovery also occurs because of a single, sometimes unpredictable event. Something happens out of the blue that is not the result of any particular effort. For example, an event in the child's life may occur that results in the recovery, as in the case of Dan and Sandy in Chapter 3, where Ruth's acceptance into college convinced Dan to contact her mother. The searching parent may get a sudden vision and call a potential contact, as happened with Ava. These are the less predictable, but no less successful, events that result in recovery.

The National Center for Missing and Exploited Children has published a pamphlet that describes what to do if your child is abducted.[20] The pamphlet lists over 50 separate steps to take and agencies to contact for assistance in locating and recovering a missing child, including contacting alcohol and drug rehabilitation centers if the abductor was in treatment or in need of treatment; checking with the bank to see if money has been transferred elsewhere; calling colleges or other degree-conferring institutions to see if a request for a transcript has been made; compelling the lawyer of the abductor to release relevant information (only occasionally successful and depending upon the judge's view of privileged communication between attorney and client); contacting credit bureaus, credit card companies, post offices, and the state department of motor vehicles; reviewing an address and telephone cross-directory; following up with the abductor's insurance company; and involving the Federal Parent Locator Service, which is a national network under the aegis of the Office of Child Support Enforcement.

Some parents have tracked down their missing children by "thinking like a bill collector." Others advise contacting the National Crime Information Center, based in Washington, D.C., which lists people wanted for felonies and can help searchers locate abductors who are criminally charged.[21] With the huge number of children missing, the continuing refrain that we hear is that a parent must take charge of the search; otherwise, the process soon will be forgotten by the authorities.[22]

Once the child is located, parents often are cautioned against doing anything illegal to recover them. Working through the authorities is the best approach to making a recovery that will be viable in the long term. In addition, at least one service is available to help parents negotiate the return of a child without legal authorities necessarily being involved. Child Find of America (call 1-800-A-WAY-OUT) may be able to help mediate the return of the child if both parties are amenable.[23] This service assists by receiving calls from abductors who may be interested in resolving the situation. After a screening during which certain criteria are met, a professional family mediator, working for Child Find of America on a *pro bono* basis, will become involved with negotiating for the return of the child. In cases where warrants are outstanding against the abducting parent, entering the mediation process does not prejudice the left-behind parent's rights to have law enforcement officials search for the child, and Child Find of America does not guarantee the abductor that legal charges will be dropped. Mediations have been resolved within as short a period as 24 hours or may drag on for months. Over a three-year period, 31 children have been returned as a direct result of this program.

From extensive interviews with the parents left behind, we have found five other scenarios that describe most of the recoveries. These five involve recovery through (1) police or FBI efforts, (2) work by private investigators or a hired team, (3) the dissemination of posters that include the missing child's picture, (4) the abductor turning the child over voluntarily, and (5) the searching parent having a vision or intuition. In addition, a *guardian ad litem* may be appointed by the court to locate the missing child and to assist in bringing the child home and helping determine custody. Later in this chapter, one such *guardian ad litem,* Dr. Ken Lewis, provides an example from his work in locating and bringing a missing child home.

Police or FBI Efforts

The majority of recoveries occur because of the involvement of the police and FBI in enforcing a custody decree. In most of these situations, the searching parent has located the child and calls the police for help in arresting the abductor. Sometimes a missing children's organization has been instrumental in locating the child through anonymous tips they have received, through posters they have printed, or because of advice they have given to the searching parent. Occasionally, legal authorities have been the primary force in locating and taking the abductor and child into custody. This usually happens through the efforts of one detective or someone else on the force becoming especially interested in the case. A lack of knowledge by lawyers and judges about various federal and state laws has been cited as an obstacle in the location and return of abducted children.[24]

Parents' experiences with legal authorities in our study varied: Some parents reported that police were helpful from the beginning, others claimed authorities were reluctant to become involved in domestic matters until custody of the child was clearly established, and still others maintained that the police avoided involvement despite an existing custody decree. In approximately one-fifth of the cases where the police were a primary force in recovery, the abducting parent was being sought by the police for some reason other than the abduction. In one situation the abducting mother was suspected of being in possession of a large cache of weapons, which apparently spurred the police and FBI to become involved. In another situation a father was wanted for having gone on a crime spree after he abducted his child. In a third case the father was arrested for crossing an international border with a large amount of cash hidden on his body; when the border patrol ran a computer check on him, they discovered there were abduction charges pending and took the children into custody for return to their mother.

The following cases illustrate in detail how the police become involved and help with recovery. In both instances, the searching parents themselves located the abductors.

Case History

Tom's four-year marriage ended with an agreement giving him and his ex-wife joint custody of their three-year-old daughter. Two years later, after his ex-wife finished her tour of duty in the Navy, she abducted their daughter, then five. Tom called the police and a local child search organization. He suspected from the start that his ex-wife's parents, who were living in North Carolina, were assisting their daughter. Of the attorney he hired, Tom says, "[He was one] with political clout who got the police to treat it as a regular abduction, not a parental abduction. The Missing Person's Bureau in North Carolina told me who to contact." Tom was directed to the sheriff's department in the county in which the grandparents lived. They watched the house around the clock for two months until his ex-wife and daughter arrived late one night. They were arrested on the spot, and his daughter was returned.

Since the abduction Tom has agreed to allow his ex-wife frequent visitation. Although he fears she will abduct their daughter again, he says, "I allowed this amount of visitation because I was afraid the courts would be anti-male and give her back joint custody if I did not let her visit a lot."

In this case the parent was able to get the police involved by shifting the focus of the case away from a parental abduction. His own detective work narrowed his ex-wife's potential location, and he was able to direct the police to her. In the next case a similar cooperative effort was mounted by a searching mother and the Australian equivalent of the FBI.

Case History

Lauren had been unhappy with her marriage to Steve for a long time. High school sweethearts, their marriage fell into a pattern often seen when there is domestic violence. Steve would hit Lauren on occasion, then apologize profusely. He began abusing drugs and alcohol. After ten years in an abusive marriage, Lauren found the strength to flee with their two children to her parents' house. Steve rushed over the next day while she was at work and snatched them, starting a two-year period of running across the globe. During her search, Lauren contacted police, the FBI, and the missing children's network. She hired a lawyer and a private investigator. She even got in touch with Interpol and Scotland Yard.

Steve would call Lauren occasionally, tell her he had moved to Australia, and beg her to return to the marriage. At first, she did not believe he was really there until she had his call traced. Once she located him, she called him back and was pleasantly surprised when he answered the phone. She couldn't believe she had located him. He realized his blunder and moved out of the apartment he was renting. "But he had put the children in a school using their real name. I contacted the federal police there, who were excellent. They located my children in three days. Our FBI, with only one agent in that part of Australia, was no help."

Lauren and her children were reunited one week later. Almost like a relief pitcher coming out of the bull pen when the team is ahead, the police put the finishing touches on many situations set up by searching parents. It is their legal authority that finally ends the game.

Private Investigators' Work

While it is often parents who succeed in locating the child and the police who complete the recovery process, some parents in our sample spoke highly of the assistance they received from private investigators. These investigators usually charge on an hourly basis if the search is conducted within their office or within their own city. If they have to travel out of town to conduct a search, they may charge a per diem fee plus expenses. Their fees can run into the thousands of dollars as the search drags on, and it is, of course, the wealthier parents who are more likely to hire them.[25]

The private investigators often have contacts in distant cities where the abductor is believed to be hiding, and they may subcontract with other investigators to pick up the trail there. In addition, they often do the legwork necessary to track down clues, follow sources who might lead to the abductor, and stake out houses, sometimes with surveillance vans equipped with the latest high technology equipment.[26] Travel is not always needed. A great deal of information can be learned about an abductor through computer searches conducted in the office of the investigator.

Case History

One parent, Alex, tells of locating his children after a three-year search, thanks to the efforts of a private investigator. Apparently, Alex's wife, Judy, left with their four children in part because she wanted to show support for her brother, who was also abducting his children at the same time. Alex and Judy's marriage had not been especially satisfying to either partner, but none of the violence or substance abuse that marked so many other failed marital relationships was present. After the abduction, Judy communicated with Alex through her parents, who, despite Alex's efforts, refused to divulge her whereabouts. An investigator found the children 18 months later, and Alex got his first glimpse of them through binoculars (he did not want to reveal himself to his children at that point, fearing it would upset them).

Having finally located Judy, Alex called and asked that they go into counseling to try and reconcile the relationship. She told him she would think about it and give him an answer when he called the next day. When he called back, she had vanished. The private investigator began tailing Judy's parents. They were going through elaborate steps to avoid being followed to Judy's house, including taking separate buses and changing clothes and cars before each visit. The investigator followed them anyway, and the police recovered the children. Alex did not find the police especially helpful during his search: "They just do not have the time or resources. The missing children's organizations were supportive of me and helped put out flyers. It was the investigator that found them, though."

*   *   *

Alex's story provides a typical example of the work of private investigators. The one Alex hired was able to track down the mother twice and was not distracted by her parents' attempts to throw him off the trail. A second father, James, needed a private investigator because the police balked at helping him. Because James had a drug charge pending when he went to the police for help in recovering his son, they didn't believe he was telling the truth. When a private investigator located James's wife in Nevada, the police refused to act. James began tapping her phone calls to him. During one conversation she bragged about how she had set him up for the drug bust. When James played the tapes for the police, they arrested her for framing him with the false drug charge and for abduction. Without the detective, the 18 months James was away from his son might have stretched into a much longer period of time.

Though in our study it tended to be the men we interviewed who utilized private investigators, our discussions with police and private investigators indicate that women also use this resource, though at times for different reasons and with different levels of emotional investment. For example, hiring a male private investigator may provide a sense of protection some women may feel they need in dealing with a male abductor. In addition, women clients, often with limited resources, have been described as being willing to sacrifice anything to be able to pay the private investigator's fees, recovering the child is of paramount importance to them. In contrast, some men who have sought help from private detectives leave the impression that they are more interested in getting back at the abductor; locating the abductor and child often seems more important than recovery. Once they are located, some men have been known to focus more on trying to get the wife to return to the marriage or on gaining revenge than on recovering or obtaining custody of the child.

One company headquartered in North Carolina, Corporate Training Unlimited (CTU), has received considerable media coverage for recovering children abducted to foreign countries. While CTU's primary business is providing training to police special weapons and tactics (SWAT) teams and consultation on security measures to businesses,[27] it receives 50 to 100 inquiries a year about international parental abductions. Of these inquiries it accepts a very small number because of the enormous expense involved, which relatively few parents can afford. Hiring CTU to snatch a child from another country can cost anywhere from $30,000 to well over $100,000, depending upon the geographic location, the countries bordering the target country, and the length of time necessary to complete the recovery. By the time parents call CTU, they may already have exhausted their resources on private investigators who have been unsuccessful. And CTU must be paid a retainer in advance, another reason why so few inquiries turn into actual contracts. A spokesperson for CTU, Judy Feeney, states that her organization will assist a parent in recovering a child only if that parent has a legal document and the blessing of the court to proceed and if the U.S. government is unable to enforce the custody order.[28] CTU would be content to never have to recover a child again, since that would mean the government is doing its job in protecting its citizens. CTU has recovered 10 children in the five years it has accepted parental abduction cases.

Disseminating Posters

One of the more uplifting experiences for the parents in their attempts to recover is when a missing children's organization assists the search effort by disseminating posters with the child's picture, name, and identifying characteristics on it or by placing a child's picture on a milk carton. The National Center for Missing and Exploited Children has been involved in such efforts since 1985, when it began featuring one child a week on ADVO cards, postcards showing a child's identifying information along with an advertisement for a product. People who receive the cards are directed to call the National Center if they think they have information about the child. ADVO, a private company, pays for the mailings by selling advertising space on the other side of the card. Approximately 50 million such cards are mailed out to homes each week. By the end of the first five years of this program, 260 children had been featured and 50 recoveries were credited to this approach (46 of the 50 children had been abducted by one of their parents).[29]

There is a long waiting list to get a child's picture on an ADVO card, and a number of criteria have to be satisfied once it is established that the child is missing. One important criterion for selection is that media exposure must be considered potentially helpful in recovery of the child. Sometimes, new information on a case will help push that case higher on the priority list. No child's picture may appear twice.

Since 1990 the abducting parent's picture also appears on the cards in cases where there is a federal arrest warrant for that parent. Growing children change in appearance more quickly than do adults, and the addition of the parent to the ADVO cards is believed to be an aid in recognizing and recovering the children. To make the children more recognizable, their pictures are "age enhanced" through the efforts of an artist at the National Center working on a computer; some remarkable likenesses of children who were located years after the abduction have been generated through this process.

Posters also are produced and distributed by searching parents. This often is done on a statewide basis and through mailings to local self-help organizations in other states. While there is no easy way to document the effectiveness of sending out posters (either statewide or nationwide) because this approach often is done in tandem with other efforts, a few parents in our study directly credited these posters with the recovery of their children.

Case History

One parent who owes the recovery of her children to the influence of posters is Cecilia. After 10 years of marriage Cecilia moved out with her two young children. Her husband, Joshua, had been taking care of the children while she worked, a situation that she believed was strapping them financially. Joshua wanted counseling to try and repair their marital rift, but Cecilia was convinced it would not help. In the custody battle that followed, the more typical gender roles were reversed: Joshua thought he should have custody because he had been the full-time caretaker, and Cecilia believed she should have it because she had been the breadwinner. Cecilia prevailed, and Joshua was awarded liberal visitation.

A few months later, Cecilia remarried. While she was on her honeymoon, Joshua abducted their children. She did not see them for one year. Joshua moved to a nearby state but, to throw her off the track, arranged to have letters mailed to her from England. The FBI determined that the paper for the letters was American made, so Cecilia proceeded to search for her children in the United States. She contacted all the major talk shows for help in the recovery, but none was interested in her story. The FBI entered the case when it was determined that Joshua had left the state with the children, but it could not locate Joshua. With the help of a missing children's organization Cecilia began circulating posters of the children.

During his time on the run Joshua had joined a Seventh Day Adventist church. When a member of the church showed a poster of his children to him, Joshua knew his days in hiding were numbered. He called Cecilia offering a fairly typical bargain: He would return the children if Cecilia dropped criminal charges against him. She agreed and recovered the children.[30]

* * *

In a similar situation another father turned himself in after seeing his children's picture on one of 30,000 posters his ex-wife had disseminated in the state where he was living. She had traced his phone calls to the state, but could not pinpoint his exact whereabouts. In both cases, a missing children's organization was very helpful in coordinating the efforts.

Disseminating posters can help in the two ways illustrated here: They can inform other people about the abduction and they can put pressure on the abductor to return the children.

Voluntary Return of the Child by the Abductor

For a variety of reasons, an abducting parent may decide to return the child before being located. Organizations like Child Find of America may help, or the return may be more informal. Because of the traditional family roles of fathers and mothers, we believe fathers are more likely than mothers to return children voluntarily; it is still a rare occurrence for fathers to be raising children alone, and many who do feel uncomfortable in their role.[31] Some fathers may return children because they believe they will be better off with the mother. Others may return children because they never really wanted them, having abducted them initially in the hopes of forcing a reconciliation or because they were angry at their ex-wives.

Case History

Denise ended her marriage to Mark against his wishes. Two years later he had remarried and was living in Texas. When their daughter, Tammy, visited, he refused to send her back. "Texas is a very chauvinistic state," Denise said. "I could not get her back." Tammy, eight at the time, had been having relationship problems with Denise and was not eager to return to her. Mark fed into the strained mother–daughter relationship by telling Tammy that her mother did not want her anymore. But after living with Mark for a year, Tammy began developing extreme school and psychological problems. "He grew tired of her and sent her back," Denise said. "He never really wanted her anyway. It was all done to get me."

*   *   *

Case History

Elaine recovered her son, Alan, after five weeks. Her husband, Nat, left her for his secretary, then became jealous of the time Elaine was spending with Alan. One day Nat, during his scheduled visitation, called his office to say he was not returning and not to look for him. A friend from Nat's office called Elaine to warn her, and she called the police. The police, acting in response to what they judged to be a weekend abduction (described in Chapter 3), called to warn Nat not to leave the state. The next day he left anyway.

Elaine contacted everyone she could think of during the next few weeks but to no avail. "The FBI and police were very slow in responding to my needs. But one day I returned from work and found a message on my answering machine saying to pick up Alan at the airport the next day at 3:00 P.M. I headed out with the police, hoping to arrest Nat. He wasn't there, but at least I got my son back."

Elaine believes Nat abducted Alan because of a desire to be with him and because of anger about the breakup. When the anger subsided, he came to his senses and returned Alan. Pressure also was being applied by the FBI, and Nat may have believed it was only a matter of time before he was apprehended. Since then, Nat has maintained contact with Alan, reinforcing Elaine's belief that he does care about his son.

The Searching Parent's Vision or Intuition

The final scenario that we have seen linked to locating and recovering children involves parents who have a dream or a vision relating to their child. In those visions they either hear a voice telling them to call someone who knows about their child, as in the case of Ava in this chapter, or they have an inspired thought about some clue that becomes essential in tracking down the missing child. It is usually women who report these experiences, either because women are more apt to have them or because men are more hesitant to admit that they have them. Men may be reluctant to admit to their visions because they feel more comfortable focusing on the logical side of their recovery attempts. Some men may believe visions are not masculine because they express the more intuitive side of their personality.

Such visions or inspirations often are born of months or years of frustrated searching, when other approaches seem to have failed. They also are sometimes related to strong religious beliefs. In Ava's case, she had not seen her children in years and had established a new life with a husband and baby. She had also become very involved in a church, and she attributes the voices she heard to her renewed faith.

Case History

Carla credits a dream with breaking open the five-year search for her son, who was 18 months old at the time he was taken. In her dream a voice woke her up. Carla describes the voice as "bothersome" and persistent enough to arouse her from a deep sleep: "The voice talked to me as if I were a child. It was very matter-of-fact. It said to me I had to talk to the last victim. At that point I did not know what the voice was talking about." Carla contacted the authorities who had jurisdiction over the case. She learned at that point that her ex-husband had gone on a crime spree after the abduction. They could not release the name of his last victim during his crime spree but did put her in touch with a police detective. Fortunately, the detective was the one who had been involved in a shoot-out with Carla's ex-husband, and he remembered that a woman and a young child had been with her ex-husband at the time. This new bit of information, concerning the presence of a woman, enabled Carla to guess who she was and reason that her ex-husband still might be with her. Recalling that the woman had a history of medical problems, Carla and the detective traced hospital computer records until they located her and the ex-husband and son.

For Carla, the dream was the key, just as the voice had been for Ava. It is not only recovering parents who have these visions. Some parents who have not recovered report dreams that led to locating the child, although attempts at recovery failed. In addition, parents have had dreams or visions about their children that have led to dead ends in their search.

*   *   *

Dr. Ken Lewis, a *guardian ad litem*, was asked to describe his experiences as a court-appointed guardian in recovering abducted children. He offers a perspective from outside that of the immediate family members:

THE ROLE OF THE *GUARDIAN AD LITEM*

The purpose of a *guardian ad litem* in a child custody case is to serve as an advocate for the child's best interests during litigation. This is different from an attorney for the child, who represents a minor child in a custody case. There is an important difference between these two appointments. The attorney for the child client maintains the same type of relationship as with an adult client; the relationship is marked by the attorney–client privilege, and the attorney "works" for the child client. The advocacy in this instance usually is for what the child client desires, irrespective of the child's best interests. Sometimes, however, the desires of the child and what is best for that child are two quite different things.

In a custody dispute the guardian may be aligned with the attorney for one of the parents on one issue and with the attorney for the other parent on another. A custody case usually is decided on a variety of factors. In short, the *guardian ad litem* at one time may stand with one parent and at another time may stand with the other parent but at all times must stand with the child.

In case preparation, the *guardian ad litem* has an advantage over either of the parents' attorneys. He or she is able to discuss the details of the mother's case with her attorney and the details of the father's case with his attorney. He or she may also make inquiry from independent sources. The composite picture drawn from these several sources is often more complete than that of either of the parents' attorneys. Consequently, the opinions and recommendations presented to the court by the *guardian ad litem* often are given considerable weight.

When I am appointed *guardian ad litem* for an abducted child, I usually am given specific instructions by the court. My duties often include locating the child, evaluating the environment from which the child was removed, evaluating the environment in which the child has been living, and recommending to the court a custody arrangement that will best serve the child's interests. The appointment order makes it clear that my advocacy is for the child and not the adult litigants.

In my work as *guardian ad litem* in child abduction cases, I often have the advantage of observing the child in the "abduction home environment" as well as the "return home environment." These comparisons have led me to focus more on the child's experiences than on the abduction alone, as so often is done in post abduction cases without a *guardian ad litem.* These comparisons provide an understanding of the child's needs.

All states have a provision for *guardians ad litem,* and family court judges have the authority to make such appointments in the interests of protecting minors under their jurisdiction. Even when the child is missing, the court has subject matter jurisdiction over a case properly filed. The cost of the *guardian ad litem* usually is not paid for by the courts. For example, I may have my fees paid by the searching parent until the child is located. At that point the costs will be redistributed between the searching parent and the abductor as court costs. While the *guardian ad litem* approach is admittedly novel, it offers promise for providing a needed service for interstate and international custody abductions.

Bringing Jessica Home

Dr. Lewis continues with a case example in which he acted as *guardian ad litem* for a little girl.

Jessica was sitting next to me, looking through the small window of the huge 747 jet. She was flying through the clouds for the second time in her life. Her first airplane trip was six months before, when her mother took her from Michigan to California for what she thought would be a visit to Disneyland. Eight-year-old Jessica didn't know then that her trip to California was supposed to be one-way only. Jessica's mother was a schoolteacher in a small rural town in northern Michigan. Her father ran his own garden supply business out of the family home. Jessica spent most of her after-school time around her father's shop, helping him and learning all about plants and flowers.

The return trip home with me was quiet for the first hour, but later the child became more talkative. "I still love my mommy," she told me in a shy whisper, "but I really miss my daddy. Does he know I'm coming home?"

Her parents had been married for nine years, but the last two had been filled with sadness. While there was no physical violence, their verbal assaults were sometimes overheard by Jessica. Mom complained that Dad didn't like parties and never wanted to go out on the town. Dad complained that Mom had too many outside interests and didn't spend enough time with the family. Jessica was their only child.

The parents had worked out a "friendly" divorce, with child custody being shared. Mom took an apartment in town, close to Jessica's school, while Dad stayed at the family home and continued with his business. Jessica stayed at her dad's house from Monday after school until Friday morning. After school one Monday, when Jessica did not come home, Dad called Mom's house. No one answered. Mom would later claim she took Jessica because she suspected she was being abused. Within a week Dad was in court.

The judge appointed me *guardian ad litem* for Jessica, and my duties included finding her, returning her to Michigan, and filing a written report on her general welfare. I was to include a recommendation for custody that would best benefit Jessica. But first I had to find her. Doing research on the family background, I learned that nine years ago, Mom's father sent a portable typewriter to Mom and Dad as a wedding gift. Mom had not had much contact with her father, so Dad never knew where he lived. Dad showed me the typewriter, and I copied down the serial number. Through contact with the manufacturer, I was able to obtain a copy of the check used to purchase the typewriter. The check was written on a California bank, a discovery that led me to a city where, in fact, Mom was in hiding.

When I finally tracked down Jessica's mother, she was shocked to have been found. The first thing she told me was that she was planning on returning but had not decided exactly when she would be going back to Michigan. Since I had cleared my court appointment with the California court and since I had in my possession an airplane ticket for Jessica's return, with another seat reserved under Mom's name, she had two choices: She could either return with Jessica and me or come back to Michigan at a later date. She chose the latter.

Jessica was a clean and neatly dressed child who had been well taken care of during the abduction. (In some cases I have been involved with, abducted children were grossly maltreated.) While Mom, Jessica, and I waited for the plane, Jessica was full of questions about Michigan, the snow, and the garden supply store. She was careful not to mention Dad in Mom's presence. She carried her little suitcase to the airport and easily separated from her Mom, giving her a kiss good-bye.

Our flight back to Michigan had a change of planes in St. Louis, so Jessica and I had several hours on the ground. We went to the airport restaurant, and it was there that Jessica and I had our "big talk." She told me all about Disneyland, and then described her new home in California. Jessica talked a lot about her new school and her new friends. Then she said that she really missed her old friends, her old school, and her father. The worst thing about California, she said, was that she could never answer the telephone. Her mother had instructed her not to pick up the phone under any circumstances.

Being eight years old is not supposed to be hard on a little girl, but it certainly was for Jessica. Her abduction was a complete surprise to her. Her mother told her that it was better to live in California and that, after a while, she would be able to talk to her father on the phone. That time never seemed to come. One month led to the next, and she was not able to even write to her friends back in Michigan. The answers her mother gave her seemed to make sense at the time, but the real answers were never given. As we talked, it became clear to me that Jessica was very confused. "Was I really missing?" she asked. "If Daddy wanted the divorce [Jessica had been told that her father was not interested in being with her or her mother], why did he send you to bring me home?" she asked, looking me straight in the face. "Why did they have to fight so much?"; "Will I have to talk to a judge?"; "Will I get to see my mom again?"—these and a thousand other questions were put to me. (I once had a physics teacher who said that anything, no matter how difficult, could be explained in simple language, but my physics teacher had never traveled across country with Jessica).

We walked by a gift store on the way to the next plane, and I bought a child's book for Jessica. The book was about kangaroos, and we read it together on the next flight. During the last half hour of the journey, Jessica fell asleep. When we landed at the small airport near her home, I carried Jessica off the plane. Her dad was at the airport when we landed. When I gave her to him, Jessica was still asleep. While Dad sat rocking her gently, I telephoned Mom in California to say that we had arrived safely and that Jessica was well. It was out in the parking lot that she woke up, and then came the hugs and kisses.

I remained in Michigan the following day to help get Jessica settled back home. I interviewed Jessica's minister, schoolteacher, doctor, and several other reference persons. Jessica adapted well to her postabduction return, but she was somewhat concerned regarding how to explain to her friends her six months' absence. I did not feel that she needed professional help at the time, but I told her that I would call her each week and we could talk about any of her problems. Jessica knew that she had gone through an unusual experience, but it would be a long time before she would fully understand the full meaning of what had happened to her.

Custody was assigned to Dad, with supervised visitation allowed for Mom. Mom also was ordered to pay child support. She visited once and then dropped out of sight. Two years later, having remarried, she requested that visitation begin again. With her remarriage, the court decided that she could have unsupervised visitation in California if she posted a security bond. Visitation resumed and continues to this day.

DEALING WITH THE INTANGIBLES

Whether parents recover through the aid of police or on their own, recovery becomes one of the high points of their parenting experience. The date of recovery is one they can recall immediately, and the experience usually can be described in exquisite detail. For many, though, recovery does not guarantee peace of mind; 84% of the left-behind parents in our study worry about another abduction.

It is not always easy to predict who will recover a child and who will not. Working toward the goal of recovery is often a long and painful process. Once a parent has taken the usual steps to try and locate a child—contacting local police, the FBI, friends, relatives, and missing children's organizations—he or she has to decide who, if anyone, to contact next. For example, is a private investigator going to help in the case? What about hiring a lawyer? Should the searching parent contact all of the possible magazines the abductor may subscribe to in order to see if they have the abductor's address? The ultimate question becomes, How much time should a parent devote to the search? Should the searching parent quit a job and search full-time? Should the parent spend some time every night calling all over the country? The choice is an individual one, driven by the personalities of the people involved. There is no exact amount of time a parent should spend searching. A parent who believes a child is in immediate danger will be more alarmed and search harder than one who hears from the abductor every so often and is told the child is doing well. In the same vein, a parent who believes in the chance to recover will work harder for it. Each parent has to deal individually with decisions about the time commitment to recovering the child.

ADVICE FROM PARENTS WHO HAVE RECOVERED

We conclude this chapter with advice that individual parents who have recovered their children offer to parents who still are searching.

Ken advises parents to not give up hope in the system. He has nothing but praise for the local police and the FBI and encourages searching parents to be assertive but not aggressive toward authorities. "I had to keep reminding myself that although this was the most important case in the world to me, it was just one of many others to those who were supposed to be helping me."

Anna found that publicity was most helpful to her in recovering her children. "It was the posters and the networking that were the most critical. I know that computer-enhanced aging pictures can be good, too, if the children have been missing for a while. I also had to work to get myself (psychologically) healthy so that I would be ready for them when they returned home. You need to have someone to talk with to deal with your grief."

"Hang in there," John advises. "I have seen a lot of parents quit during my work [with a missing children's organization]. Act immediately if there is an abduction by filing paperwork to get custody. Don't let people push you around or ignore you."

Carla thought that keeping busy was the most helpful technique for her while she was searching. "I am a hyper person and I needed to do something every day to help get my son back, even if it was just mailing out a flyer a day."

Jeff suggests that parents "get with people who can help you, like the church. Also, use every organization you can. I was in touch with Child Find, the National Center for Missing and Exploited Children, and Child Rights of America in Florida. My children's pictures were on the Oprah Winfrey Show. It all helped!"

CHAPTER 5

How Children Experience Abduction

The effect on children of life on the run is not easily washed away by their return home. Whether a child is away from home for a few days or for a period stretching into months or years,[1] there is potential for the abduction to have a profound impact. Most often, that impact is negative.

Consider the following composite case presented from the child's perspective. A four-year-old girl has been living in a family strained by the tension that often precedes a marital breakup. As she has grown, her loyalties have been divided between her parents. She has never felt that it is completely safe to be close to a parent and knows that closeness to one sometimes incurs recrimination from the other parent. She feels like an accordion, pushed and pulled by each parent as they have their ups and downs. As the marriage breaks up and the tension escalates, the child witnesses both parents becoming increasingly upset and angry. Whatever sense of stability the child received from either parent is threatened further when they become temporarily unable to nurture her as they turn inward, focusing instead on nursing their own wounds. As a result, the girl's capacity to cope diminishes as her environment becomes less trustworthy.

The parents separate, and the girl begins spending most of her time with one parent. In many families of divorce this can begin a stable period for the child; new routines are established and the child's and parent's coping abilities slowly return. But in families where there is an abduction, this stage may usher in a new level of conflict, one often marked by threats of abduction, visitation disputes, or violence. Suddenly, the girl is snatched, perhaps from the parent with whom she has begun to form a closer relationship.

The girl then begins a life of hiding. She may be encouraged to lie about her identity, her hometown, siblings, and the other parent. She begins to form a new relationship with the abducting parent, but often it is a relationship based on fear and anger and rooted in a life of ever-changing homes, schools, and friendships. It is not the stable and nurturing environment she needs, particularly after a family breakup. Weeks, months, or years later, perhaps when her life has finally begun to stabilize, she may be located, wrenched away from the abducting parent and her new routine, and returned to a mother or father she may not remember, has been taught was unloving, or believed was dead. She must then attempt to form a new bond with that parent and to devalue the previous existence with the abducting parent. Is it any wonder the child suffers from this disorienting experience?

As gruesome as this scenario may sound, it still does not reflect the full potential for damage in the many cases where a child has been severely mistreated, neglected, beaten, or sexually abused by either the abducting or the searching parent. When such treatment is included in the abduction equation, much more severe difficulties often follow recovery. The simpler scenario also does not do justice to situations where the abducting parent is on the run from a battering spouse. In that case, the negative consequences of remaining in the home may outweigh the emotional consequences of abduction for the child, who has seen her parent being victimized repeatedly. The legal consequences may be another matter.

The conclusion to be drawn about the effects of parental abduction is not that all children are irreparably damaged by the experience. We know from studies of other traumatic experiences that positive relationships and nurturing can help undo many of the stresses related to particularly horrible events. Whether a child has been held captive by a terrorist with a bomb, as was a group of schoolchildren in Wyoming in 1986,[2] or whether a child has been living in one of the world's war zones from Belfast to Cambodia,[3] many remain resilient.[4] Whether a child's experiences in an abduction are positive or negative depends on factors unique to the family, the child's personality, the earlier life experiences of the child, and what the alternatives might have been.

WHAT IS LIKELY TO AFFECT THE CHILD'S ADJUSTMENT TO AN ABDUCTION

It is known that children of divorced families are often at psychological risk.[5] With a child snatching, the risk is heightened because, in part, of the extreme nature of the situation and to the total lack of contact with one of the parents. At different stages of development, children tend to form stronger bonds with one parent than the other. How a child is affected by being cut off from contact with a parent will be influenced by many factors, chief among them being the age of the child and the strength of the child's bond with the parent left behind and with the abductor.

The age of the child is a major factor in how the child will integrate the abduction experience. John Bowlby's work with infants separated from their mothers and placed in hospitals during World War II documented the negative impact on the child's development when he or she was left virtually unattended except at feeding time.[6] More recent work has supported the conclusion that young children need a consistent caring adult in their lives, whether that adult is a mother, father, grandparent, or adoptive parent.[7] What is likely to happen to a two-year-old who is removed from contact with one parent and placed in the hands of the other naturally will depend upon the kind of relationship the abducting parent has with the child. If the abducting parent has not formed as strong a bond with the child as the left-behind parent, the child is more likely to have difficulties adjusting. This is especially true given the context of abduction, in which the abducting parent is constantly looking over his or her shoulder, focusing on avoiding capture. This is not the best of circumstances for raising a child.

A two-year-old is at the stage of just beginning to develop a cognitive understanding of the outside world. We focus on this age in particular because there were more abducted two-year-olds in our study than children of any other age. It is at this age that the child begins to have a sense of time and sequence, and behavioral differences between the sexes appear.[8] The child notices when something is broken and may react with anxiety to pictures of people with distorted faces. Jerome Kagan, a developmental psychologist, believes that children become upset when events violate their grasp of how things are supposed to be.[9] Children at this approximate age also can tell when a parent is angry, and they believe that adults can read their thoughts. It is Kagan's impression that children, believing bad thoughts can be read, see themselves as being bad for having those thoughts. Thus, a number of things are apt to happen in the tense atmosphere that accompanies an abduction. The very young child is apt to be acutely aware of something having gone wrong and of the parent being angry. The child may turn that anger inward, particularly if she or he feels responsible for the parent's anger or does not understand it. When separation from a parent occurs, the child's anger can be great. The child believes the abducting parent senses the anger, may feel he or she is bad for having the anger, and may begin to assume the identity of someone who is "bad."

In our study the average age of abducted children was between five and six; the five to six-year-old has great emotional needs, also. Approval is vitally important, and six-year-olds, in particular, love to impress adults with their intelligence. The six-year-old's sense of time is quite sophisticated, and the child will show great interest in learning about his or her younger years. Relationships outside of the family are expanding, as is the child's sense of himself in relation to others. Feelings about death and the fear of losing a parent become acute at this age.[10] In addition, there is a great deal of comparison of self with others. Children are able to rank themselves in terms of popularity, attractiveness, and so on. Finally, the ability to feel guilt, which begins at the age of four,[11] is solidified by this age.

For abducted children in the five to six age range, the potential for difficulties is acute. Their awareness of time allows them to mark how long they have been on the run. If enrolled in school, they may be discouraged from achieving to their fullest potential in order not to draw too much attention to themselves. They are extremely aware that they are different from their new classmates.

Their growing sense of right and wrong, as evidenced by their feelings of guilt, informs them that their parent has done something wrong in leaving with them. Being trained to avoid legal authorities and lie about family names may seem like a game at first, but eventually it will test the child's moral development and ability to trust either parent.

In our sample a few older children, 7 to 10-year-olds and even adolescents, also were abducted. The typical 7 to 10-year-old is in the process of establishing a firm sense of identity and, usually, a clear differentiation of right and wrong. The abduction, with its frequent demands for anonymity and avoidance of authority, jeopardizes the child's moral growth. The child's sense of ethics is undermined as he or she becomes an accomplice, sometimes unwittingly, in the abduction by avoiding escape to the searching parent, by not telephoning home, or by not going to the legal authorities.

At adolescence the peer group becomes a primary source of identification as the teen seeks to break away from parents. In the cognitive realm, the adolescent is capable of trying to understand the order of a complex world.[12] The abduction can be extremely confusing to adolescents who are striving for cognitive mastery in a situation where both parents are strenuously arguing their sides.

Adolescents rarely are forced into an abduction because of their physical size and the ease with which they could escape or telephone home. They may be willing accomplices or may beg the abductor to take them. While this would reduce the potential psychological damage they experience, particularly if they are escaping an abusive parent, it does not leave them free of the guilt of choosing to leave in such a manner. Loyalty conflicts often remain as they wonder why they were not able to work out their relationship with the parent left behind.

In summary, the age of the child at the time of the abduction can have a profound effect because it sets the stage for the child's role in the abduction and for how he or she is treated. Age is a key variable in the abduction equation but certainly not the only one.

Other questions to consider when thinking about the potential impact on a child are the following: Was the child snatched by the parent with whom the child was most closely bonded? What was the nature of the relationship between abductor and child before and during the abduction? How long was the child on the run? Was the child in contact with other family members, like the abductor's parents? What was the nature of those relationships? How frightening was the experience of going into hiding? Was there a great deal of residential instability? Was there abuse? Was the child told negative things about the parent left behind? Were other siblings involved? How does the age of the child interact with each of these variables?

In learning about the facts of the abduction we can gain a clearer understanding of how the child may have been affected. It must be remembered, though, that there are as many variations as there are children. At one end of the spectrum are children being taken away from an abusive situation by the parent to whom the child feels closest. This may not be damaging to the child, especially when compared with the alternatives. At the other end of the continuum are children who are removed from a parent with whom they have formed a close bond and are placed in an abusive or neglectful environment where life is chaotic. One could predict that the latter situation would be damaging to a child of any age. The cases we have come to know fall along this wide spectrum.

THE EXPERIENCES OF CHILDREN ON THE RUN

Research about children who have been abducted is scant. What other researchers have learned is that while on the run many are exposed to a range of upsetting behaviors as well as to confusing attitudes and norms. The ordeal may begin with the terrifying experience of being snatched out of the home when the other parent is out of the room or with being taken at gunpoint.[13] The children are taught to avoid police and other officials. They may not attend school for months. Names are changed. For young children this may appear to be a game, while for older ones it raises issues of guilt because they are aware that they are accomplices in a crime.[14] Travel and residential instability may become commonplace. One case study describes a three-year-old girl who lived in five different states during three and a half years and slept in houses, apartments, rooming houses, and cars. She was physically abused by her father's girlfriend during that time. When she asked her father about her mother's whereabouts, she was given a vague answer, as are many abducted children.[15]

Children may live with a suitcase always packed and may flee from the law or from the parent left behind as a legal net closes on them. Attempts to call home may be thwarted by the abducting parent or by ignorance of the telephone system. Young children may know the number at home but not the area code. When they call from a new state, they either find the number is inoperative or hear a strange voice answering the phone, fueling the belief that they have been abandoned by the other parent. Some children avoid calling even though they are familiar with the phone system because they do not want to stir up animosity between the parents.[16]

It is not uncommon for a child to be told the other parent no longer loves them or is dead,[17] a prostitute, or a substance abuser. This obviously can work against the searching parent recovering the child since the child comes to see the abductor as the only one who cares. One child who was taken to Amsterdam by his father screamed at his mother when she located him that he hated her, the result of his being told for months that she did not want him.[18]

Children cope with the battles over them in a variety of ways. If abductions occur frequently (some children in our study had been abducted at least six times and sometimes snatched back and forth within a short period of time), the child may withdraw to avoid showing any reaction. He or she learns to wear a mask over feelings as a form of self-protection. Children who live with their abductors for a period of time may attach themselves very closely to that parent. The abductor takes on the persona of rescuer from the parent left behind. Such an attachment becomes, for some children, a psychological defense against the pain of having lost one parent. The children, like hostages or other victims who develop the Stockholm or hostage syndrome,[19] overidentify with the captors. Abductors may even try to have the child think of the other parent and legal authorities as agents of Satan (as discussed in Chapter 3). If there is a reunion, adjusting to the parent left behind is especially difficult in these situations.

Children who are recovered may also be subjected to the experience of being taken into protective custody and sometimes into foster care.[20] They may witness violence as police handcuff and take their parent into custody. They may be asked to testify against their parent or to make a choice about the parent with whom they want to live. They may be given little chance even to say good-bye to the abductor, especially if the recovery entails another snatching.

Finally, in rare instances, abducted children have been killed by the abductor.[21] These are usually parents who have had a long history of mental illness and violent behavior.

The Parents' Report

In well over 90% of the situations we studied, parents reported that their children were in good health before the abduction, were behaving well at home, and, if old enough to attend, were behaving well in school and receiving satisfactory grades. In fact, the children were described as having been models of decorum and scholarship. Given the probability of strain in the home environment during this period, it is likely that these descriptions are tinged with at least a little parental hyperbole. Why would this be? Parents who have not recovered their children may be inclined to describe them in more positive terms, since increased absence makes the heart grow fonder. Parents who have recovered their children and whose children are not faring well may feel the need to argue that since all was well before the snatching, the abduction must be the reason their children now are having difficulty.

Our findings show that children on the run are definitely at risk for physical or sexual abuse (not to mention the broader category of emotional abuse, which includes continually being screamed at or teased or witnessing violence).[22] In situations where there is abuse, the abuse may occur for a variety of reasons: The child may remind the abductor of the other parent and, as a stand-in, may become the recipient of hostile feelings. Sexual abuse that had begun while the parents were together may continue when the parent and child are on the run. It may also occur because the child becomes a sexual stand-in for the other parent or because of inappropriate sexual feelings the abductor holds for the child that are unrelated to the other parent. Abuse by another adult involved with the abductor is not uncommon. In some cases abuse may be alleged but never substantiated.[23]

One example of sexual abuse in our research occurred at the hands of a boyfriend who was dating an abducting mother. Another case of sexual abuse and physical neglect was confirmed by a mother who learned of it after she recovered her six-year-old daughter and had her psychiatrically evaluated. Six years later, the daughter still has severe difficulties in distinguishing reality from fantasy and handling any changes in her routine.

About one-third of the parents who recovered said their child was abused while with the other parent: 23% reported physical abuse, 7% sexual abuse, and 5% both physical and sexual abuse. Almost one-third said the abductor had been accused of abuse before the abduction (this does not mean it was substantiated.) Female abductors were more apt to have been accused of child abuse before the abduction than male abductors.[24]

Parents and children describe a range of other experiences while on the run, some that border on the abusive, depending on the definition.[25] Carrie was abducted by her mother when she was four. Carrie's mother, a former drug addict, was strongly encouraged by her mother to take Carrie after she lost custody owing to her drug-related problems. Ten months later her father recovered her in another state 1,000 miles away. It was a year before Carrie was able to talk about her mother's boyfriend, who would throw food at the wall and rip out doors when he was angry. Carrie's father thinks that although she witnessed a great deal of anger and may have been rather harshly treated, she was not abused herself.

Carla, introduced in the previous chapter as someone who recovered her son following a vision, reports that he was exposed to extensive violence as his father was committing various crimes. She also reports that he was given hallucinogenic drugs. The time with his father was so upsetting that it took him many years before he was able even to talk about some of his experiences.

* * *

Max, now 35 years old, was abducted by his father when he was four. In a long interview with us, he recounted his own experiences being snatched. He and his younger sister became the pawns in their parents' divorce. His mother and father, both of whom were in their teens when Max was born, had a stormy life together that ended when his mother returned home to her mother with the children. Max's father immediately struck back by snatching Max and going to California in an attempt to get Max's mother to return to the marriage. It was the early 1960s, and Max's mother had heard that California was a "crazy" place to live. She refused to join them there. For the next 20 years Max had virtually no contact with his mother and only occasional telephone conversations with his sister. When he asked about his mother he was told she was a bad person and that the past was not important. He learned the subject was forbidden in his father's home.

Max's father remarried, and Max developed a contentious relationship with his stepmother. She wanted him to tell her he loved her, which he, still feeling a sense of loyalty toward his mother, refused to do. Looking back at that period, Max reports, "In many ways I was a model child on the outside. But inside there was the more than normal depression and anger."

During his absence Max's mother had also remarried and had given birth to two more children. She made an initial attempt to regain custody of Max but was told by a lawyer to forget about him and have other children (advice that Cathy, in Chapter 3, also was given by an attorney). The new marriage did not prove to be happy for her. Problems developed as she spiraled into drug abuse, and she eventually was kicked out of the house, taking only Max's sister with her. (Max has never met his two half brothers.) She then went through a long period of substance abuse and prostitution. During their early years apart, Max and his sister were in sporadic contact through the efforts of grandparents, but his sister never was told who Max was. Each thought the other was a distant cousin. Essentially, the message Max received growing up was that his mother was unable or unwilling to fight very hard to regain custody of him. As Max explains later in this chapter, this caused problems for him as an adult when he attempted to establish intimate relationships.

*   *   *

Whereas Max was only four when he was abducted and did not put up a fight, older children can be much more difficult to raise if they are being taken against their will. In one situation a 9-year-old boy and a 10-year-old girl who were snatched by the father demanded to be returned immediately. The father said he would return them as soon as they learned Spanish (they had been flown to South America). Then the father began to brainwash them that their chronic health problems were the fault of their mother. As time wore on, the children's relationship with the father became more complicated. They began to threaten him physically if he did not return them. He tried a different tact, saying that if he returned them he would go to prison and never see them again. As is sometimes seen in the hostage syndrome, he was eventually able to gain their sympathy, making their adjustment after their recovery much more arduous.

*   *   *

Another example, from a family introduced in Chapter 3, provides a further picture of the complicated relationship that can develop over time between a child and the abductor. Ruth, you may recall, was the child who was living in hiding with her father, Dan, for 12 years before being reunited with her mother, Sandy, who was told of Ruth's whereabouts after Ruth received word of her college admission. Ruth describes her time with her father:

> He just asked me one day if I wanted to go for a ride with him and that I might not see my mother again for a while, and I said okay. I was six at the time. I don't really remember how close I was to my mom or dad at the time. I was very young at the time and didn't really think it was that strange that I was going to live with my father and not my mother. Kids would ask me in school where my mom was and why I was living with my dad, and I would just tell them she lived in another city and couldn't see me right now. I always believed she was alive, though.
>
> I remember when I was 11, I began asking him about her. I think subconsciously I stopped asking after that because of his reaction. He said my mother would see me if she could but that she can't right now. Then he would ask me if I was happy living with him. I'd feel guilty about that and stop asking. Bringing her up made him defensive. I thought at the time that he had custody and that she knew where I was living.
>
> I knew something must have been weird though because I was reading a novel about an abduction and I began to figure out that that was my situation. I began asking him again when I was about 14 and he said I could write to her if I wanted to. That's become a big thing for me now because I didn't do that. I feel real guilty about it because if I had written my mom she would have gone through a lot less pain. I guess I didn't write her in part because of how I thought it might make my dad feel. It all came to a head when I was accepted into college and he called my mom to tell her the news. Then it came out that I had been taken and that my mom really couldn't have seen me if she had wanted to. He told me and I was in shock and we were both crying and everything.

For Ruth, the issue of guilt has been a stumbling block in her own growth and development. Like many children who were missing at an older age, Ruth believes she could have acted in some way to end the abduction or at least to have lessened her mother's pain. It is common that people who are victimized blame themselves both for their own victimization and for the pain they inadvertently may have caused others. Victims of crimes or abuse may begin to believe they deserved what they received. It is difficult to wrest this way of thinking from them even after the victimization has ended. In addition, as has been suggested from the previous discussion about the hostage syndrome, Ruth and Dan formed a very close bond, with daughter assuming a protective role. When Ruth mentioned wanting to see her mother, Dan became upset. Ruth then felt guilty about making him upset; as a result, she became protective of his feelings. In normal parent–child relationships it is the parent who is more protective of the child, not the reverse.

HOW CHILDREN ADJUST FOLLOWING RECOVERY

We have focused thus far on the experiences of children on the run; however, once children have been recovered, the problems do not go away. Accounts suggest that although kidnapping can have a severe emotional impact on some children, others, depending upon the circumstances, do not fare as poorly. One study of five children found that those who were gone for a short period of time and were treated well tended to regard the experience as an adventure. These children reacted with short-term symptoms such as worrying, crying, and fearfulness and were often helped by psychotherapy. Children gone for longer periods of time had nightmares, were suspicious of strangers, did not want to be left alone, experienced difficulties getting along with other children, and tended to mature more quickly than other children of the same age. This maturation is believed to be related to a lifestyle where they moved about a great deal, were left alone, and were occasionally given responsibility for other children's welfare.[26]

In a study of 17 children who had been returend it was found that the negative impact of the abduction was most severe immediately following recovery and lessened over time. While functioning was never impaired to a pathological degree, it did not return to the level it had been before the abduction, according to parental reports. No strong connection was found in this study between the children's adjustment and their age or the length of time they were missing.[27]

One review of the literature cites such consequences for children of snatching as fear of men and anger at women for not being protective (when the abductor was male), play where the abduction is acted out in different settings, extreme fear of getting lost, and depression. In addition, when the parent flagrantly disregards the law, the child's sense of protection is further shattered because even legal authorities are believed to be ineffectual.[28]

One clinical evaluation of 18 children who were recovered found 16 of them to be suffering from at least one of the following: emotional trauma; the aftereffects of being brainwashed; grief or anger; and overidentification with or, conversely, rejection of the abductor. The two children of the 18 who were not significantly affected by the abduction were in telephone and occasional personal contact with the parent left behind. One hypothesis set forth is that in long-term abduction children may actually perceive kidnapping as being removed from the parent who abducted them many years before. When a bond has been formed with the abductor, the child who is located and returned to the other parent may suffer severely from the loss of contact with the primary psychological parent, who in this case is the abductor.[29]

One case in the literature centers on a two-year-old child who was abducted by his mother for five weeks. The child was returned by the mother when the child regressed and became fearful and distant from the mother. The separation, though lasting for a relatively short time, had dramatic consequences for the young child. He had difficulty falling asleep and staying asleep, refused food, soiled the floor, and would cry uncontrollably for no apparent reason. "During the day, he led his stepmother around the house, searching fearfully for his natural mother. When the doorbell rang, he became very frightened and tearfully called out his natural mother's name."[30] Therapy was successful with this child, though at one year follow-up he still had some anxiety associated with the anniversary of the abduction.

Summing up the literature on the effects of abduction on children who were recovered is not easy; researchers' impressions tend to differ. Common reactions to be expected in children include the following: regression, bedwetting or refusal to use the toilet in young children, interrupted sleep, clinging behavior, fear of windows and doors, extreme fright, grief and rage about parental abandonment aimed at the parent left behind, anger at and rejection of the abductor, depression, and a desire to return to the abducting parent if a strong bond was formed. While all agree that abductions result in adverse reactions in the children, impressions of the extent of those reactions differ.

Our Findings

According to parents' reports concerning 181 children who were recovered, functioning in the children declined in 54%, stayed the same in 21%, and improved in 24% of the cases. In order to determine this, we compared parent ratings of recovered children's functioning before and after the abduction in the following four areas: behavior at home, overall health, grades, and behavior in school. In cases where the children were not in school before the abduction because of their ages, we compared the before and after reports of behavior at home and overall health. This approach to assessing children's functioning has research limitations.[31]

As mentioned earlier, the preabduction descriptions of the children appear to be quite favorable, with 93% to 95% of the parents reporting satisfactory or very satisfactory scores for their children. Satisfaction with the children after the abduction is lower. Satisfactory grades were reported by 85% of parents who recovered, and 84% reported satisfactory school behavior. The overall health of the children was also good, according to 88% of the parents. Behavior at home caused the greatest concern of the four areas, with 73% of the children rated as behaving satisfactorily. These responses need to be discussed further because they provide only a partial, and perhaps misleading, picture. It may be that parents gave their children high ratings, considering what the children had experienced. In other words, when parents report that children are doing well in school, they may be making allowances for what the children may have experienced while on the run.

Other information provided by the parents paints a picture of children who were having more difficulties. For example, half of the children who were recovered received mental health counseling. Almost half of the children were believed to be afraid of the abducting parent. When the parents who recovered were asked if the time the child spent with the abductor was emotionally upsetting, 48% said it was very upsetting and 45% said it was somewhat upsetting. Only 7% believed the abduction had not been emotionally upsetting to the child.[32]

Our interviews with the parents over a two-year period provide further signs of children's psychological distress stemming from the abduction. Approximately 75% of the parents we interviewed said that the abduction had some negative effect on the child that still persisted. According to our follow-up interviews, almost all of the parents reported that their children were receiving help by then, indicating continued difficulties with adjustment. We heard descriptions of children, at one end of the spectrum, who were in therapy initially after the recovery but who seemed to be coping fairly well at the time of our interview; even with these children there were occasional problems related to the memory of the abduction or to visits with the abductor. Other children were reported to be confused about the whole episode. Some had problems readjusting to being back with a parent they did not remember. At the other end of the spectrum were children who were experiencing severe emotional problems: some needed psychiatric hospitalization or were suicidal. Few children appeared to have escaped completely unscathed from the experience, according to the parents' verbal reports.

Stories of reunions and adjustment by children vary greatly from family to family and even within families. Predictions of how children will adjust are problematic regardless of age. Teenagers, because of the developmental stage they are going through and their tendency to connect more with peers than with adults, can be difficult to interview. Depending upon their experiences while on the run, they may have learned to fend off any type of questioning.

Case History

Abby, 13, was in hiding first with her mother, Betty, and then with her grandmother and great grandmother for almost 10 years.

Betty was abandoned by her husband (Abby's father) soon after Abby was born. Betty moved in with her mother-in-law, Claire, who had become very attached to Abby. Eighteen months later, Abby and Betty left Claire's and moved in with Betty's mother and grandmother. When Claire began visiting, tension developed because Betty's family members increasingly resented her involvement and started to block her attempts to visit. Claire sued for visitation rights. On the day of the court hearing, Betty and Abby, with the help of Betty's mother and grandmother, vanished.

As Betty explains it, her mother misrepresented the situation so that Betty believed Claire was going to harm Abby, who was then almost four. Going into hiding was seen as the only way to protect the child. Betty and Abby moved to a different state to live with an aunt and uncle. Three years later, Betty's mother, who still had strong influence over Betty, convinced her that it was better for Abby to live with her. For the next seven years, Abby lived with her grandmother and great grandmother and saw her mother only about once a year. The child had no contact with Claire or her father. Claire searched frantically for her but with no success. She started a support group for grandparents like herself, which is how she eventually came to have contact with Abby. Betty read about the support group in a magazine article. She was becoming increasingly concerned by the way Abby was being raised by her grandmother and was growing stronger and more independent of her own mother; after reading the article she came to believe that Claire would be a good influence after all. Betty blew the whistle, and Abby was reunited with her father and paternal grandmother after 10 years.

Betty described her own coming of age as struggling to free herself from the psychological bonds her mother had placed on her. Her mother had made her feel incompetent to parent, and it was only after being away from her that Betty was able to stand up to her in the end. Betty and Abby increased their contacts, and both agreed that Abby would leave and live with Betty. Betty's mother tried to stop Abby from leaving, and Betty went to the police, setting off a chain reaction of court cases, which are still pending. Abby is living with Betty now. A second child of Betty's is still living with Betty's mother and is currently the target of a custody battle.

Abby's development appears to have been negatively affected by living with her grandmother, according to Betty. Betty depicted Abby as being a shy girl who was never allowed out of the house and who was afraid to sleep alone in a room. Betty said she was socially immature and, now that she was free from her grandmother, was enjoying playing outside for the first time in years. "She is like a little girl when she goes out now," Betty said. "She has to catch up on all the play time she has missed."

When Abby was interviewed, she had been living with her mother for five months. She gave short replies, was not eager to fill the silences in the conversation, and appeared unimpressed by her own experiences. "I like living with my mom more than my grandmom now because it is not as boring. My grandmother wouldn't let me go out very much," she confirmed. "There were dances that were over at ten that I couldn't go to because my grandmother wouldn't let me stay out past nine." When asked if she knew she was in hiding, Abby said the only thing she remembered was being sneaked out of the house in a box. Her last name had been changed, but she never asked why. Even after moving back with her mother, Abby maintained contact with friends from her previous neighborhood. "My mom lets me do things that I couldn't do before, like going to dances and sports." Of her grandmother Abby said, "I couldn't even go to get the mail or cross the street at her house and she had no money to go to the movies."

Abby said she sees her father sporadically: "It's okay when I see him occasionally. He is the kind of person who does stuff when he feels like it." When probed further, Abby described him as unpredictable in his behavior, leaving the impression that he does not maintain regular contact with her and is hard to count on to maintain the visitation schedule.

Abby has become the subject of news reports (the magazine article, a newspaper article, and a TV interview with Claire), receiving attention she never expected. She seemed bewildered by it all: "Because my grandmom never told me that we were in hiding [from her father and paternal grandmother], when I found out, I freaked out. I got this look on my face like, 'What? I was in hiding?'" Later, in talking about what she missed while being in hiding, she said, "I wished I had known my other grandmother when I was little. She's nice."

What advice does Abby have for other children who are in

hiding or have been in hiding? In her reply is a hint of the obvious turmoil she had gone through in being fought over by three generations:

> How can I put this? They should ask the person they are stay-ing with why they have to stay with them and not with the other people. And stay out of the middle of the fights. Like if my mother and grandmother begin to fight over whether I should stay here or go back there, I'd stay out of it and the only thing I would say is where I want to stay. My mom has helped me by saying if I don't want anything to do with it, I don't have to get in the middle.

At the end of the interview Abby was asked where she got the strength to cope with the experiences she had. She quickly responded, "My mom."

Aside from occasional glimpses of them, Abby's reactions to the abduction are well hidden. Clearly, she has learned that saying little is the best way to cope with what has been a tempestuous situation. During the interview she downplayed the significance of the events that had occurred. But from descriptions of her behavior provided by her mother, Abby is now coming out of a shell within which she has lived for many years. She does not seem to have been aware that her situation was unusual, perhaps to her benefit. Her mother sees positive changes in her and is hopeful that in being exposed to more opportunities, Abby will catch up on many of the things she missed while on the run.

Case History

Not only do children's adjustments vary between families, but they also vary within families. For Ava (see Chapter 4) there were great differences. When her daughter, Susan, at age 6, was recov-ered four years after she had been abducted, she initially did not remember Ava. "She had been staying in a foster home and was flown back to be with me. She had thought I was dead. But when she got off the plane, we ran to each other and hugged and cried. It was like in a storybook. My [new] husband hugged and cried, too.

It took her a few days to adjust to us, but she has done real well since then."

We interviewed Susan on three separate occasions. At the first interview, within a few months of her recovery, she was an attractively dressed, shy child of six. She sat very close to her mother and gave us the bare minimum of details about her life. She was bright-eyed and answered appropriately, but she clearly had learned to keep her own counsel. She had spent half of the previous year in a foster home before Ava recovered her. Her home schooling, initiated by Ava to catch up on the time she had missed with her children, was going well. Susan also was adjusting well to her new half sister. She greatly feared her father, though, and had no desire to hear from or speak with him.

The experiences of David, Ava's 7-year-old son, left him in a more precarious position in terms of readjusting to his mother. He was missing longer and was having a very hard time being back with Ava, Susan, a new half sister, and a stepfather. David had been separated from Susan for months prior to his recovery and had been sexually abused (Susan had not). In addition, while Susan had been living with one foster family, David had been placed in a group home following his father's incarceration. As Ava reported:

> He was very difficult. He did not know right from wrong. He threw tantrums constantly. He would beat his head against the wall for hours. He cried fifteen or twenty times a day if he did not get his way. We went for counseling at a Sexual Assault Center and that helped us a lot. He has really improved over the last few months.
>
> At first he talked about wanting to go back with his father. Now he mentions it only on occasion. His father writes the children these letters from prison about us getting back together. Crazy stuff. The lawyer gets them and mails them to me, as their father doesn't have our address. I just read the kids the good stuff. I try to tell them he is a good person but that he just has done some bad things. The counselor said David can write him in a few years if he wants to, but it is too soon now.

When David was interviewed two months after reuniting with his mother and sister, he was extremely outgoing. For our second meeting, six months after the first, he ran out to the car to meet us and continued to be very talkative, loving the attention he received from us. Like many children with his experiences, he had learned to get attention through being affectionate and responsive to adults. Because David was very young when abducted, critical stages in his development had been missed and needed to be experienced with a loving parent like Ava. In addition, his moral development was stunted by the experience of living with a father who constantly broke the law. David's sense of right and wrong was not appropriately developed for his age. While he went to great lengths for attention at our first meeting, there was a marked improvement by the second time we met. He had learned more clearly where boundaries between adults and children should be drawn. He was continuing in therapy and had become much more manageable at home. Despite the gaps in his early experiences, David was able to build a more positive sense of self once he was given an appropriate home environment and professional help.

By our third interview with the family, more than two years after the first, David's behavior was appropriate for his age and he had completed his therapy. However, he was in a stage of idealizing his absent father, who had been released from prison and was telephoning occasionally. In reply to the observation that he appeared to be thinking a lot about his time with his father, he replied seriously, "It rings in my head like a bell!"

*   *   *

David is not alone in asking to see his father. According to the parents who recovered, 18% of their children frequently ask to see the other parent and 31% ask occasionally. The wish not only to visit but to return to the abductor also appears occasionally in these families: one in seven children was reported to want to live with that parent. We learned from a preliminary analysis of our follow-up data that this desire lessens over time.

For Ava, as for the vast majority of the parents who had recovered, the fear of another abduction is great. In fact, 53% of the parents said they feared it very much and another 31% said they feared it somewhat, leaving only about one parent in six without fear of reabduction. With time, this fear tends to diminish, according to our follow-up interviews.

As would be expected, the fear of reabduction is less for the older child. But some of these children have to cope with other fears having to do with their own well-being and that of their parents.

Case History

Jean, a 16-year-old, discussed her fears with us during an interview. She asked four poignant questions when she learned that we had experience talking to other families who had been through an abduction: "Is it okay for me to be angry at my father [the abductor]?"; "Is it okay for me to go for therapy and to talk to someone about my experience?"; "How do children who have been abducted fare over time?"; and "What happens to parents who abduct?"

These questions arose from her own traumatic life on the run. Jean, her older brother, and her younger sister were abducted when they were 10, 8, and 6. Their father, who had been divorced from their mother for three years and had remarried, lost a series of custody battles and asked the three children if they wanted to live with him. The children had been unhappy living with their mother and agreed. "My mom was on a health kick and all we ate were peanut butter sandwiches for months. The thought of living with Dad sounded pretty good at the time," Jean told us. They went into hiding in the Poconos, in central Pennsylvania, where Jean's father and stepmother searched for work in the vacation industry there. Jean reported the experiences of being on the run:

We stayed out of school for about the first ten months we were with my father and stepmother. He was afraid we'd get found out. When we went back to school, it was real hard. All of the kids we met just thought my stepmother was my mom, and we called her Mom, so no one ever suspected we were in hiding. We were told not to tell anyone. It was real hard on us because we were so poor. We stayed in a two-room shack with an outhouse at one point. Another time we slept in the car. We moved around a great deal and were always changing schools. Social services helped us out and never asked us any questions about being in hiding.

During this time the children's mother, Carol, had searched for them unsuccessfully. She also was stricken with cancer, which inhibited her investigation efforts. When the father heard through various sources that Carol was ill with cancer, he told his children that their mother had died. Three years after the children were taken, Carol located them. She did not pursue getting them back at the time, though, because she was too ill. "I also believed that when they wanted to come back to me, they would," she told us.

It was two years later, after they had been on the run for five years, that Jean's brother, remembering the phone number of their grandparents, called to say they wanted to return. "We wanted to go home," Jean said. "When we were first with my dad, it was fun. But it changed and it stopped being fun. They got tired of us, and we started to get whippings."

The children have been back with their mother for three years now. Carol reported that about 24 hours after the children's return they seemed to have "just slipped into the groove." There is one thing that hasn't changed, though. Carol is still a vegetarian, and the children are not thrilled with the food that is put on the table.

Jean's adjustment has not been easy since reuniting with Carol. She has difficulty with peer relations and with school:

> Because we moved around a lot when we were in hiding, my brother and sister and I had trouble making friends, so we hung around together a lot. I have trouble picking friends now because people can't relate to what I went through. Sometimes I feel caught between two groups of kids—those that are the fast crowd who like to party and those who are real serious and work hard at school. I am not sure where I belong sometimes and who I am. I feel like I've been putting up a front and have a secret identity under it all. I'm also not sure if I want to be in school now or work so I can get some money together.

Jean's experiences caused her to raise the four questions she posed to us. The anger she felt toward her father was slow in coming, in part because she initially chose to go into hiding and in part because he has suffered emotional problems. Jean reported that her father tried to find work but because he was unsuccessful, their lifestyle became more traumatic. As his problems manifested themselves in rejection and harm of Jean and her siblings, she became more conflicted in her feelings toward the parent she initially believed was her savior. Now Jean is attempting to sort out her emotions. One of them is anger, a normal and healthy reaction, given the experiences she has had. She and her siblings visit their father occasionally but find it emotionally difficult to stay for more than a few days. It is during those visits that the negative and mixed feelings are most likely to surface.

Jean went for therapy after being reunited with her mother; however, she did not find it helpful because, according to her, the therapist did not seem to understand what she had experienced. After we counseled her, Jean decided to return for additional treatment in her hometown. Unfortunately, many clinicians lack the special background needed to treat adolescents who have had experiences like Jean's (see Chapter 7).

For Jean and her siblings, experiencing poverty and deprivation, being physically abused and neglected by their father and stepmother, having to cope with their father's erratic behavior, and constantly moving made life on the run an extremely traumatic experience. While Jean describes the last few years with Carol as being "pretty good," concerns about her future clearly remain.

*   *   *

For other children who were abducted, the impact may be less dramatic but no less painful. Max, introduced earlier in this chapter, is struggling in middle adulthood with forming lasting relationships. He finished high school, went to college in California, entered sales, and married a year later. When he was 26 he became a father. The marriage did not last, and two years later Max and his wife separated. Work also has not been easy for him:

> I had problems with authority. I probably had a chip on my shoulder. In addition, I had a hard time being intimate with my wife and with women I have met since then. I'm sure it is all connected to my abduction in some ways. I got into therapy and then decided to train to do mental health counseling. But even in my work I sometimes wonder if my problems don't get in the way of some of the advice I give.

Max eventually reestablished contact with his mother and sister. His sister arranged a family reunion a few years ago, when Max was 33. She had been married and divorced and had given up custody of her first child, following in her mother's footsteps. "I saw my mom for the first time in years," Max said. "She had gotten off of drugs and found religion. She was better than I had ever seen her. Now I try and see her about once a year. I am working on things, but self-esteem is still a problem."

Ruth, at 22, also reports that she has had problems sorting things out for herself. Her relationship with her mother, for instance, has had its ups and downs, while there has been a slight deterioration in her relationship with her father:

When I first saw my mother, it was very strange. We didn't know what to say to each other, and yet we had a lot to say. I think we were both very nervous and have had to work very hard on our relationship over the past four years. I visited her that first summer and have tried to spend time with her ever since. Then I visited again over Thanksgiving when her whole family was there, and it was terrible. We fought the whole time. Since then it has been much better.

One issue that came between my mother and me was that I was very protective of my father. It was like I was waiting for her to say something bad about him so I could come to his defense. But she didn't. Her family also never said anything bad about him either and that made it easier for me to be with them. They still treated me as if I were six, which was the last time they had seen me. That took some time for us to get used to, also.

Another issue for me has been the guilt I have had to deal with. I know I could have made things easier for my mother if I had written her. I think it kind of spills over into my relationships now and my own self-esteem. When I went to college I would talk to everyone about my being abducted and after a while my friends suggested I see a therapist, which I did. So I don't feel as responsible for my mom's happiness as I did. And I think over time I've gotten a lot closer to my mom and am not as close with my father as I used to be. My mom and I are very much alike. We like the same books and the same kinds of art, which is really interesting given the fact that we did not see each other for so long.

My folks still have problems dealing with each other and certain issues still come up for my father. When he heard I was about to get a TV from my mother for my new apartment, he had to send one that was bigger and make sure it got to me sooner than hers did. He still needs to prove to her that he has been a success.

The task for Ruth now is to sort out the mythical impressions she had of her mother as she was growing up, that is, to differentiate the mythical noncustodial mother who would not visit from the real mother who could not visit. A complicated message for anyone to sort out, this requires that Ruth attempt to reevaluate both parents while also attempting to understand her own part in not contacting her mother. Ultimately, Ruth will have to find a position for herself that is removed from the continuing competition between her parents, a task she is now making clear strides to accomplish.

Not all children who are abducted end up living with only one parent after they are recovered. Kathleen, who was snatched by her father in 1968 when she was five, had no contact with her mother for six months while they were in hiding. When a court decision gave her father custody, Kathleen began seeing her mother on an occasional visitation schedule. A year later Kathleen's parents reconciled and remained married for another ten years before a final breakup and remarriages for both. Thus, for most of her childhood, Kathleen was living with both her parents, even though there had been an abduction, an experience she remembers as frightening:

> My parents had separated at the time, and I was visiting my father. After the time came for me to go home, I told him it was time to leave. He said, "You are not going back." When I started to question him, he shut me up. I was scared at the whole situation, and my father was not someone you questioned. He had me call my mom over the next few months to tell her I was okay, but he did stuff like tap the phone so he could show in court how upset I was talking to her about the thought of going back. Two years after they got back together she had a nervous breakdown and was hospitalized for being suicidal. He was ten years older than her and controlled everything. It was real strange growing up because on the outside we seemed like a picture-perfect family.

For Kathleen, growing up meant dealing with a father she feared and a mother she often viewed as incompetent. While the abduction was frightening for her, it was not the crisis event it was for many other children in part because her parents reconciled. The experience Kathleen had was perhaps closer to that of children who grow up in a family where parents temporarily separate, reconcile, and finally split up. Yet even in this situation, where the reconciliation lasted 10 years, the individual identified herself as someone who had been abducted more than 20 years earlier.

SPECIFIC ISSUES FACED BY RECOVERED CHILDREN

There are a number of realities to which a child who has been recovered has to adapt, particularly if that child was missing for a long period of time.

Changes in the Life of the Parent and Child

As the weeks and months on the run turn into years, the parent left behind is inexorably moving on with life. This may result in a new relationship and, as in Ava's case, even a new husband and child. The searching parent's significant new relationships necessarily influence the parent's way of accommodating to the returning child. The new child may resent having to share the parents with the returning child. The new spouse may have difficulty establishing a relationship with the recovered child.

If a sibling is left behind, as happened in about one in eight of the families we studied, the abducted child will try to sort out the possible reasons why the sibling was not abducted. Did the sibling refuse? Was the sibling not wanted? Was the sibling unavailable at the time of the abduction? Was the sibling not the biological child of the abductor? These questions will be raised again when recovery of the abducted child necessitates reintegration into the family.

The searching parent may pour all of his or her energy into the returning child to make up for lost time and to assuage that parent's guilt over the abduction. Thus, a whole family's attention may be intensely focused on the returning child. Of necessity, this means a great deal of adjustment for all family members.

Simultaneously, the missing child has matured. Such changes are inevitable. Even in typical family situations parents and children struggle to adapt to the child's new developmental stage, where old patterns of behavior are shed and new ones attempted. When the child and parent have been separated by an abduction, these normal changes can become impediments to the restoration of the parent–child relationship. Ruth, earlier in this chapter, complained that her maternal grandparents treat her as if she were six, the age when they last saw her. Upon recovery, the parent learns the child is not the same as when the abduction occurred. Some of the changes, particularly if they are perceived as negative ones, may be blamed on the abductor. If it is difficult for the recovering parent to accept the behavior that he or she associates with the abductor's negative influence, it may be harder for that parent to accept the child.

Other adjustments also are needed. The child may have idealized the searching parent or, more likely, may have pictured the parent as an ogre. The child then has to adjust this internalized image of the parent to reality. In addition, normal routines of living have to be established upon recovery. The child may be accustomed to a set of expectations different from those established in the searching parent's home. The child may resent the new expectations, particularly if they are more restrictive.

In some cases children may have been taught to avoid all authority figures and not to reveal anything personal when questioned. Immediately after recovery, children usually are compelled to talk first to legal authorities and then perhaps to a mental health counselor, to whom they are expected to reveal intimate secrets. Coping with these changes is a slow and often painful process for children who already may have learned to keep their own counsel while their parents were breaking up.

Missing the Searching Parent: The Sense of Loss

In many cases a significant psychological loss has to be dealt with by the abducted child. As was discussed earlier in this chapter, young children in particular often form a close and important attachment to one parent. This bond becomes a key building block in their identity and self-esteem. When that block is taken away by the abduction, the child's internal sense of self may suffer. While the damage is not irreparable, it certainly can put the child at psychological risk. The result is that new tasks may be harder for the child to achieve; tasks such as schoolwork, socializing, and separating from the parent may be more difficult than they normally would be.

Some young children deal with early loss by turning inward, looking for affection and stimulation less and less from people and social activities and increasingly from their own fantasy world. Abby, for example, was described as being very immature and shy. Other children deal with early loss by having an exaggerated reliance on others, so that they have trouble forming an identity of their own.

The older the abducted child, the more likely it is that the sense of self already is solidly formed. For older children, however, other potential issues emerge, such as the feelings of guilt described by Ruth. Older children have a greater intellectual awareness of the meaning of the abduction for the family and for their own lives, as is evidenced by the questions Jean posed. In ideal situations, they may have formed emotional defenses for coping with the actions of their parents. This would be more likely if they had time to prepare for their parents' breakup.

Some children will survive the abduction without being greatly stressed. There have always been children who prove resilient throughout the ordeal they encounter, whether it be life in a war zone in Ireland or in a divorce zone in the United States. It is not a certainty that all children are hurt by the experiences they have at the hands of adults. The loss some children experience in separation from their parent can be overcome.

Anger at the Searching Parent for Not Having Prevented the Abduction

As mentioned earlier, children may be angry at the searching parent for not having located them sooner. The parent, supposedly the child's protector, is viewed as having let the child down. In situations where children have been treated harshly, abused, or neglected by the abductor, the anger is likely to be much greater. Depression can sometimes accompany anger if children believe that they were somehow to blame for not being located sooner. They may come to feel that they were not worthy of being found, that the searching parent did not love them enough to locate them. If the abductor and child have been fleeing an abusive situation, anger toward the searching parent will have another basis. Abused youngsters also blame themselves, believing they have not been good or lovable children.

Anger at the Abductor

Similarly, children have to sort out feelings they have for the abductor. These feelings can become quite complicated. Often children will be angry and frightened if removed from a parent with whom they were close. Lost contact with friends, relatives, and siblings provides fuel for this anger. Maltreatment feeds it further. A strong bond may be formed with the abductor if the abductor is seen initially by the child as saving the child from the parent left behind. It may be learned later, though, that the abductor committed crimes or was lying to the child. The child then becomes unsure whom to trust, and if the evidence mounts against the abductor, the abductor becomes the object of blame.

In some cases it is even more complex: The child returns to the searching parent, begins to believe that parent's version of events, but then finds elements of truth in the abductor's version also. Abducted and recovered children have to sort out for themselves the same difficult issues that children deal with in custody disputes, where no side is the clear hero or villain. For young children who need to see things in all-or-nothing terms, this can be quite confusing.

Fear of Being Abducted Again

Just as the vast majority of parents fear that their child will be abducted again, so too do many of the children experience this fear. According to the parents who recovered, only approximately one child in seven wants to go back with the abductor (the number may actually be higher, but the children may not have conveyed that wish to the recovering parent for fear of upsetting them). Many of the other children constantly look over their shoulders and worry that they are going to be at the center of another snatching. Their lives after recovery may revolve around this fear. They are coached about how to avoid capture and what to do if they are taken again. Some are quizzed frequently by their parents to make sure they know how to call them and how to contact the police; others are watched during holidays or anniversaries, periods that seem to be especially likely for the abductor to attempt another snatching.

If visitation is allowed, the parent's and child's fears may be even greater because the opportunity for another snatching is ever present. When visitation occurs away from the child's home, the parent and child often worry that the abductor potentially has at least a few hours head start in escaping. Finally, the child may be interrogated constantly about discussions he or she had with the abductor during visitation. The custodial parent may wonder if the child is being questioned about which parent the child feels a greater allegiance to or which parent the child would prefer to spend time with, signs that the abductor may be considering another snatching. The child who is asked such questions inevitably is being forced to choose between parents, every child's nightmare.

Part of the child's fear of being abducted is related not only to a distaste for a lifestyle in hiding but to a general fear of the abductor. Almost half of the children who are recovered are reported to have such fears. Children who were abused by the abductors are much more apt to fear them than those who were not.[33] In addition, violence is apt to have been present in many of the families where the child fears another abduction. For example, fearful children are more apt than others to have lived with parents who had a violent marriage[34] and are more apt to have been abducted by force.[35] Given the frightening nature of violence, this relationship would be expected.

In the same vein, we know that women are injured in family violence more often than men. So it is not surprising that female parents who have recovered are more likely to report that their children have fears than are male parents who have recovered.[36] Closely associated with this is the finding regarding the gender of the abductor and the gender of the child: We learned—by comparing cases of female children abducted by females, females abducted by males, male children abducted by females, and males abducted by males—that parents who recovered believe their children are more apt to fear male abductors regardless of the sex of the child who has been recovered.[37]

Considering the children's experiences in the context of our typology of five abduction patterns, recovered victims of violent visitor abductions fear the abductor more than do children in other situations.[38] Victims of nonviolent shared custodial abductions (where we hypothesize that in some cases the left-behind parent may have been abusive to the child or abducting parent) fear the abductor the least.[39] Because these abductions frequently involve abducting parents who have established a strong bond with the child before the snatching, it is to be expected that the children would fear them less, particularly if the searching parent was abusive.

Lost Time at School

A very practical problem for the child who was enrolled in school before the abduction is getting back into school life (approximately one-half of the children who were abducted were five or older at the time they were snatched.) Some parents we interviewed mentioned abducting their children during the summer so that it would interfere less with their school experience and give the parent a chance to find a new school in the fall.[40] Other researchers have noted that abductions take place throughout the year.[41] Certainly, if the abduction is an impulsive event, it is not apt to follow any particular seasonal pattern.

If children are not enrolled in school while on the run (Jean and her siblings were not enrolled for months), educational gains will be lost. If recovered children were in school while on the run, a certain amount of adjustment to the former school will still be needed. A number of parents who had recovered mentioned school problems, including an inability to attend to the work, trouble with friends, and poor grades. Some of these problems could be linked to the child's experiences while on the run, especially if those experiences were upsetting.

Issues Related to Physical and Sexual Abuse

For nearly one-third of the children, having been abused by a parent puts them at risk for a multitude of other problems, as was true for Ava's son, David. Children subjected to serious violence often have trouble making friends and are more likely to have temper tantrums, academic and discipline problems in school, physical fights with children at school or at home, and problems with the law stemming from destructiveness, stealing, and substance abuse.[42] Sexually abused children often evidence unusually sexualized behavior, including public masturbation, drawing or reenacting sexual acts with toys, and displaying sexual overtures or aggression toward other children. Other common problems include difficulties with sleep, bowel and bladder control, concentration, and school performance. Self-destructive acts, from frequent accidents to attempted suicide, also occur.[43]

When we compared key experiences of the recovered children who were reportedly physically abused (40 families), sexually abused (12 families), or both (8 families) while on the run with those who were not abused, we found a number of differences. We must caution here that we do not have detailed information in all cases about the extent of the abuse, its duration, or who the perpetrator was (the abuse may have been committed by the parent, a lover of a parent, a babysitter, etc.). Thus, children who were reportedly abused perhaps only once or occasionally were grouped together with those who were reportedly the victims of frequent abuse. As such, we are referring to abuse in the broadest sense. In addition, it is only the account of the recovering parent that we are using. What one parent considered abuse, another may not.

With these caveats, we can say the children who were abused were somewhat more apt to have received mental health counseling after recovery than those who were not abused.[44] Given the possible aftereffects of abuse, this is appropriate because these children are potentially at greater risk for behavioral and emotional problems. And the recovering parents, being aware of this or perhaps observing the aftereffects, were more likely to seek outside help. The children who were abused also were much more apt to be afraid of the abductor,[45] less likely to ask to visit the abductor,[46] and, in fact, visited less with the abductor.[47]

It may not be only the abusive behavior the children wanted to avoid. The abusive abductors were often involved in other illegal activities and were more likely to have spent some time in jail[48] than were nonabusive abductors. The abductor was clearly someone these children did not want to see for a variety of reasons. Girls were no more likely to have been abused than boys, and children who spent time with male abductors were no more likely to be described as being abused than children who spent time with female abductors.

In one unfortunate example of sexual abuse, two young girls who were abducted by their father for a year were located after a neighbor called child protective services (CPS). The neighbors had been alarmed by noise emanating from the father's apartment. CPS took the girls into custody because of neglect, and the mother was telephoned by an anonymous caller who told her where to find them. Upon recovery the girls did not remember their mother and refused to talk about their father. After extensive therapy, the children disclosed numerous incidences of sexual abuse where the father "peed" in their mouths. Three years later both girls still exhibited behavioral problems for which they were receiving therapy. The father served two years in prison and has not seen the children since his release.

Being Emotionally Triangulated Between Parents upon Recovery

Just as the child often was caught emotionally between the parents before the breakup, so too is the child torn between them upon recovery. While in an ideal situation parents do not include children in their arguments, during a breakup parents frequently pull the child toward them as a source of emotional support and in an attempt to justify their position when arguing with the other parent. This can happen after abduction and recovery, whether or not there is an ongoing custody battle. If the abductor is visiting (as happens in over one-third of the recoveries), the child may be manipulated to side with one parent. When there is no visitation, the ghost of the abductor can still become a factor. The child may feel very defensive about the abductor and can be upset easily by an angry reference to the abductor by the custodial parent, as was Ruth. This often places the child in an untenable position: whichever parent the child sides with, the other will be angry. If the child chooses not to side with either, he or she fears losing the affection of both.

Feeling Like a Financial Burden to the Parent Who Recovers

Some parents have spent in excess of $400,000 to get their children back. Even an average expenditure of about $10,000 places most families in a financial hole from which it takes years to emerge.[49] Attempts by the family to return to a normal routine and put the abduction behind them are thwarted by the financial burden they are under. If the custodial parent has remarried, the new spouse may resent deeply the amount expended to recover the child. The child may feel guilty about the burden that has been placed on the family by the abduction.

Wanting to Return to the Abducting Parent After Recovery

Children are not always happy being returned to the searching parent. As mentioned, one in seven parents in our study believed their child wanted to return to the abductor.[50] In a handful of cases we interviewed, the children had already returned to them. These children may have formed a closer bond with the abductor, may have been brainwashed to believe the searching parent is not a good person or does not like them, or may have had good reason to avoid the searching parent (child abuse, neglect, etc.). In addition, life on the run—playing "cops and robbers" and avoiding school—can be exciting to some children.

Janet, a 55-year-old teacher, recounts her struggles in which she regained custody of her son only to have him leave again. After she ended her marriage and refused numerous attempts by her husband to reconcile, he snatched their 10-year-old son, Bill. She found him four months later through the help of her husband's mother. Bill became a behavior problem upon his return and remained in constant contact with his father through a secret telephone arrangement. Therapy was unsuccessful when Bill refused to return to sessions. Two months later Bill was abducted again. This time it took Janet four years to find him. He had been living in a different state, alone but in an apartment adjacent to his father's. Bill did not want to return to Janet, accusing her of having abused him, a charge that was dropped after child protective services investigated it. Life with Bill was difficult for Janet. During one argument he pushed her down the stairs. After that she gave him his choice of where he wanted to live. He returned to his father and has not spoken to Janet for three years.

Children express their lack of desire to stay with the parent who recovers in various ways. Sometimes, extreme misbehavior can make life difficult during the period when parent and child are trying to reestablish their relationship. Other times, it is not so much misbehavior as difficulties the child and parent have in adapting to each other. Physical custody after recovery sometimes changes hands as this difficult adjustment period is worked through. Ellen provides one such example. She was living in hiding in England with her father for ten years before his parents finally tipped off her mother as to her location. After her mother agreed not to prosecute, her father sent Ellen back home at her request. She was not faring well psychologically when she returned. She was bedraggled and unkempt and, at 14, had become sexually promiscuous and a drug abuser. Ellen and her mother spent a turbulent year before Ellen was given an ultimatum: straighten out or leave. During that year Ellen had beaten up her mother, shunned therapy, refused to come home at curfew, and had maintained her drug habit. She left to live with her paternal grandparents, with whom she stayed for a year. Her mother was told by state authorities that unless she took back custody, Ellen would become a ward of the court. Her mother gave up custody at that point, and the grandparents were awarded guardianship. Then Ellen's father came back into the picture, and his parents decided to relinquish guardianship to the state. Ellen's mother again was contacted and agreed this time to try custody one more time on a trial basis. Although the outcome is not clear at this point, this example illustrates the kinds of difficulties children and parents can have reestablishing a relationship after a long separation.

These traumatic periods of readjustment and custody changes appear more frequently with older children. It is the adolescents who, because they clearly have a voice of their own, are more able than the four- and five-year-olds to fight back and disrupt the family. Both Bill and Ellen in the examples just given were physical threats to the mothers. Both refused to continue in treatment. When younger children are recovered, it is easier to compel them to go to treatment (although, as will be discussed later, they are less apt to enter treatment in the first place). Older children also have reached the stage in their development when it is natural to break away from their parents. Thus, trying to forge a strong relationship with a child after a number of months or years runs counter to the needs associated with the adolescent's own developmental stage.

The cases in our study in which the recovered children wanted to return to live with the abductor (14%) were explored further.

This is an important minority to discuss because these children were very difficult for the recovering parent to raise. The recovering parents in these situations perceived that they were not seen in the role of savior, unlike parents of children who want to stay with them. Thus, their relationship with the child had the potential for being quite thorny.

Some of what we have learned by comparing those who want to return to the abductor with others can be inferred from our previous discussion. Those children in the nonviolent shared custodial abduction group, who were reported to fear the abductor the least, were most apt to want to return to them.[51] Almost half of the children in this group wanted to return. In addition, the children who wanted to return were more likely to have been snatched by the abductor at least two times.[52] One way to interpret this is to infer that these children had spent a number of different periods of time with the abductor and had formed a strong bond with him or her. Another interpretation is that the children believed in some cases the abductor had continually shown concern and caring for them through the abductions. A final explanation supports our hypothesis that this pattern of abduction sometimes involves removing children from abusive or violent parents.

Finally, the situations where the children wanted to return to the abductor tend to be, first, those where a female was abducted by a female parent and, second, where a male child was abducted by a female parent. In only 10 out of 109 cases were children reported to want to return to abducting fathers, as compared with 14 out of 60 situations where children wanted to return to abducting mothers.[53]

One frustrated father wrote to us about his son's desire to return to his mother. The boy was abducted when he was three and was on the run for five years before the father located him. The boy did not know his father and was quite confused when he returned to live with him and a new stepmother and half brother. "My son's mother felt it was wrong to take a child away from a mother, regardless of the quality of life the mother can provide," the father wrote us. "My child fears his mother but seems to have a split personality, which changes depending upon which parent is present. He gets the best of care from us yet feels a strong bond towards his mother who took everything away from him for very selfish reasons."

Entering Therapy

With half of the recovered children receiving some mental health counseling upon return (and a much higher percentage at the time of our follow-up interviews), the therapeutic relationship becomes an important aspect of these families' lives. Therapy tends to be used by the parents and children for two purposes: to ascertain if emotional problems have arisen as a result of the abduction and to assist with any specific emotional problems that have developed. The first instance is usually associated with shorter-term, less traumatic situations. These children often are seen for a few sessions to explore what their reactions might be. The parents send them for treatment because they are unsure how they are adapting.

Treatment is also provided to children who have had the more unusual and more troublesome experiences. Children may have extreme reactions to being back home and may be in need of therapeutic intervention to help them adjust. The parents of such a child are keenly aware of the trauma experienced by him or her and will seek professional help. David and Susan are two children who were in therapy for over a year at a center specializing in treating sexual assault victims. Ruth continues in treatment for help with sorting out her past and with improving her current relationships. Max entered treatment as an adult. Some children stay in treatment for years, and therapy is used by the family members as a key healing process.

The children who had entered therapy by the time of our survey tended to be children who were abused.[54] In addition, they were more likely to be children who were afraid of the abducting parent.[55] A child's experience of abuse and fear of the other parent are compelling reasons to enter him or her into therapy.

Also suggested by our findings is the fact that older children, those ten and over at the time of the abduction, are the most likely to enter counseling, with those in the five to nine age range next likely and those in the one to four age range the least likely.[56] One reason for this may be that very young children are not always good candidates for treatment because they are less able to verbalize their concerns. Although play therapy can be used with some children as young as two, treatment approaches with younger children tend to emphasize the role of the parent in learning how to handle the child's reactions. Older children who are abducted, as in the cases of Janet and Bill described earlier, may pose great behavioral problems for recovering parents. The child may be ambivalent about being recovered, and he or she may have been a willing participant in the abduction. The parent, when seeing aberrant behavior, may feel a greater sense of urgency in getting the child into treatment because teens have a greater potential for self-destructive behavior (drugs, sex, violence, suicide, etc.) than do younger children.

Denying the Abduction Ever Occurred

In some families discussion of the abduction and the abductor becomes taboo. It is as if the family wishes to forget a painful yet important part of its own history. As a result, children may learn to avoid talking about negative feelings related to other parts of their lives. Yet reminders exist every day about the abduction: Their friends ask them about their mother or father, television shows and news reports discuss abductions, and mailings from the National Center for Missing and Exploited Children fill the mailbox. Such secrecy and denial can increase the child's feeling of shame and of being a victim.

These issues face the child and family. Their impact is varied as they unfold over a period of time. The parent–child relationship is key to helping the child deal with these issues and, like all relationships, needs time to develop. We discuss therapeutic interventions with families in Chapter 7.

STAGES OF RECOVERY

What tends to occur when parent and child are reunited is a slow process of accommodation by both. This process, although it may vary, tends to go through stages that are similar to the stages experienced by families who go through other separations. Whether it is a soldier returning from war, a convict who has served time and is going home, or a child who is reuniting with a parent, first there tends to be a honeymoon period, then a more difficult time of reassessment of the relationship, and ultimately (and hopefully) an adjustment to the changes that all have undergone.

With parents who have recovered after a substantial period of time, the stories are legion of teary reunions in airports and police stations. Parties often are held for the returning child. Local newspapers feature stories on the parent who has located the long-lost child. This is the honeymoon period. The bloom does not stay on the rose forever, though, as the rigors of parenthood and childhood, often exacerbated by the abduction, come crashing in. The honeymoon period is soon over; the child must be disciplined, and the parent begins to deal with any emotional problems that have resulted from the abduction experience.

This second stage, when the honeymoon is over, we call the reality stage. Whatever behaviors it was possible to overlook initially, perhaps in the hope that being back home again would erase these reactions, no longer can be ignored. It is also in this stage, which can begin within a few days or weeks of the recovery, that the child is often back in school. The parent may begin hearing concerns from teachers, friends, or relatives about the child's behavior. While those concerns may have been voiced earlier, the parent was not ready to hear them then. Therapy may begin in this stage. Anger between the parent and child may come up at this point also. This stage may continue for a long period of time or might lead more quickly to the third and final phase, the readjustment stage.

In the readjustment stage the family members accommodate to their new reality and begin building a life together based on the present and their hopes for the future. This includes accepting the changes each member has gone through during the absence. It means that the parent realizes that the eight-year-old who has been recovered has needs different from those of the four-year-old who was snatched. Not all families reach a stage of readjustment. Some that do not are those in which the children may want to or actually do return to the other parent. They also may be the ones in which the hurt the child has experienced has been so great that a much longer period of time is needed for readjustment. Ideally, though, some mutual acceptance is reached and the family members are able to move on with their lives and place the abduction in a perspective where it is acknowledged but does not become the sole focus of the family's future.

SUMMARY

What we have learned about the children who were recovered confirms earlier impressions that their adaptation can be problematic and that their experiences while on the run do play an important role in their adjustment. Abuse, violence in the family, fear of the abductor, the sex of the abductor, the bond that has been formed with the abductor, the bond previously formed with the other parent, the length of the abduction, and a multitude of other variables all have an effect on what happens when the child is reunited with the searching parent.

We could hypothesize from our findings, from what others have found, and from what we know about child development that children who are abused, who are missing for a long period of time, and who witness violence are likely to suffer the most and to have the hardest time when recovered. This is not to say that these children will not adapt. Many do so with or without counseling. But from talking with a number of adults who were kidnapped as children, the effects are not easily shaken off. If problems appear in later life, the kidnapping often is seen as a cornerstone in the development of that problem.

CHAPTER 6
International Abductions

Like David Balfour in the stories by Robert Lewis Stevenson, the first youngsters to be termed "kidnapped" were snatched and taken abroad for some adult purpose, usually to work in the American colonies.[1] Today, international abduction is a major problem, although now the kidnapper is most likely to be the child's parent. Between 1973 and 1991, about 4,000 American children were reported to the U.S. State Department as having been abducted by a parent and taken across an international border, and estimates of the actual total run as high as 10,000.[2]

This chapter examines the questions of why abducting parents flee abroad and which ones are most likely to do so. It discusses parents' experiences with international abductions in light of other literature, particularly studies of interracial and international relationships (both types of marriage are overrepresented in our sample). This chapter then introduces the major international convention for deterring and resolving abductions, the Hague Convention on the Civil Aspects of International Child Abduction.[3]

GOING OUT-OF-BOUNDS

In our study of parental abduction, children were known or believed to have been taken to another country in more than one-fifth of the situations. Because the targets of international abductions included fewer single children and more sibling groups, almost 23% of the 519 children were involved in suspected international abductions. Destinations reported by the parents left behind in abductions included 27 different countries, three of which—Canada, Mexico, and the United Kingdom—accounted for 41% of all the international abductions to known countries. Other regional destinations included Central America and Puerto Rico (19%); Arab nations, Iran, and Pakistan (10%); South America (9%); Australia and New Zealand (7%); and continental Europe (7%). (The remaining abductions involved two to Israel and one each to Japan and South Africa.) There is no reason to think that the proportion of international abductions in our study is unrealistically high; another investigation found that 40% of abductions crossed international boundaries.[4]

A number of differences appeared between abductions with domestic and international destinations and, as will be discussed, between United States–born abductors and foreign-born abductors who go abroad. The children taken outside of the United States tended to be older, accounting for one-third of the victims over the age of eight and only one-sixth of those age two or less.[5] The abducting parents as a group also were older by almost four years, with an average age of 36.[6] Finally, the parents left behind in international abductions were less likely to have pressed legal charges against the abductor, probably because it was more difficult for them to bring charges outside the bounds of U.S. legal jurisdictions.[7]

The abduction patterns relating to custody and violence that are introduced in Chapter 2 and discussed further in the succeeding chapters are not particularly useful for explaining which parents abduct abroad. Families fitting all five of the patterns are found in the group of international abductions, and no pattern is represented disproportionately. Instead, our investigation reveals two types of international abduction that cut across the categories already discussed. The first features an abducting parent with no close ties abroad who attempts to throw pursuers off the track by escaping, perhaps only temporarily, to a nearby country such as Mexico or Canada or to another English-speaking destination. The second pattern revolves around a parent born outside the United States who, when a marital relationship sours, returns with the children to a country where the culture is familiar and where family and legal help may be available. In the following sections each pattern is discussed, and a family is profiled.

The Case of Harold:

HIGH-STAKES HIDE-AND-SEEK

Harold is typical of parents who up the stakes in abduction by fleeing to a place where it is difficult and expensive for the other parent and the authorities to follow. After a marriage of 13 years, Harold and his wife Jean felt they had little in common except for their two sons, ages 12 and 10. Of the two parents, Jean, who had been an abused child, had the more troubled background. When she was 16 she met Harold and saw in him a way out of her dysfunctional family. Harold's childhood involved few family problems, but he was aimless, unemployed, and unmotivated when, at 19, he met Jean. They married six months later, after Jean got pregnant. The conflict that they each had in their own lives spilled over into the marriage. While Jean worked to support the family, Harold eventually attended college and started a business. He began abusing cocaine, marijuana, and alcohol, and Jean sometimes joined him. He was periodically abusive to her (something she never expected because there had been no violence in his own family), but he did not mistreat his two sons.

When legal problems relating to his drug use caught up with Harold, Jean finally suggested divorce. Fearing the loss of custody and unwilling to leave his boys with their mother, whom he saw as unstable, Harold picked up the boys from school and disappeared with them for several weeks. After Jean got a temporary custody order and located them, the local police helped her recover them. A month later Harold snatched them again.

Part of Harold's strategy during the second abduction was to lay a false trail by telling friends he would take the children to Bermuda, where the family had vacationed and to which they dreamed of retiring. Instead, he took the boys to Canada, eluding authorities for 18 months. When he was caught shoplifting and arrested, Harold tried to conceal his identity, knowing there were drug and kidnapping charges pending in the United States. Canadian authorities notified the FBI, and Jean was contacted concerning the children, who were staying with friends during the few days their father was in jail. Jean brought the boys home to New Jersey, while Harold spent two months in jail for shoplifting in Canada. The state's attorney's office advised Jean not to press charges in the abduction, an all-too-frequent request based on hesitancy by states to pay the costs of extradition for prosecution; some state's attorneys believe their limited budgets can be better spent extraditing more dangerous criminals, like murderers and rapists.

The ordeal has been difficult for Jean, who has been hospitalized twice for depression, once before and once since recovering the children. The second time, she agreed that the boys should go to stay with their paternal grandparents, who live nearby. That arrangement has proved satisfactory to everyone, and the grandparents now have custody. The two boys tend to regard their time in Canada with their father as an adventure because they did not attend school, moved around frequently, and had lots of unsupervised time. Harold, who remained in Canada after his release from jail, is not currently in contact with his family. Jean worries that the ordeal will begin again with another abduction.

*   *   *

Like Harold, the American-born abductors in our study who took their children to another country were better educated than the total sample,[8] but in most other ways they were indistinguishable from other abductors. For example, they were as likely to be male (55%) or female (45%) as the abductors as a whole, and they showed no other unusual demographic or family patterns. The only exception was a tendency to abduct groups of siblings; 57% abducted two or more children whereas in the rest of the sample 29% did so.[9]

In other ways—including the incidence of violence in the marriage or toward the children, past psychiatric history, drug use, and criminal records—the parents born in the United States who abducted abroad were similar to the other abductors. The abductions themselves also followed the usual patterns. Abduction had not been threatened by the abductor or feared by the other parent more than in other cases, and the use of force in the abduction itself was not a distinguishing characteristic. There were patterns in the foreign destinations chosen by abductors born in the United States, and these tended to be based on convenience. For example, about 40% of abductors chose destinations in Canada, Mexico, or England, and many returned to the United States after a time. Children taken abroad by United States–born abductors were as likely to be recovered as children never taken out of the country.

There are several probable reasons for the similar rate of recovery. First, many of the preferred destinations for this group of abducting parents are countries subscribing to the Hague Convention, which is discussed in greater detail later in this chapter. Second, most of these abducting parents had no special advantages abroad in terms of financial support, family or legal help, or employment possibilities. This may be why many of them returned to the United States. If they remained abroad, they frequently stood out as foreigners to neighbors and law enforcement officials, and as such they were unlikely to receive special protection or preferred treatment. The United States–born international abductors were willing and able to take extraordinary steps to elude pursuit in a high-stakes game of hide-and-seek, a game plan that for them was not particularly successful.

Our study included an unexpectedly high proportion of abducting parents born outside the United States; 13.2%, compared to 6.2% in the general population.[10] Abductors born abroad fled to their country of origin in almost three-quarters of the cases in which they crossed international borders.

The Case of Paul:

HOME FREE

One case of international abduction involves Paul, born in the United States; Carmen, a native of Chile who retains that citizenship; and their daughter Elena, eight years old at the time her mother abducted her. Paul's family history is unusual when compared to the other searching parents we have come to know in that he was a victim of abduction as a child and he also admitted having previously abducted his daughter.

The youngest of several children, Paul was five at the time of his parents' bitter divorce. His mother tried to prevent his father from visiting with the children, and she tried to influence their feelings about him by using brainwashing tactics that Paul later came to see as a form of psychological abuse. However, Paul does not recall violence between his parents or physical maltreatment of himself or his siblings. When Paul was seven, his father refused to return him from a weekend visit, an act Paul attributes to frustration over visitation problems. After about a week the police arrested his father. Paul remembers an interview with a woman at the police station who asked how his parents treated him and where he preferred to live. Paul remembers that he was the one who chose to return to his mother and to spend every other weekend with his father, who was not prosecuted. The remainder of his childhood was uneventful.

At the same time, Carmen was growing up in a very traditional middle-class Chilean family. Her father died when she was 13 and by age 16 she was married and had a child. The marriage did not last. Carmen lived with her baby and her extended family and had the help of servants until she moved to the United States in her twenties, leaving her son with her family.

It was not long before Paul and Carmen met on the west coast. She was a few years older than Paul and worked as a cocktail waitress at the bar where he was a bouncer. Their first date ended in a motel room, and soon they were living together. After about a year they married. Paul describes the marriage as difficult from the start, with regular verbal fights and threats by Carmen to return to Chile. Neither spoke the other's language well, and they had frequent misunderstandings. Things deteriorated further after Elena's birth when Paul lost his job and they had to move in with his relatives. Carmen didn't work during this time, but she was taking classes to become a hairdresser. Paul remembers that she was unsure of herself as a mother and that he, who grew up in a big family and was close to his nieces and nephews, often could comfort their baby better than she.

Dissatisfaction with the situation eventually overwhelmed both of them, and they agreed to separate. While they each were looking for places to stay, Paul took Elena to his mother's house and never came back. Carmen got a custody order in her favor at a hearing Paul didn't attend because he didn't know about it (someone lied about having served him with notice). A private detective snatched Elena back for Carmen, who went into hiding with the 8-month-old baby. Paul pursued the matter in court and eventually won joint custody; a relatively stable period began. Paul had Elena with him part of every week, and within a couple of years he remarried. Things began to sour when Elena at age five began calling her stepmother Mommy and when the two households disagreed about parenting matters (Carmen also had remarried).

Carmen eventually accused Paul's wife of child abuse because of a minor injury, but after about a year of proceedings in the juvenile and divorce courts, Paul and his wife won custody. Carmen reacted very badly, making repeated false child abuse complaints and threatening to abduct Elena. She also had a new baby with her Chilean-born husband (her oldest son remained in Chile with his grandparents). Finally, when Elena was eight, Carmen did not return her from a weekend visit. Her husband claimed at first that she had left him, abducting their baby daughter as well as Elena, but he later joined his family in Chile, as may have been the plan from the start.

For almost a year Paul did not know where his daughter was. Then a tip from her family led him to Chile, where he found and tried to recover Elena. It was a hopeless task. There were felony charges against Carmen in the United States, but the United States had no extradition treaty with Chile. That country has not ratified the Hague Convention, and pursuing custody in the Chilean courts proved impossible. Paul was advised that it was unheard of for fathers to obtain primary custody, especially of daughters. In Chile he probably could not have obtained even overnight visitation with his child. He thought of snatching her back, but the idea of ending up in a Chilean prison deterred him; the U.S. State Department advised him to give up and return home. Out of money and hope, he eventually did so. Elena is now almost 12, and Paul knows little about her. She is not allowed to write him.

Like many parents who exhaust all avenues without success, Paul has given up and gone on with life. He says his best way of coping is not to think about his daughter or the abduction, but the detailed story he told us shows he has not forgotten. He and his second wife now have two children, and his new family is his lifeline. He told us, "If we didn't have each other, we'd collapse."

*   *   *

Parents born abroad were no more successful than others when abducting within the United States, but when, like Carmen, they left the country, they eluded capture and recovery of the child much more frequently.[11] They also avoided recovery more frequently than did United States–born parents who went abroad; recovery rates were 35.7% and 59.2%, respectively.[12] One of the probable reasons for their greater success is that they fled to countries not recognizing the Hague convention more often than did their American-born counterparts who engaged in international abduction.[13] Other reasons may include the willingness of family and friends to hide them and a tendency for courts to favor their own nationals when deciding custody cases. One United States–born father reported feeling that French officials declined to help him because of an uncooperative attitude toward Americans in general.

Parents left behind, like Paul, are at a serious disadvantage when attempting to recover children abducted by spouses or ex-spouses born abroad. In most cases, the abductors have no intention or need to return to the United States. They can live and support themselves relatively easily in their home countries, while the searching parent may be hampered by lack of fluency in the language, lack of long-term visas and work permits, and shortage of money and leave time from jobs. The most difficult situations arise when the legal system favors the abductor because of gender, religion, or some other factor. For example, we know of three abductions to Egypt, two of them by Egyptian-born fathers. Relatives of the searching parents have told us about groups of mothers, many of them Americans, living in Cairo and trying to recover their children in a legal system that strongly favors a father's right to custody. One grandmother answered our survey on behalf of a daughter whose search had led to pursuit of her son and his Arab father. Ironically, the abductors in these situations may have fled the United States with their children in part because they perceived mothers to be favored in custody awards made by American courts.

Abduction to some Middle Eastern countries has been especially difficult for those attempting recovery, according to some sources.[14] When an abducting father of Middle Eastern origin returns home, an American wife who pursues him there in an attempt to gain custody encounters a system that may not help her because of legal and cultural assumptions that fathers make the major decisions affecting their children. The pain and powerlessness of that situation has been portrayed dramatically in a popular book and movie that chronicle the experiences of Betty Mahmoody, a mother who escaped Iran with her daughter.[15]

GROUND RULES AND SIGNALS

Most, but not all, parents who abducted their children and returned to their countries of birth in our study were leaving United States–born spouses or former spouses. Although not every abduction from such cross-cultural marriages involved children taken abroad, families where there was intermarriage (i.e., international, interethnic, or interracial partnerships) appear to be at higher risk for international abduction. In this section, we focus on the nature of those high-risk families and the stresses that may lead to abduction. Included in our discussion are related issues about intermarriage in general.

Our study reveals surprisingly high rates of international and interracial or interethnic (Hispanic/non-Hispanic) marriage. In the U.S. population as a whole, 8.4% of marriages involve partners who differ in race or Hispanic ethnicity,[16] while our study found 12.7%. Some of these marriages were also international. Marriages between people not born in the same country (including the U.S.) made up 15.9% of our sample, and while the U.S. Census Bureau no longer reports marriage data by country of birth, that rate is more than two and half times the percentage of the total population born abroad in 1989.[17]

In all, in our sample more than one-fifth reported marriages that were international, interracial, or Hispanic/non-Hispanic. Neither this study nor the U.S. Census Bureau offers data about other types of ethnic or religious intermarriage. It should be noted that our research does not suggest that parents from ethnic groups of color are more apt to abduct than other parents; Hispanic, Asian, and African-Americans are underrepresented among the abductors in this study when compared with the general population.[18] It is intermarried families that are overrepresented, especially in international abductions.

Cultural differences in marriage and childrearing are explored in this chapter because of the insight they may provide into the larger than expected number of intermarriages in our study sample. The rate of international abductions was dramatically higher for both interracial/ethnic and international marriages than for couples who had the same race, ethnicity, and nationality.[19] U.S. borders were crossed by almost half of the racially or ethnically intermarried abductors and by more than half of those from international marriages, compared with the overall foreign abduction rate of one-fifth.

The literature concerning cultural issues in marriage is not well developed, and the ways in which different backgrounds affect parenting is explored even less.[20] However, there is some literature that may help explain why intermarriage is overrepresented in a sample of families who have experienced parental abduction. It should be noted that few parents in our study initially identified cultural conflict within their marital or parenting roles as contributing to the abduction. In follow-up interviews, however, many more did so; between 12% and 27% of the parents identified conflict in their marriages as due to differences in national origin, race/ethnicity, social class, or religion. In addition, culturally based expectations and patterns may be present even when the couple remains unaware of them.

The Case of Martin and Sandra:

A LACK OF TEAMWORK

Martin and Sandra are an ethnically intermarried couple who experienced a traumatic international abduction. Married eight years, they had a preschool daughter at the time of their divorce. Sandra got custody of two-year-old Tammy, and Martin, who lived nearby, had frequent 24-hour visits, although Sandra had told the court that he had been violent at times and had threatened abduction. Two months later, during court-ordered visitation, Martin left with Tammy, taking with him assets from cashing in an insurance policy.

Martin's family background was Mexican-American and Catholic, although he no longer practiced his religion, while Sandra came from a mainline Protestant family of Anglo-European ancestry. Neither had close or known relatives abroad. Martin had wanted his daughter reared as Catholic, but Sandra took Tammy to her own church and Sunday school. While that was the only overt instance of cultural conflict during the marriage, Sandra felt that their different backgrounds contributed to poor communication and frequent misunderstandings. She thought Martin had unrealistic expectations of her as his wife, based in part on his mother's role in his family of origin. Women, in Martin's view, should be the strong central force in family life, meeting everyone's needs and at the same time beautiful and feminine, worthy of being "on a pedestal." When Martin's expectations were not met, he became verbally abusive and threw objects, although he did not become physically violent toward Sandra until she insisted on divorce. As a child, Martin had experienced harsh physical discipline administered by his mother.

Sandra's parents, who had lived close by, were a major source of emotional support to her after the divorce and abduction. Her family was a close one that lived for years with the secret of her father's alcoholism. Although her father's drinking led to his recent death, Sandra denied that alcohol had had a significant impact on her family life. Part of Martin's initial attraction for her was that he drank little alcohol. Sandra had completed college and worked at a professional job whereas Martin had completed high school and had worked steadily for the telephone company until he resigned just before their divorce.

When Martin left the Colorado community where he and Sandra had grown up and lived most of their lives, he took Tammy to a city in the interior of Mexico. Although he had no special connections with that city and had never been there, he spoke Spanish, had a substantial amount of money with him, and believed he could find work. He also knew it would be hard for his ex-wife to trace him and Tammy there. Sandra hired a private investigator and sought help from local authorities, the FBI, and a missing children's organization, but she heard nothing of Martin and Tammy for over a year. She believed that Martin's mother knew where they were and visited them, but law enforcement officers told Sandra they could not follow the mother-in-law because she was not a suspect.

Sandra recovered Tammy when Martin returned to the United

States and went to work in Albuquerque, leaving Tammy unattended at home. When child protective services were notified by neighbors, they found serious child neglect and placed Tammy temporarily in foster care. Sandra received an anonymous call (she never found out from whom), telling her where the child was. When she rushed to claim her daughter she found a nonverbal, emotionally bruised child of three and a half who did not remember her and had been told she was dead. For several months afterward, Tammy asked her, "Are you really my mother?" There was strong evidence from medical examination and from Tammy's behavior and statements that she had been sexually abused by her father. Martin was convicted on charges related to the abduction but was not prosecuted for child abuse because Tammy was considered too young to testify. Tammy has received extensive therapy for developmental and behavioral problems, and at age seven she remains an insecure, depressed child.

*   *   *

Martin and Sandra fit the pattern we call the violent visitor, involving abduction by a noncustodial parent with a history of spouse abuse. That pattern is the only one of the five we found to be significantly more common among racially/ethnically intermarried couples,[21] although all of the other patterns also are represented.

There were several ways in which interracial/ethnic or international marriages differed from others. As the overrepresentation of the violent visitor pattern suggests, the parent left behind in the abduction was more likely to have been a victim of violence in marriages between partners who differed in race or Hispanic ethnicity.[22] This was not true of the international marriages. In the international marriages, but not in the interracial/ethnic ones, the abductor was perceived by the other parent as having been significantly more involved in two aspects of childrearing—physical care and supervision—than was true for the general sample.[23] In the three other aspects of childrearing investigated—recreation, discipline, and school work—less pronounced tendencies toward greater involvement also were found. Couples who intermarried, either internationally or interracially/ethnically, were more likely to have sought professional help for family problems, though not for individual ones, perhaps suggesting a higher level of stress around relationship issues.[24]

Another striking finding was that the partner left behind in an international marriage reported having had a greater fear of abduction,[25] an anxiety that apparently is not unrealistic. A section of a U.S. State Department publication—"Cross-Cultural Marriages: Should You or Your Child Visit the Country of the Other Parent?"—reads in part:

> Many cases of international parental child abduction are actually cases in which the child traveled to a foreign country with the approval of both parents but was later prevented from returning to the United States . . . A person who has assimilated a second culture may find a return to his or her roots traumatic and may feel a pull to shift loyalties back to the original culture. A person's personality may change when he or she returns to the place where they grew up.[26]

The State Department's advice to parents is offered because of the connection between international marriage and international abduction.

As we noted earlier, there is some information in the professional literature concerning interracial/ethnic and international marriages,[27] but there also are many unanswered questions. For example, the evidence is mixed concerning the stability of marriages among white, black, and Hispanic partners.[28] In some cases intermarried couples may bring to their relationships heightened appreciation of each other's culture. Diversity of backgrounds in marriage may demand a level of acceptance and tolerance that transcends what is typical in other marriages.

It appears likely that rates of racial/ethnic intermarriage may increase because of greater social equality and increased social acceptance[29] and that international marriages also may increase owing in part to slightly higher rates of immigration and easier international travel. Forces such as World War II and the Vietnam War produced large cohorts of international marriages; unless there is another major conflict involving countries whose customs are compatible with the American lifestyle, such marriages may decline. In the past, interest in military intermarriage has produced some of the literature that provides insight into international marriages in general.[30]

For anyone interested in parental abduction, one of the most salient questions is whether cultural differences concerning marriage and childrearing become sources of stress in marriages that cross racial, ethnic, or national lines. One interesting clinical study of women in interracial relationships suggests that societal racism is a major stressor, requiring self-protective behavior that frequently must be learned.[31] The same author discusses conflicting childrearing expectations and patterns in interracial families, differences that may help explain the overrepresentation of intermarried couples in our study of parental kidnapping. The pain of losing custody of one's child in the breakup of a relationship may be intensified by seeing that child brought up in a cultural tradition different from one's own.

Interesting insights into parental conflict over childrearing also may be gleaned from several studies suggesting that while national groups differ greatly in parental expectations of children, fathers and mothers within each nationality do not.[32] These findings about parenting differences have clear implications concerning the intermarried couples we have come to know. Patterns of ethnic belief and behavior do not change just because someone emigrates. In fact, such patterns may persist for generations, but they certainly are strongest in the immigrant generation. The literature suggests that differing assumptions about intimate relationships and the upbringing of children may underlie marital disruption, struggles over children, and, ultimately, abduction by one parent. Culture has been called the "grammar" that regulates interpersonal behavior; one result in a marriage between partners using different cultural languages is that important signals may go unrecognized.[33]

RULES OF THE GAME: THE HAGUE CONVENTION

The problem of parents abducting their children and fleeing abroad is not new or uniquely American, and the international legal community has struggled for many years with the difficulty of enforcing custody and other domestic court orders across national borders.[34] It is very important, at least symbolically, that the recently adopted United Nations' Convention on the Rights of the Child declares in Article 11 that subscribing states "shall take measures to combat the illicit transfer and non-return of children abroad."[35]

Traditional remedies to the problem of international kidnapping involve criminal extradition proceedings or custody contests in foreign courts, both difficult avenues.[36] An international accord on kidnapping first was proposed by Canada at The Hague in 1976, and by 1980 the Convention on the Civil Aspects of International Child Abduction had been drafted.[37] As of the summer of 1992, the following 24 nations have taken all the steps necessary to implement the convention: Argentina, Australia, Austria, Belize, Canada, Denmark, Ecuador, France, Germany, Hungary, Ireland, Israel, Luxembourg, Mexico, the Netherlands, New Zealand, Norway, Portugal, Spain, Sweden, Switzerland, the United Kingdom, the United States, and Yugoslavia.[38] New Zealand, where Hilary Morgan was living when she was located, was at that time one of the few English-speaking countries that had not adopted the Hague Convention. This well may have been one of the reasons she was taken there.

The definition of abduction used in the Hague Convention is similar to the one we chose to apply in our study. The convention provides for children to be returned to their preabduction country of residence, regardless of whether a custody order is in effect. In addition to abduction by a parent who lacks legal custody, the convention covers abduction by a married parent, by a separated parent when there is no court decree, and by a parent with joint custody following divorce. It also includes provisions concerning visitation rights across international borders.

Although the goal of the convention is to return children, courts in the country to which the abductor has fled (i.e., a country that has accepted the convention) may decline to do so for a few limited reasons.[39] For example, if proceedings for return are begun more than a year after the child's removal to the new country and if the child has settled into the new environment, return may be denied. Other grounds empower courts to refuse to return children to situations that carry grave risk of harm to the child, such as abuse or persecution. The Hague Convention applies only to minors under the age of sixteen, and it allows a court that is deciding whether to order a return to weigh the wishes of younger children who are sufficiently mature to express preferences about their custody.

Use of the convention is hampered by the fact that the number of countries that have taken all the steps necessary to put it into effect is small, although the number to have done so recently is encouraging. The United States signed the convention in 1981 and the U.S. Senate ratified it in 1986, but its provisions were not implemented until July 1988 when the International Child Abduction Remedies Act took effect.[40] That act provides specific mechanisms that enable the United States to comply with the Hague Convention and makes the U.S. State Department the agency in charge of enforcement.

THE SCORE ON INTERNATIONAL KIDNAPPING

Whether international abduction is a successful game plan depends in large measure on the players and the field. While United States–born abductors in our study appeared to gain no special advantage by fleeing abroad, except perhaps to delay recovery and make it more expensive,[41] the parents who were born outside the United States do appear to have benefited from the strategy. They were markedly more successful in preventing recovery of their children (for the variety of reasons explored in this chapter).[42]

One of the major differences between the two patterns of international abduction we have identified has to do with the destinations chosen by the abductors. United States–born abductors were more likely to choose English-speaking countries, most of which subscribe to the Hague Convention. Those countries also share with the United States a common legal heritage that may have fostered respect for each other's custody decrees and other legal mechanisms even before the convention was adopted. In contrast, abductors who were born abroad gravitated toward their home countries. Of the 24 different countries that were the birthplaces of the non–United States born abductors in our study, only 9 now follow the Hague Convention and many have legal systems very different from that of the United States.

Because numerous factors concerning international abduction are interrelated—including the places of birth and destinations of the abductors, the differing legal systems, and subscription to the Hague Convention—it is difficult to sort out the circumstances that make recovery of children less likely when an abductor was born abroad. The number of those abductions in our study does not permit controlling for the many different variables involved. However, our findings suggest that the Hague Convention is an important factor in the recovery of children who are abducted and taken abroad. Three destination countries in our study subscribed to the convention at the time of the abductions: Canada, the United Kingdom, and Australia. Eighty-four percent of the abductions to these countries after the Hague Convention rules were in effect resulted in recovery, compared to a recovery rate of 43% for international abductions to non-Hague destinations.[43]

When a parent takes a child abroad, the difficulties in effecting recovery are compounded: Information is hard to obtain, language may be a barrier, and distance alone makes all communication more difficult. In addition, a new legal system must be learned and navigated, sometimes against resistance from local authorities. The parents, fearing they will never see their children again, face what they consider to be the worst of parental abduction scenarios. Although the Hague Convention now holds promise for recovery of children from countries that participate in it, the only hope for many parents is that more countries will subscribe and enforce it in the future. Unfortunately, such international cooperative efforts sometimes are made on the basis of national political expediency, rather than on consideration of the welfare of children and families.

CHAPTER 7

Helping Families Survive an Abduction
Therapeutic Approaches

To understand fully the treatment needs and approaches suggested here, clinicians must travel, at least through their reading, some of the ground of those seeking help. The previous chapters of this book, where the experiences of the 371 parents whose children were abducted are described, will begin that process. If the clinician does not prepare in advance for work with this population, valuable time may be lost in treatment. Families seeking help, often frustrated by what they perceive to be a lack of effort by the police and FBI, will be further frustrated by having to educate mental health practitioners about the problems they face. This chapter identifies important issues and suggests ways that social workers, psychologists, psychiatrists, family therapists, and other practitioners can help families that have experienced an abduction.

These parents and family members seek help in one of two time periods: after the abduction or after the recovery. Before we discuss treatment issues within these two time frames, the role of therapy in preventing abductions merits mention. Timely individual, marital, and family therapy; divorce mediation; or court-mandated treatment programs[1] are approaches that should be tried with families who appear at risk for an abduction. Families at particular risk are those where there is marital violence, where threats have been made about abduction, where one or both of the parents previously have abducted a child, where the partners come from different cultures and one or both maintain strong ties with their country of origin, or where one parent clearly is unhappy with a custody arrangement or a divorce. Other warning signs include the following: difficulty related to employment; a change in family circumstances, for example, the death of an abductor's parent, so that the abductor no longer has a need to remain in a certain geographical location; extreme dissatisfaction with the court system; mounting financial debt; change in residence to more temporary housing (e.g., a motel); and any behavior that indicates a quick departure from the area is possible.

In working with these situations, whether the couple refers itself or is referred by the courts, the clinician may have to move swiftly to prevent an abduction: Communication between parents must be clarified; an acknowledgment of both parents' pain has to be conveyed. Techniques for reversing the violent nature of the relationship and the victim–victimizer roles should be applied when needed. Such techniques might include an acknowledgment of the differential economic and power positions of men and women in couples. An understanding of divorce laws has to be communicated. Cultural boundaries have to be bridged if the parents come from different countries of origin; this is true for the clinician, too, if he or she is unfamiliar with the role expectations inherent in one or both of those countries.[2] Finally, the needs of children after separation have to be made paramount and in such a way that abduction is discouraged. Access to the children must be made available, as appropriate.

Countertransferential issues (when the clinician has negative feelings toward the client that interfere with the ability to help) may loom large for the clinician working with divorce-related issues,[3] violent couples, and with partners from ethnic groups or cultural backgrounds different from the clinician's. Changing patterns of immigration and international alliances may call on clinicians to reassess their feelings about clients with cultural backgrounds different from their own.

If treatment continues past a few sessions, family-of-origin issues should be addressed. One of the abductors described in

Chapter 3 felt her own childhood pain being recreated when access to her child was blocked. Had her past been discussed in treatment, the chance of an abduction might have been reduced. Clearly, some abductions can be prevented with skilled clinical interventions. When an abduction has not been averted, treatment shifts to the family members left behind; if there is a recovery, the child may also be a candidate for treatment.

TREATMENT AFTER THE ABDUCTION

In the first time period (after the abduction and before the child has been recovered) it is usually the parent left behind who seeks help. Other people related to the parent may be prime candidates for treatment also. In taking a family systems perspective, those needing treatment may include anyone potentially connected to the child, that is, siblings left behind, grandparents, other relatives, even the new spouse or significant other of the parent left behind. If we broaden the scope of treatment further, depending on the situation, we might include friends, schoolteachers, baby-sitters, and other mental health professionals involved with the family. The strength of the connection to the child tends to dictate the potential need for treatment. For purposes of discussion, we will focus here on the immediate family—the parent left behind, the new spouse or partner, and the sibling who was not snatched— while recognizing that others also may benefit from treatment at some point. The literature on treatment of posttraumatic stress and on helping those experiencing divorce and remarriage provides the underpinnings for our discussion.

The Parent Left Behind

As discussed in Chapter 2, parents left behind often experience a host of reactions following the abduction, including rage, sense of loss, anxiety, depression, guilt, lack of sleep, health problems, and, occasionally, the need for psychiatric hospitalization. Treatment in many of these situations can focus on dealing with the stress reaction and attempting to reduce it, on helping the parent examine past events that may be exacerbating his or her current behavior beyond the expected level of a stress reaction, and on assisting the parent in mobilizing to search for the child, when appropriate.

Some parents experience something akin to posttraumatic stress, the reaction sometimes felt by soldiers who have been traumatized by battle and by civilians who are caught unexpectedly in a life-and-death crisis such as rape, an airplane crash, or an automobile accident. Common reactions to a severely stressful incident include reexperiencing the event, numbness to external stimuli, problems falling and staying asleep, hyperalertness, physical symptoms,[4] and feelings of shame and guilt.[5] Posttraumatic stress also can include the fear of harm or threat (e.g., torture or kidnapping) to a person's loved ones, as well as attempts to avoid thinking about an event.[6] In some pathological expressions of posttraumatic stress disorder an intrusion–denial cycle is established in which thoughts about a missing child cannot be stopped; that is, such thoughts affect daily routines (intrusion) and cause numbness or distancing from feelings or behaviors (denial).[7]

The potential impact of a stressful event is greater when there is little or no time to prepare for it, when there is danger involved in the event for the person or for a loved one, or when the event seems overwhelming.[8] In considering the impact of abduction on left-behind parents, we can hypothesize that those who were prepared for it (i.e., when it was threatened in advance or when the parent believed it to be a possibility) and those who believe the child is not in physical danger would have an easier time coping.

It is not only the event itself that determines the impact the stressor will have on a person. In the case of an abduction, a parent's personal makeup and past experiences dealing with stress also may influence how well he or she will cope with the abduction.[9] One means of coping with a stressful event is seeking and accepting the assistance of social support, that is, being able to rely on others when in need.[10] This has been defined further in the literature to include the stressed person's receiving encouragement, emotional support, advice, companionship, and tangible aid. Parents whose children were kidnapped are likely to cope better with the situation when key persons in their life provide hope and inspiration, care, love, comfort, specific problem-solving techniques, and practical resources (such as money to conduct a search).[11]

Intervention with the left-behind parent should begin with a full assessment of the parent's current functioning, as well as an exploration of past coping patterns (especially if the parent was a victim of abuse as a child)[12] and of experiences that might be related to current functioning. A differential diagnosis, which sometimes can be aided by personality tests, may need to be made to help distinguish between anxiety, depressive, and adjustment disorders.[13] The goal is to help the parent transform his or her adverse environment into a more nurturing one built upon his or her existing strengths. If the child returns, he or she will have a better chance of adapting if the parent is coping adequately.[14] Whether to involve other family members in the initial stage of treatment depends upon the issues the parent is facing. While long-term adaptation is more likely to be assured through family interventions that reinforce encouragement, emotional support, advice, companionship, and aid, early sessions may have to focus more on helping the individual transform himself or herself from victim to survivor.[15]

This transformation may be facilitated through catharsis and a working through of the anger, guilt, and feelings of isolation the parent might have. In addition, cognitive restructuring (e.g., helping the parent realistically appraise the part he or she played, if any, in the abduction) can be helpful.[16] Reframing the situation to one that will mobilize the strengths of the individual both to cope with the situation and to search for the missing child becomes a key part of the healing process.

The amount of effort a parent feels compelled to expend in searching must be considered. A parent who is feeling particularly guilty may leave no stone unturned. But as the length of the child's absence stretches from weeks to months, some professional help in discussing limitations to spending a great deal of time searching may be necessary. One parent, after searching 40 hours a week for months, found himself completely depleted. He adapted by promising himself he would spend one hour every day involved in recovering his child; his efforts have come to include providing support for other parents who are searching as well as carrying out his own search.

In addition to help related directly to the abduction, divorce therapy for the parent may be indicated. Whether the abduction occurred as the culminating event in a marital breakup or years after a divorce, marital issues may need to be discussed. For parents whose separation was precipitated by the abduction, issues about being single again have to be broached. In addition to the loss of the child, the parent may be angry about the breakup of the marriage, the loss of the partner, and the dissolution of the fantasy of a happy marriage. The parent may feel guilt or shame about not working harder to save the marriage or about having made a poor choice in a mate (friends and family may reinforce these feelings by saying that they had always thought the abductor was a poor choice). Depression, anxiety, and numbness are common reactions to a marital breakup; when the breakup is coupled with the pain of an abduction, these reactions may increase greatly.

If the abduction occurs many months or years after the marriage has ended, it may dredge up memories or feelings that the parent has not had to face for a long period of time. Adjustment to divorce is not a single event; it usually requires years of sifting through feelings, relationships, and memories before the marriage is placed in a perspective that is comfortable to the people involved. Adjustment can be made more difficult by continuous wrangling over custody and financial matters. Important events in the children's lives (graduations, marriages, etc.) can trigger unresolved feelings in a divorced person.

When an abduction occurs a number of years after the breakup, it is usually within the context of an unresolved divorce or parenting situation. (Abduction occurs rarely, if ever, when both parents are content with their individual lives, are on amicable terms, and are satisfied with their relationship with their child and with the way the child is being raised.) Whether the abduction is sparked by problems that are out in the open or smoldering beneath the surface, it, in turn, exacerbates those difficulties. For some parents, the abduction brings back unpleasant memories related to the marriage and breakup that they may not have dealt with for years. In treatment the therapist needs to be attuned to the meaning that the abduction has in relation to the marriage. This issue needs to be addressed directly. Patterns from early childhood relationships may reemerge and need to be discussed. For example, parents who were upset by their own parents' breakup may have felt they had come to grips with their own divorce only to find years later, with their child's abduction, that much still was unresolved for them.

Because of the availability of support groups for divorced people and the lack of groups in most communities for people who have experienced an abduction, referral to a divorce group may be appropriate as the best option. This is particularly true if the parent conceptualizes the abduction in divorce-related terms. The searching parent may also see the abduction as related to the abductor's substance abuse, emotional problems, or patterns of victimization or other criminal behavior; in these cases, groups targeted for these populations should be considered. Learning the parent's view of the events is the determining variable in deciding how to approach treatment recommendations. A group can be an obvious benefit to the isolated left-behind parent who may feel more connected if he or she sees that other noncustodial parents are struggling to have more contact with their children. Certainly, referral to support groups run by local missing children's organizations would be most appropriate. Searching parents often have to be helped to see that they are not to blame for what happened. Groups can help parents recognize what a normative reaction to an abduction might be. This feedback can help searching parents view their own reactions as understandable and normal. However, due to the trauma that the parent left behind often experiences, group treatment should not be the only modality considered.

Treating the New Spouse/Partner

If there is a new spouse or partner in the life of the parent left behind, that person is affected by the abduction in at least one of three ways. First, as was discussed earlier in terms of the definition of posttraumatic stress disorder, seeing a loved one hurt causes pain; the left-behind parent's anguish is experienced by the new partner as painful. Second, the new partner may experience additional anguish from the loss of contact with the child if a relationship between them had been established. Third, the interaction between the parent left behind and the new spouse is changed. Because each is hurting, their abilities to handle their daily routines are diminished. It is not unusual for one or both partners to be less able to work, less interested in sex, or inclined to withdraw in other ways, or to be angry and lash out.

Whatever the reaction, the clinician must be prepared to reach out to the new spouse. He or she may be angry at the parent left behind for any number of reasons: for not preventing the abduction in some way; for being involved with the abductor in the first place; for having to use family resources to pursue recovery or for losing that parent's income if time at work is missed; for losing the companionship and attention of the searching parent while he or she is in crisis; for having to negotiate with others on behalf of the searching parent; for having to talk to the legal authorities (if the partner has a history of negative interactions with the law); and for worrying about the recurrence of any previous problem of the left-behind parent, such as substance abuse.

These are issues for couples therapy as well as for individual sessions with the partner. For example, the partner can be asked by the clinician to explore the relationship between reactions to the current situation and earlier conflicts in the couple's relationship. Such an approach can begin to bring some perspective to how the couple will handle this crisis. Past successes at coping with problems can be used as a blueprint for dealing with the present. In addition, the partner's role in assisting with the search for the missing child needs to be defined: Will all decisions about expenditures for the search be made jointly? Will the couple divide up the work of notifying various police departments, contacting missing children's organizations, and sending out flyers? When the nuts and bolts of working toward locating and recovering the child are left up in the air, the stage is set for misunderstanding, which will hurt efforts by the couple to pull together when they most need each other. For example, if a mother whose child was abducted is accustomed to taking care of herself in her new marriage, attempts by her new husband to protect her from painful experiences or to help her search may be interpreted by her as interfering with attempts to recover the child.

Treating the Sibling Left Behind

A sibling who was not taken by the abductor also may need to be included in a treatment plan. The snatching potentially will have affected that child on a number of levels. At the most immediate level, the sibling will have lost the companionship of the abducted child and is witnessing the adults in the house in a highly agitated state. The greater the violence used at the time of the abduction, the more upsetting the experience can be. Siblings have been left behind for a variety of reasons: Some resisted being taken; others were taken but escaped before the abductor got far; still others were not sought because it was known that they would not go or did not have a good relationship with the abductor or because they were too young or too old or were not wanted.

The left-behind sibling may react with feelings of anger, rejection, relief, guilt, confusion, or fearfulness of another attempt. Added to the normal competitive feelings that occur between siblings, these feelings are quite difficult for the child to understand. Sometimes the child's reactions go unnoticed. At this time of crisis, when the child needs the support of parents, one parent is distraught and the other (the abductor) has left; there may not be anyone available to be reassuring and helpful. Such reassurance is especially important because children may feel that the parent who was unable to protect the missing sibling from the abductor also will be unable to protect them.

The primary goals of therapy with young children are to increase their guardian's ability to nurture them and to provide an opportunity for them to safely express any disturbing thoughts and feelings they may have. With older children the emphasis shifts slightly toward encouraging the child's increasing independence from the family, once the stability of the parent–child relationship has been established. Regardless of the child's age, some sessions should include all relevant family members. Like individual sessions, family sessions can be a venue to discuss feelings, taboo areas, changes the family has undergone, and the family's plans for the future, whether or not the missing child is recovered quickly. The emphasis should be on enhancing the family's strengths and on helping its members cope with the rigors of searching for the missing child. Individual sessions should be low-key in approach and should allow the child to ventilate any disturbing feelings about either parent.

TREATMENT AFTER RECOVERY

The longer the child is away, the more likely it is that professional help will be needed. In this section we focus not only on issues in work with the parent left behind, the new spouse, and the sibling but also on treatment for the recovered child. Families involved in abduction tend to go through three time phases (though there are great variations) after the recovery: First, in the honeymoon period, the recovered child and family are often excited to be reunited and are unusually patient with each other. Behaviors that normally would not be acceptable are excused because the parent is happy to have the child returned. Occasionally, the initial period is not a honeymoon. The child may be frightened of being returned to a parent about whom he or she has heard terrible things. In those situations the child may be quiet and withdrawn, needing a great deal of reassurance. Next comes the reality period, when the differences that exist between the child and the parent are confronted and when problems that were initially ignored or unrecognized surface. Finally, in the readjustment period the family, ideally, finds new patterns of interacting that integrate the changes the child and the family have undergone during the abduction and since the child's return.

The importance of describing these stages is that they help the clinician understand and anticipate what the family may experience at different points in time after the child has been located and returned. Families tend to seek help either as soon as the child has been recovered (during the honeymoon period) or when problems with adjustment start to occur (in the reality period). Some parents send their children for evaluation so that they can be "checked out" by a professional to see if there is any trauma that needs to be treated. Others see a disturbing reaction immediately and seek help to ameliorate it. Still others do not consider treatment initially; they attempt to return to their previous lives as quickly as possible and deny that anything untoward has happened that may require treatment. When adjustment problems arise, they then may seek help.

Children's Reactions and Treatment

The literature describing the adaptation of abducted children after they have been recovered is sparse, consisting of single case studies and research using small samples. One study of 17 recovered children, 5 of whom were again living with the abductor, found that while the abduction was linked to an increase in problem behavior in the child, there appeared to be a diminution of negative effects over time.[17] The impression the researchers had from parents' reports was that the negative reactions were not permanent. In a study of 18 children seen for treatment, there were signs of posttraumatic stress, such as play that included repetitive motions and fantasies about kidnapping; other reactions of the children included a hostile relationship with the recovering parent, rejection of the abductor, early involvement in sexual activity, extreme secrecy, weight gain, and confusion about the identity of the searching parent.[18] Neither of these studies focused on treatment issues. Available advice for clinicians has focused generally on being alert to parents who may be considering abduction, on trying to counsel deterrence, and on acquiring a knowledge of the legal context in which abductions occur.[19]

One case study that does describe the treatment process in depth centers on a two-year-old boy taken from his father and stepmother for five weeks.[20] The mother voluntarily returned the child because of his regressed behavior: He had difficulty with sleep, refused to eat, demonstrated mood swings, and urinated and defecated on the floor. The initial short-term thrust of therapy included reassuring the father and stepmother and medicating the child to sleep better at night. The child returned for further treatment almost a year later for a sleep disorder and anxiety reactions, the initial interventions having been unsuccessful. The child was then seen for play therapy sessions, sometimes accompanied by his stepmother. Meanwhile, the stepmother and father were seen separately for reality-based psychotherapy. In play therapy the therapist slowly introduced dolls representing the child's family structure; during one play sequence an adult female doll removed one of the child dolls. After a period of time away from the family of dolls, the child doll was returned. In reaction, the boy destroyed both the house of the female doll and the house of the family of dolls. When the therapist repeated the sequence, only the adult female doll's house was destroyed. This proved to be a breakthrough for the child. Further sessions with the boy and work aimed at assisting the parents in providing a supportive atmosphere facilitated further change, although it was a number of years before the child was problem free.[21]

Treating abducted children is a tricky process that first requires gaining as complete a knowledge as possible of the events surrounding the abduction and recovery. Key issues that need to be explored include the following: the reasons the child believes the abduction occurred; the length of the abduction; and the experiences of the child during the abduction (e.g., whether the child moved around a lot, received adequate medical care, was in school, or changed names; what responsibilities the child was given; what the child witnessed in terms of aberrant behavior; what type of relationship the child formed with the abductor, etc.). Particular issues requiring exploration are whether there was sexual or physical abuse; whether the child was willing to go with the abductor or even assisted in the abduction; whether the child was brainwashed (e.g., did the child believe the recovering parent was dead or did not love her or him anymore?); what sense of right and wrong the child was given concerning behavior and legal authorities; what the child was told would happen if the abductor and child were ever located; and whether the child wants to be back with the abductor.

CHILDREN WHO WANT TO RETURN TO THE ABDUCTOR

In our interviews with children and with adults who were abducted as children, some expressed mixed emotions about returning to the searching parent, especially if they had been gone for long periods of time. Yet when the experiences of abducted children are frightening or when the child is abused, the situation is often quite different. While some children form a close bond with an abusive parent, the relationship is not a healthy one. As the child's self-esteem increases after being recovered, the desire to return to the abductor may decrease. Helping the child to relinquish the need to be loved by someone who has been hurtful is one goal in helping abducted children.

Treatment in situations where the child wants to return to the abductor should be initiated carefully to deal with the child's potential resistance and ambivalence. The clinician must avoid being caught between warring camps of two parents. Depending upon the child's relationship with the abductor and the searching parent and the situation surrounding the abduction, the child may be better off with the abductor. A psychosocial assessment is needed for the legal determination of what would be in the child's best interests.

CHILDREN WHO DO NOT WANT TO RETURN TO THE ABDUCTOR

Other children cannot wait to return to their searching parents. When children are happy to be free of the abductor, the course of treatment is straightforward. The aims of treatment in these situations include helping children who feel guilty for not having resisted the abduction more vigorously, who are disappointed if the long-awaited reunion is not perfect, and who fear another abduction.

However, the course of treatment, even when the child wants to be with the recovering parent, is not simple. The clinician in these situations also must be careful to avoid being caught between the searching parent and a child who is resisting professional help. Children may maintain some allegiance to the abductor regardless of the treatment they received while on the run. They may feel upset about being compelled to reveal important and potentially damaging information about the abductor. They also may not want to further inflame the battles over them and may interpret therapy, which often focuses on talking about the abductor, as being inflammatory. That is, when a clinician attempts to treat a child who is extremely upset from having been at the center of great acrimony for an extended period of time, clinician and child may appear to have opposite goals: The child may want to put the experience in the past, to deny it, while the clinician wants to help the child examine and integrate the experience.

In addition, the question of an abrupt versus a gradual reunification should be weighed.[22] Some children and parents will need time to adjust to being back together. Forcing them together after months or years of separation may be problematic; other, interim, placements may need to be considered. Differential assessment can help in this process.

WHEN THE CHILD HAS BEEN ABUSED

When an abducted child has been abused by either the abductor or another adult, treatment for the abuse is imperative. Depending on the age of the child, the length of time that has elapsed between the abuse and the start of treatment, and the extent of the abuse, it may be difficult for the child to clearly remember it. The literature concerning treating physically and sexually abused children is not summarized here as it is extensive and has been well described by others.[23] Treatment should, though, include other members of the reunited family. The clinician needs to be aware of the potential legal ramifications of involvement in these situations because of the probability of a future custody contest and of abuse charges being leveled against the perpetrator.

SUMMARY OF ISSUES IN THE TREATMENT OF ABDUCTED CHILDREN

Thus, issues the clinician may confront in the treatment of an abducted child include the child's denial of the abduction (or being forgetful about it), triangulation between warring parents, lost time at school, anger at being abducted, fear and anger toward the abductor or concern about what will befall the abductor, resentment toward the parent left behind for not preventing the abduction, guilt for causing the parent pain and for being a financial burden, and regret at having missed changes in the family's life.

These issues need a therapeutic response that is supportive and cathartic. Play therapy with young children, as in the aforementioned case of the two-year-old boy, can provide an effective outlet for expressing frightening feelings. With older children, an open and nonjudgmental approach, one that does not force the child into treatment but leaves the door open for a return in the future as the child and family go through different stages of adjustment, is indicated. Finally, the confidentiality of the sessions must be discussed at the outset. Without clear ground rules as to how information given by the child will be used, trust cannot be established. Confidentiality may be a child's greatest concern. Refusing the therapist's request to video- or audiotape sessions, for example, may be one way for a child who feels little control over other aspects of his or her life to assert some healthy control in the therapeutic environment.

Some children will not overcome the pain of the abduction easily, particularly if it was a stressful experience and there is ongoing and confusing contact with the abductor. One California girl, who was taken to Israel by her father when she was five and recovered by the mother one year later, still has difficulties talking about the experience after seven years. Hindering her progress is her belief that she is constantly being manipulated by her father. She occasionally receives letters from Israel, ostensibly from her 18-year-old sister; in the correspondence she is invited to visit. A careful reading of the letters, though, has revealed to the girl and her mother that it is actually the father who is authoring the invitations. The girl believes she will be trapped there if she does visit. The choices she is considering for how to extricate herself from this emotional web include not responding at all to the letters, confronting the father in a letter and asking him to stop playing games with her, and inviting the sister to come visit her instead. Regardless of her response, this girl's feelings are an example of how the pain of abduction lingers. The role of the recovering parent in being supportive and in helping the child to sort out responses becomes vital.

Treating Other Family Members After Recovery of the Child

THE PARENT LEFT BEHIND

The most common scenario facing the clinician in an abduction case is the referral for evaluation and treatment of the recovered child, but the therapist's task is also to widen the scope of treatment to include other family members when possible and appropriate. The therapist may have to convince the parent and others that while missing the child may have been the most painful aspect of the experience for them, reunification carries with it its own set of tasks, which are not accomplished easily without professional assistance. Drawing connections between the recovered child and the other family members so that they will recognize the importance of their involvement in treatment can be done by explaining the parent's crucial part in the child's adjustment and by explaining how adaptation often means change on everyone's part.

Therapy with parents who have recovered a child entails working with them on their own feelings about the abduction, helping them parent the child, and assisting them, as the hub of the family, in bringing the whole family together. Seeing the parent, and not the recovered child, as the hub of the family is beneficial in that it reinforces the parent's role as nurturer. In the family hierarchy the parent should be in charge, providing the child with the structure that may have been lacking during the abduction. Many of the issues facing the searching parent (anger, anxiety, depression, etc.) also confront the parent after recovery. In addition, the parent may need to deal with the fear of another abduction, with ongoing legal battles with the abductor, and with the guilt of burdening a new spouse and other children in the family with abduction-related problems.

After the honeymoon period following the child's return, the child and parent have to face the hard reality that each has changed during the abduction. The longer the abduction, the greater the change. The parent may need information about what is normal behavior for the recovered child's age, knowledge parents may lack even when living with a child.[24] When a child has been away for a number of years, the parent has not had the opportunity to observe the slow changes that come with each new stage. All of a sudden he or she is faced with a child who has needs quite different from those that existed before the abduction. Grandparents who have not seen the missing child for years may have similar problems. Ruth, who is described in Chapter 5, said her mother's parents still called her the same young child's nickname she had when she was six and that they attempted to treat her as if she were still a little girl.

The parent who has recovered an older child may be angry that he or she did not try to establish contact. This needs to be addressed, as does the child's anger at the parent for not coming to the rescue sooner (if that was desired). Each may have fantasies about how easy it would have been for the other to make contact.

The myth of the perfect child also must be laid to rest. A parent who does not see a child for a period of time may forget some of that child's characteristics, and the child may be glamorized during the search. Upon location and return, the child turns out not to be the perfect child the parent has been seeking but, rather, a normal child—or even one with more problems than average. The parent may require assistance in mourning the loss of the myth of that child's perfection.

Parents of younger children who are returned need reinforcement of their competence to provide nurturing and structure for the family. The parent must be reinstated as the protector of the child. The parent of the older child remains a nurturer, but owing to the child's great need for individuation the parent–child relationship is slightly different. The independence of the child needs to be respected, with the parent providing support and protection when the child asks for it.

In some situations the parent is attempting to incorporate the returning child into a new family. If the parent has remarried, a new half sibling or stepsibling may be living in the home. Trying to balance the demands of the returning child and the new family can cause excruciating dilemmas for parents who attempt to meet everyone's needs in a fair way. The parent may have to focus a great deal of attention on the returned child, seemingly neglecting the adult and child from the new relationship. The child has to be reenrolled in school; examined by a pediatrician; clothed; reacquainted with friends, relatives, and grandparents; and prepared for potential court proceedings concerning custody or criminal prosecution.

When the new spouse is supportive and has been able to establish a good relationship with the children, the return proceeds much more easily. But things may not always go so well. In one family a searching mother's six-year-old daughter was taken to Australia for four years before being returned. The mother remarried and gave birth during her daughter's absence. The returned 10-year-old daughter had a great deal of trouble adjusting to her mother's family and remained very attached to her father, who was still abroad. After three years of battling with the daughter, whose behavior was highly disruptive, and despite the enormous support she received from her new husband, the mother feared her new marriage was going to fail. In attempting to maintain a stormy relationship with her daughter, who wanted to return to Australia, she risked separating from her new husband and child. She returned her daughter to Australia and has not heard from her for a year.

In addition to the general help provided during therapy, parents who recover need to be given specifics about the following matters: how to deal with a child who has been brainwashed against them or believed they were dead; how to handle the fear of a new abduction; how to deal with telephone calls, letters, or visits from the abductor; how to cope with family members who make inappropriate comments; how to explain changes in living arrangements (some children return to a different house or find they have to share a bedroom with a sibling they may or may not have known before they were abducted); and how to depict the abducting parent in a way that does not undermine the self-esteem of the child who may have a strong attachment to or be confused about the abductor. Parents also need to be advised of the importance of receiving legal counsel.

While interventions vary with the circumstances, the therapist can reassure the family by describing to them some of the common problems of parents who recover children. A knowledgeable clinician then can form a partnership with the family by helping them anticipate potential problems and cope with the ones that arise.

THE NEW SPOUSE/PARTNER

The recovering parent's partner is a key participant in the healing process that goes on after recovery. By accepting the child into the home and by being supportive of the child and the parent, the significant other in the parent's life greatly improves the chances that the family's adaptation will be successful. The clinician will be working with significant others who knew the child before the abduction as well as with those who did not. The treatment issues are slightly different based on this relationship. In cases where the spouse knew the child prior to the abduction, there are fewer unknowns with which both have to contend. The spouse can give advice and support based on knowledge of the child while he or she also works to reestablish a relationship with the child.

When the child and new spouse have not met before the abduction, the fantasies that each has about the other have to be addressed. The child may believe or may have been told that the new spouse is an ogre who was responsible for breaking up the parents' marriage or preventing them from reuniting. When dealing with any stepparent–stepchild relationship, lines of communication and issues of authority have to be clarified. Such mundane questions as who will discipline and which parent will be in charge of overseeing the completion of chores are the types of issues the family will need to consider. While these seem less important than decisions dealing with who will be available to the child when there are nightmares or phobic reactions related to the abduction, they must be addressed nonetheless. They can form the basis for dealing with the more sensitive areas.

Because of the trauma suffered by many children who are abducted, the stepparenting issues become intensified. Family loyalties are strained more than usual. The difficulties of stepparenting may be magnified if there is an ongoing custody battle or if a child is not adjusting well. The financial strain placed on a searching couple, as well as any continuing battles with the abductor after the child has been located and returned, take their toll. Excellent resources on stepparenting issues are available and should be consulted;[25] the clinician must remember that with abduction, however, family adaptation is often more difficult.

The new spouse may have to be seen separately for a few sessions. Various issues may have to be faced: He or she may feel neglected by the other parent and rejected by the child but be too embarrassed by the obvious pain of the returning child to ask for help. The new spouse may feel torn between loyalty to his or her own child and the needs of the returning child. He or she may want to protect the searching parent from any animosity expressed by the returning child and may intervene between them inappropriately rather than assist them in working out their relationship. In some instances, the returning child is more difficult to parent than was anticipated and comes home with many problems. If a quick solution to the child's problems was expected but has not arrived, a new source of stress will have been visited upon an already-depleted family system. If the couple's efforts at parenting are thwarted, they will feel increasingly angry and incompetent and may wish the child had not been recovered. In these situations, parents often are unsure how much negative behavior to allow from the child before disciplining. Parents are loath to be harsh toward a child who has had traumatic experiences. At the same time, they have to balance that tendency with the need to provide structure, something many returning children seek. In fact, the child's acting-out behavior may be a request for structure.

Setting up concrete parenting goals for the family can help to clarify some of these issues and reduce the strain around parenting. One of the first issues to address could be behavioral expectations for the child concerning, for example, TV watching, curfew, bedtime, and household chores. Later, the thornier issues, dealing with the abductor and reactions to alleged or actual abuse, for example, can be approached. Boundaries around the couple may have to be redrawn as the boundary between the child and the parent is being reconsidered. For example, parents who were clear about their relationship with each other when there was no child present now will have to address their new parental relationship. It should not be assumed that difficulty parenting the returning child will affect the parents' marital relationship negatively.[26] Many of these families, having gone through a great deal, now have enormous reserves that help them weather most crises.

THE SIBLING

The final family member to consider in treatment is the sibling. This may be a sister or brother who was left behind or a child born of the new marriage or brought into the new marriage by the stepparent. In the first situation, where the sibling was left behind, many of the issues described earlier for treating the sibling after the abduction apply. Other issues to consider include the following: the need for the sibling and the recovered child to get reacquainted after the absence; any jealousy or guilt that might exist because one sibling was abducted and the other was not; the preabduction sibling relationship and its usefulness as a predictor of the current one; the sibling's expectations about what the recovered child's behavior will be and how that child may have changed; and the need for siblings to work out anew the sharing of bedrooms, bathrooms, homework space, TV time, household chores, old and new friends, and so on.

Other issues need to be considered, some of which are specific to a new sibling being in the home. One is the need to establish rules for each child that are sensitive to the trauma the abducted child may have experienced and yet provide a structure that is fair to each child. Another concerns monitoring the time spent solely with the returning child so that the sibling does not feel neglected. Helping the sibling and returning child understand their new relationship is important. If they are half siblings or stepsiblings, they may have no history together and might benefit from being given specific things to do together that would increase teamwork. Finally, the parent(s) may need help in responding appropriately to the children's expressions of anger, anxiety, and jealousy.

This final point is especially important because the parent, weary of fighting with the abductor, may want to downplay any expression of anger or any differences that occur between siblings. Yet expressions of anger are a normal part of sibling and childhood relationships and should be allowed. The sibling should not be expected to welcome the returning child home with the same joy the parent feels. The sibling may not want to share the parent, may not have had a good relationship with the child, and may have constructed a negative image of the missing child, resenting all of the trouble that child has caused the family. These feelings must be allowed to be expressed so they can be worked through. With open communication and understanding from all members, scapegoating of the returning child, the parent, or the sibling who grouses about the returning child can be avoided. The literature about helping siblings is not extensive, but it does offer the practitioner some guidance in planning interventions with reunited brothers and sisters.[27]

THE ABDUCTOR

The clinician also has to guard against being caught between the parent who has recovered, the child, and the abductor. In some circumstances (in over a third of the families in our sample), the abductor remains a presence in the child's life, having supervised or unsupervised visitation. Through his or her continued involvement in the child's life, including comments to the child concerning therapy, the abductor has an influence. The abductor should be viewed as a potential partner in the child's treatment because he or she is still a part of the child's life whether there is any contact or not. The clinician must gauge carefully whether and how to include the abductor in treatment. Abductors who have acted out of a desire for revenge or who hurt the child would not be good candidates for inclusion initially. As in work with abused children and with children caught in custody battles, the child's welfare within the family context must be paramount. Ideally, as in most divorce-related therapy, if cooperation in continued parenting can be fostered, the child will benefit.[28] Unfortunately, this is not always possible.

Abductors may be involved in the child's treatment or their own therapy through telephone contact, letter, or personal meetings. Owing to the high level of animosity and mistrust that often exists between the parents, treatment approaches that include seeing the child, the abductor, and the left-behind parent together soon after the child has been located are not recommended except in cases of marital reconciliation. Such a meeting usually will be upsetting to all involved. The legal implications of all of these approaches should be considered in conjunction with legal counsel and discussed with the custodial parent of the child. Many parents who have reunited with their children are reluctant to include the abductor in any treatment plan that is not required by a court, and they may need a great deal of reassurance before they feel comfortable with therapeutic involvement of the abductor. At some point, perhaps six months to a year after the child's return, supervised or unsupervised visitation may begin, which would then make including everyone in therapy more important. The reasons for the parent's desire to exclude the abductor must be respected while explaining the potential importance of making some therapeutic contact with the abductor. The parent may not want visitation, as another abduction may be feared. The child may not want visitation because of the same fear and because of not knowing how to deal with both parents again. Ultimately, the decision should rest with the parent with legal custody and with the child. As always, a careful assessment based on the needs of the situation must be made before any particular model of treatment is applied.

When working alone with the abductor, whether or not the child is also a client, a number of issues may need to be addressed. These include the abductor's (1) anger at the court system if the court outcome appears unfair to the abductor; (2) anger at the recovering parent; (3) anger or confusion about the child's reaction to or remarks about the abductor; (4) sense of loss and depression if the child is not visiting; (5) potential employment; (6) inability to move on with his or her own life; (7) need to reconnect with old systems of support that were avoided while on the run; (8) concern about the child's welfare (which may have stimulated the abduction); (9) guilt if he or she perceives that the child has suffered; (10) recognition of any harm done because of the abduction; (11) taking responsibility for the events that occurred as a result of the abduction (by reducing his or her rationalization or distortion of the facts); and (12) seeking out more adaptive ways of coping with the feelings and negative behaviors that led to the abduction and may have continued. These last three points are particularly important for the pattern of abduction we see with the violent visitor and the violent shared custodian, where the child's well-being is less likely to be the reason for the abduction.

The possibility of paying restitution may also be an issue. The abductor may be ordered by the court to reimburse the recovering parent for the cost of therapy or for the harm that has been caused.

In addition to helping the child and recovering parent, this act can support important treatment goals for the abductor. It is not always feasible to have abductors absorb costs, and families also need to explore insurance coverage and agencies and others offering sliding fee scales.

CONCLUSION

Family reconstruction after an abduction demands recognition on the part of the clinician that abduction usually is a traumatic event for all family members. Its impact on all parties must be conveyed to the family so that treatment can be inclusive. Adaptation after such a potentially disruptive event takes time, and the ease with which it occurs will vary among family members. By using the literature about abduction, the treatment of victims of trauma and abuse, and divorce and stepparenting issues, the clinician can set the stage for work to begin. Each individual's strengths, as well as the strengths of the family unit, should be emphasized. The feelings of each family member must be validated. Focusing on past patterns of coping and current family strengths can provide the clinician and the family with a positive context within which change can occur.

CHAPTER 8

Before Parents Kidnap

Preventing Abductions

George and Denise are in their early thirties, married 10 years, with a daughter and son, ages eight and six. They are having serious marital problems and have a history of brief separations, which tend to occur after George has hit Denise. Lately, the beatings have been getting worse. George recently was laid off at the town's only factory, and it galls him to have to depend on Denise's job as a store clerk for financial stability. After being the family's chief breadwinner for years, he has begun to spend increasing amounts of time sleeping. The children are showing the strain of living with the unpredictable anger, fear, and unhappiness of their parents. Overwhelmed by the battering, her job, and doing most of the child care, Denise is privately considering divorce. Suspecting that she may try to leave, George fears losing his children more than anything in the world. Is a parental abduction inevitable? What would enable these parents to confront their problems in some other way?

Earlier chapters of this book examine the experiences of different actors in the drama of parental kidnapping: parents left behind, abducting parents, parents who recover, abducted children, and families who experience international abduction. The

219

preceding chapter focused on suggestions for working with family members after an abduction and after recovery. Ways society can help prevent and resolve abductions are the topics of this chapter and the next. Although emphasis is placed on parental abduction in the United States, many of the same problems and solutions are relevant to other countries, particularly those that share with the United States common demographic trends, legal systems, or approaches to solving social problems.

THE WHAT AND WHY OF PREVENTION

Prevention can be viewed on different levels, as it must be when considering how to deal with a problem as complex as parental abduction. Here we are concerned primarily with what society, through its laws and institutions, should do to keep parental abductions from occurring. Prevention can be thought of as a two-layer task, with the first layer affecting all individuals and families who might at some point be at risk for parental abduction and the second affecting those people who are most at risk.

The first layer of prevention policy, concerned with everyone who might be affected, often is called *primary prevention,* a term borrowed from public health policy, where the goal usually is to keep well people from becoming ill.[1] Primary prevention tools include sanitation, immunization, and elimination of the causes of illness. Our goal with the primary prevention of parental abduction is to keep healthy families from developing the kinds of problems that can lead to abduction of children.

The second layer of prevention policy is concerned with those who are known to be at particular risk for having a problem. *Secondary prevention* usually involves providing special help or supports to vulnerable individuals and families to enable them to continue to function adequately. To borrow examples from the health care field again, secondary prevention might include special diets for those whose test results show them to be in the high-risk group for a particular illness or treatments (such as gamma globulin shots) to build the immunity of those exposed to a disease (like hepatitis). In the secondary prevention of parental abduction, we would want to apply our knowledge of the problem to offer special services to those most at risk, for example, families involved in bitter custody disputes.

There is a third level of prevention, sometimes called *tertiary prevention,* that is concerned with keeping those already affected by a problem from getting worse. This level is really a part of treatment, such as efforts that are made to prevent children with high fevers from going into seizures or immobile patients from developing bedsores. Tertiany prevention of abduction would include efforts to protect children who have been abducted from the worst harms of abduction, such as abuse, years spent on the run, or the threat of repeated abductions. What can be done to help abducted children and their families therapeutically is considered in Chapter 7. The primary and secondary prevention of parental kidnapping, social policy goals for helping individuals and families in the aggregate, is the topic of this chapter. Policies to address abductions that have already occurred are the focus of the next chapter, which considers how society should respond when parents kidnap.

PREVENTION AIMED AT ALL FAMILIES WITH CHILDREN

Although the population most at risk for parental kidnapping may be the one quarter of American children who live with only one parent,[2] we know from the literature and from our experience that children living with both parents also are potential victims. Ultimately, any child could be affected by the parental problems that lead to abduction. Primary prevention is directed at the whole population at potential risk, which includes all families with children.

Because the major goal of primary prevention is to keep people at potential risk from experiencing a problem, primary prevention of parental abduction requires that society deal with the root causes of family disruption, including role strain on parents, gender inequality, domestic violence, and limited access to a variety of resources. While we cannot go into detail about all of the kinds of services that would support mothers and fathers in their parenting roles, we can make some general observations about the types of help that would reduce the stress on parents so that family disruption is less likely. This stress reduction would, in turn, make parental abduction a less common occurrence.

At this point in our history many families seem to break up in response to the stress of carrying multiple roles in a pressured world, especially when there are too few resources available to let them obtain any relief. It probably never has been easy to balance the roles of parent, spouse, worker, member of an extended family and community, and so forth. It is more than some families can bear to add the demands of two work schedules, expensive and hard-to-find child care, rising health costs, racial and gender inequality, wages that do not keep up with the cost of living, and life in neighborhoods where children cannot play outside with safety and where no neighbors or relatives are at home to help out in a pinch. More than 30 years ago, C. Wright Mills wrote these words to illustrate that private marital troubles can be due to such larger social problems:

> Inside a marriage a man and a woman may experience personal troubles, but when the divorce rate during the first four years of marriage is 250 out of every 1000 attempts, this is an indication of a structural issue having to do with the institutions of marriage and the family and other institutions that bear upon them.[3]

To help parents sustain themselves and their families, a network of supportive services needs to be available in every community and must include affordable, flexible, and safe child care; affordable health care for children; some paid and longer unpaid job-protected leave for the birth, adoption, or illness of a child; and flexible work schedules for parents.[4] Such policies and services, with the primary goal of keeping families together, also would ease the pressure on single parents when families do break apart. These family supports should be delivered in ways that benefit all families with minor children, for example, through direct provision of services or vouchers used to buy services, rather than in ways that primarily benefit those with considerable resources (e.g., tax deductions). The United States as a society does very little to share and ease the burden of raising children. If we are serious about helping families stay together, that must change.

There are other facets of life in our society where change also is needed. The relationships between men and women frequently are under stress because of the rapid changes in our culture. In relatively homogenous cultures with slow change, it may be easier for partners to feel that they share core values, goals, and expectations of each other. Our society is neither homogenous nor slow to change, and families sometimes are caught in the cultural earthquake zone created by shifting realities. As many women redefine their goals, taking on roles that would have seemed impossible to their grandmothers, and as men reassess their place in the present-day family and workplace, social institutions often lag behind the pace of change.

The impact of life in the earthquake zone can be severe. Family members may resort to violence or substance abuse in futile attempts to ease their pain. Marriages can be casualties. So can children. While the aforementioned social supports to families with children would help, more basic change is required. Sex role expectations of women include pressures to be the custodial parent or face strong social disapproval and suspicion.[5] This may be one force behind the surprising proportion of abductions by mothers. Perceptions of gender bias against fathers in the legal system sustain the belief that men have difficulty obtaining custody or having their visitation rights enforced,[6] a belief that may lead to some abductions. Mothers seeking custody also may encounter bias against women who are working, who have entered into new sexual relationships, or who are struggling financially. Policies concerning custody, child support, and visitation rights are often gender-neutral in theory but not in application. We should work to eliminate the remaining gender bias in all matters surrounding child custody if parental abductions are to be prevented.

What we have been discussing so far in this section pertains to the need to decrease social stressors that may result in family disruption and the possibility of parental abduction. There also are primary prevention strategies more directly related to the threat of abduction. In our conversations and correspondence with people about parental kidnapping, we have heard many suggestions about ways to discourage parents from taking their children and to facilitate recovery. For example, we have been told that in other countries with more developed systems of personal identification and state record keeping, successful parental abduction is less common than in the United States.[7] In many Western countries, for example, people carry personal identification papers, comparable to domestic passports, that are much more difficult to alter or replace than the driver's licenses and social security cards that Americans present for identification. Many countries also have national registration systems to record the birth of children, changes of address or employment, and other personal data.

Although these means might make it more difficult for a parent to go on the run with an abducted child, we have serious reservations about recommending any increase in government record keeping concerning parents or children.[8] In the United States the constitutional commitment to individual liberty makes it necessary for the state to show that it has a compelling interest to advance before the individual's privacy rights can be compromised. Americans also are keenly aware of the potential for abuse of power by governments, and they are reluctant to place information in the hands of those who could use it to discriminate against or persecute individuals or groups of people.

To date, specific efforts to help parents prevent or prepare for abduction have been voluntary. One example is the campaign sponsored by schools or law enforcement agencies to have children fingerprinted. The State Department also advises and assists parents who have reason to fear international abductions by preventing passports from being issued or reissued to their children, and the National Center for Missing and Exploited Children advises all concerned parents of preventive steps to take.[9] We believe that decisions about fingerprinting and photographing children, about issuing or restricting passports, about advising schools and day care providers concerning custody orders, and other such preventive measures should remain voluntary steps for parents to take if they feel they are necessary. Although government agencies have an important role in informing and advising parents, requiring participation in preventive programs would violate the privacy rights that the U.S. Supreme Court has recognized repeatedly in family and childrearing matters.[10]

However, for families who come before the courts to establish custody of children following separation or divorce, it may be appropriate for the courts to take some steps to facilitate identification of the children should that become necessary because of a subsequent abduction. In other words, once a family is in a position to need the second layer of prevention, a different approach may be justified. This idea is elaborated in the following section, which includes specific recommendations to prevent abductions in the families most at risk.

PREVENTION FOR FAMILIES MOST AT RISK

Since 1975 the number of children affected by divorce in the United States has exceeded one million per year, and by 1990 more than six million children were living with a divorced parent.[11] Although our research suggests that children of divorce are the primary population at risk for abduction, the more than eight million children who live with separated or never-married parents are also potential victims,[12] as are those whose parents are on the verge of separation. It is this group of several million children and their divorced, separated, separating, or unmarried parents who should be the targets of the most specific efforts to prevent parental abductions.

Our research has convinced us that the risk of abduction springs from several different roots, namely, fear for the safety or welfare of a child; fear of losing contact and relationship with a child; the need to control the other parent or the general situation, which often is fueled by personal problems; and anger or a wish to hurt the other parent. Prevention targeted to families at risk must change these root causes by influencing the medium in which they grow. The previous section addressed some of the societal changes that could influence families now at risk, as well as all families that might risk abduction at some point in the future.

In this section the more specific focus is on how the family or domestic court system could better serve disrupting families. At the time of the abduction 87% of the parents we studied were or had been married to each other. Why did they abduct rather than seek legal custody or the modification of a custody order? In many cases it is because they despaired of getting what they wanted through legal channels, whether that was protection for themselves or the child, protection of their access to the child, or a sense of control in a new and unfamiliar situation. These are problems that potentially can be dealt with by preventive measures.

Other abductors are motivated primarily by revenge and the desire to cause pain, and in our sample more than half were accused by the other parent of having been violent at some time in the marriage. One goal of the principles and recommendations we advance in this chapter is to make it more difficult for parents with this history to abduct or to abduct successfully (some abductions will occur, despite serious efforts to prevent them).

We believe that many parental abductions could be prevented if the courts that deal with domestic matters were guided by two principles and if they implemented a number of recommendations that flow from the principles. The recommendations are not uniquely ours; many are in place in various court jurisdictions, but they are not now the norm in all U.S. family or domestic relations courts. The two overarching principles are presented here with brief rationales, followed by each recommendation and a discussion of it.

TWO PRINCIPLES CONCERNING FAMILIES AT RISK

Principle I: Children are entitled to physical safety and emotional continuity in custody arrangements decreed by courts.

Physical safety and emotional continuity are important for all children, but when the state becomes involved by granting parents a separation or divorce and awarding custody of children, it takes on a special burden to safeguard the children's physical and emotional welfare. At a minimum, children of divorce are entitled to custody decisions that are the least detrimental alternative available to the court.[13] Custody decisions should, therefore, seek to avoid placing children in situations where abuse, violence, and conflict put them at risk of physical or emotional harm.

Principle II: Children and parents in disrupted families are entitled to maximum contact with each other, consistent with Principle I.

Parent–child relationships should not end because parents cease to live in the same household. They should change only as much as is necessary or unavoidable. In most cases this principle serves the child's need for emotional continuity. One legal commentator writes that "the best interests of the child do involve continuity and stability, but also extend to a mutually responsible relationship with *both* parents."[14] However, in the case of a harmful or undeveloped parent–child relationship, where contact with the parent may endanger the child or threaten emotional continuity, this principle is secondary.

RECOMMENDATIONS CONCERNING FAMILIES AT RISK

The seven recommendations that follow are given in approximately chronological order, that is, in the sequence in which they might apply to a family experiencing separation and divorce. This is important because the recommendations are somewhat interdependent; some of the later recommendations are made with the understanding that earlier ones also have been followed in the same case. The recommendations should therefore be viewed as a package that has potential for preventing many parental abductions.

Recommendation 1: Courts should be accessible and prompt in response to parents seeking temporary custody orders.

There are several situations in which a parent might request a temporary order concerning child custody before a more lasting order is entered (usually at the time a divorce is finalized). Separating parents might want the court's sanction for their agreement about which of them is to have primary custody during the separation or about shared custody. Or, if they are unable to agree, one parent might request the court's intervention to establish temporary custody. In many cases use of the court's authority to issue a temporary order can deter abductions by making custody clear and by advising parents of the sanctions against child snatching. Temporary orders also can make recovery more likely and prompt should abduction occur. The mechanism for obtaining temporary custody in these situations is in place for those who can obtain legal counsel, although access to the courts is problematic for those who cannot afford attorneys.

What is in need of change in many jurisdictions is access to temporary custody orders in emergencies, such as when a parent or child is in danger from the other parent. In those situations parents require effective legal means of protecting themselves and their children. If those means are not available—or if the parent does not know they are available or how to obtain protection—the parent sometimes flees with the child. This often occurs when battered women escape intolerable situations by running to shelters or to friends or relatives. Although the fleeing parent shares custody, that situation can become an abduction in a criminal sense the moment the other parent obtains an order of temporary custody.[15] Then the parent running from abuse frequently keeps running in order to avoid turning the child over to the feared parent.

Flight by an abused spouse often leads to pursuit, and sometimes the child is taken by the parent from whom he or she was running. This action, too, is usually not illegal if custody has not been awarded by a court. The parent who was running from danger and who experienced such a "snatch-back" of the child usually must seek sole custody before law enforcement agencies can assist, a process that delays pursuit.

In response to the problem of the abused parent with children, courts make orders of protection available, but these do not always include emergency custody or temporary possession of the family's place of residence. All three—restraining the abusive parent from coming into contact with the family; awarding emergency custody to the parent who might otherwise have to flee; and allowing that parent and the children to remain temporarily in the home—are necessary. It is critical that protection orders be available quickly, including during hours that courthouses are closed, by some process established by each court.[16] Procedures to obtain such orders must be simple, so that they are accessible to those who cannot afford extensive legal services. Criminal laws that provide for mandatory arrest when there is probable cause to believe an assault has occurred also help alleviate the need for an abused spouse to flee.

Because emergency orders of protection are not equivalent to temporary custody awarded after notice to all parties in a scheduled hearing, it is not clear how they are interpreted by law enforcement authorities in the event of an abduction.[17] For the court's orders to stay in effect past the emergency time period, the facts of the situation would have to be established in a court with regular (nonemergency) custody jurisdiction at a hearing with notice and opportunity to be heard given to all custody contestants.[18]

Recommendation 2: Courts should require mediation in disputed custody cases, unless there is cause to believe that domestic violence or child abuse has occurred.

Mediation is a process through which disputes can be resolved to the satisfaction of both parties without the usual adversarial process in the courtroom.[19] It may not eliminate the need for each party to have legal counsel, but it often narrows the points of dispute or produces agreement so that fewer, if any, issues have to be fought out in court. This can avoid the high costs of a contested hearing by reducing both the legal fees of the parties and the state's costs for court time.

Mediation services now are available through many domestic relations or family courts, as well as from social agencies and private mediators, to help parents reach agreement about child custody and other matters that arise in divorce.[20] Children sometimes are included in the mediation process.[21] The mediators often are specially trained practitioners from one of several fields, including social work, law, and psychology.[22] The Academy of Family Mediators sponsors a national referral service linking clients with qualified professionals.

Since 1981 California has required mediation in all disputed custody cases. Mediation has been used in domestic matters long enough for its success to be evident.[23] For example, studies show that mediated divorces are less likely to end up back in court because one party petitions for a change in the decision.[24] Mediation seems to give both parents a sense of control over the process by which important decisions affecting them and their children are made. In the process, parents are encouraged to see that they and their children gain from agreements everyone can accept as serving the children's interests.

The implications for the prevention of parental kidnapping are clear; if people feel more in control and less cheated in the process of reaching custody decisions that serve the interests of their children, they are less likely to feel that there is some wrong or injustice they need to right by taking matters into their own hands.[25] If they do become dissatisfied at some time after the original agreement, postdivorce mediation also should be available (a recommendation that is considered later in this chapter).

There are situations where mediation is inappropriate, even dangerous. It should not be used in cases where there is cause to believe that abuse of children has occurred, nor should it be used when there is the kind of personal power imbalance between parties found in families where there has been spouse abuse.[26] This is because mediation requires participants who can make their wishes and needs known and who can respond to the wishes and needs of others. Angry and hurt divorcing couples can be helped to do this by a skilled mediator, but those with a history of one person dominating through violence usually cannot be expected to do so. Given the couples' history, silent intimidation by the abusive partner usually is enough to dominate the other.

Recommendation 3: In disputed custody cases that reach court children should have their own court-appointed attorneys.

Traditional thinking about legal representation for minors in family matters holds that since parents ordinarily do what is in their children's interests, children do not need independent counsel. Since the late 1960s minors have won the right to have their own attorneys in court in certain situations, beginning with cases where their liberty is at stake in juvenile delinquency proceedings.[27] Representation of minors has been established by statute in other juvenile court contests, such as child neglect proceedings and termination of parental rights cases. However, children still are rarely represented independently in their parents' divorce cases, although the decisions affect them profoundly.[28]

If the aforementioned recommendations were implemented, most of the custody cases that reached court would involve unsuccessful mediation or allegations of violence. These are likely to be situations where the parents' acrimony toward each other makes the contest bitter and ugly. In such cases it often is difficult for the court to sort out the truth or determine what custody arrangement would best serve the child's interests. In the contested custody cases where mediation is inappropriate or has failed, children should have their own legal counsel, appointed by the court and paid for either by the court or by the parent or parents the court determines should pay.[29] Independent representation is necessary to make sure that children's interests are safeguarded in a situation where it is likely that one or both parents may be more caught up in winning than in making the situation tolerable for the children. In the unusual situation where siblings appear to have different interests that require protection, they would need separate attorneys, but in most cases the same legal advocate could be appointed for all the children in a family.

In potential parental abduction situations the child's attorney can advocate for the custody and visitation arrangements that have the best potential for providing the child with safety and stability.[30] Should an abduction occur, it could be helpful to the court, as well as to the parent left behind, to have a legal advocate already appointed who can protect the child's interests in any further hearings about custody. For example, if it is necessary for the parent left behind to return to court after an abduction to seek modification of the original custody order, perhaps to establish primary custody or to modify the abductor's rights, the attorney appointed to represent the child in the divorce could speak for his or her client's interests even if the child were still missing.

Recommendation 4: Courts should consider evidence of domestic violence in making child custody decisions.

Courts in a growing number of states are required to consider evidence of domestic violence in child custody hearings.[31] In 1990 Congress considered and passed a resolution introduced by Representative Constance Morella of Maryland and cosponsored by 80 other House members, a resolution "expressing the sense of the Congress that for purposes of determining child custody, credible evidence of physical abuse of one's spouse should create a statutory presumption that it is detrimental to the child to be placed in the custody of the abusive spouse.[32]

Before passage, the resolution was amended to note that Congress "declares that this resolution is not intended to encourage States to prohibit supervised visitation" with the noncustodial parent.[33]

This resolution of Congress has no binding effect anywhere, since laws governing child custody are made on the state level, but it raises the visibility of the issue and may encourage introduction of legislation in the states that have yet to consider the issue.

In any child custody case it is important to recognize the harm that is done to children who have witnessed or otherwise felt the effects of a parent's violence in the home.[34] At the same time, it is important to be aware that spouses sometimes falsely accuse their partners of abuse in order to bring about a more favorable custody decision. The emphasis in the House resolution is on credible evidence of physical abuse, and all charges do need to be weighed carefully with the understanding that even accurate allegations often are difficult to prove.

For the prevention of parental abduction of children, it is critical that the abusive marital partner not obtain primary or joint custody of children in custody disputes.[35] One approach that would further this goal would be a rebuttable presumption (an assumption the courts would make unless it is proved otherwise) that children who witness abuse of their parent suffer emotional harm[36] and that custody should therefore not be awarded to the abusive person.

Custody status also is critical for the resolution of abductions when they do occur. We conclude that a primary reason that those abductors in our study with a history of violence and lacking sole custody were less successful (in that the children were more likely to be recovered) is that the custodial parent left behind was able to obtain prompt legal and other help in the search.

Recommendation 5: In disputed custody cases courts seeking the least detrimental custody arrangement should weigh heavily the parenting patterns of the predivorce family.

There have been many changes over the years in the legal doctrines and tests that courts have used to decide custody between disputing parents. Under the legal tradition that the United States inherited from Great Britain, fathers held superior rights to custody; then, late in the 19th century, that claim began to be modified to favor maternal custody of young children. Mothers in the United States now receive primary custody in a very high proportion of cases, most often by agreement between the divorcing parents. This has remained the case, despite the shift some years ago to the "best interests of the child" test used to determine custody. Some states make gender neutrality their official policy, either by statute, as in Colorado, or by case law, as in Alabama.[37] There is evidence that fathers obtain legal custody in approximately half of all contested cases.[38]

Within the past 20 years joint legal custody, the sharing of legal responsibility and decision-making authority, has become an option for divorced parents, although living arrangements for the children vary widely and time is not necessarily divided equally between the parents.[39] In some jurisdictions there is now a legal presumption that joint custody is in the child's interests unless one party can prove otherwise.[40] Since California first established (and later abolished) a preference for joint custody, much has been written on both sides of the issue in the professional and popular press.[41]

Joint legal custody is appropriate in situations where both parents have a positive relationship with their child, where they can cooperate with each other in making joint parental decisions, and where they are willing and able to share in regular caretaking responsibilities.[42] Yet this clearly is not always the case with divorced parents. When parents cannot communicate well enough to agree about critical childrearing decisions or when they live too far apart to share in regular child care, legal and physical custody should be awarded to one parent. To give parents joint legal custody while the one with physical custody carries most of the child care responsibilities undermines the parental authority of that parent.

We are convinced that children can maintain attachments to more than one "psychological parent" after divorce when such a relationship was established in the intact family.[43] In families where both parents participate actively in the day-to-day care of children, it is to be expected that children will relate to both mother and father as psychological parents. In many of the cases where divorcing parents who have emotionally close and healthy relationships with their children make their own agreements about custody, either through mediation or without it, we think joint legal custody with shared physical caretaking will be a popular choice, one that should be encouraged.

In disputed custody cases, where mediation was inappropriate or unsuccessful, courts should base custody decisions on the parenting patterns of the predivorce family.[44] When parents both have been highly involved with the children, although not necessarily in exactly the same ways or roles, joint legal and physical custody is the arrangement that most closely mirrors the predivorce family.[45] In situations where one parent has been substantially more involved, and especially if the other parent has shown little interest in the children or family, the arrangement that provides the most continuity is for legal and physical custody to be placed with the more involved parent, with the substantially less involved parent having visitation rights. Determination of the most appropriate custody arrangement requires an exploration that goes beyond an assessment of who has spent the most time with the child and takes into consideration the nature of the relationship between each parent and the child.

In seeking a custody arrangement that is the least detrimental alternative for the child, courts should make case-by-case determinations of the parenting patterns of the predivorce family. There are several reasons for this. First, that criterion responds best to the child's need for continuity and emotional stability during a difficult transition. Second, it recognizes that families allocate roles and responsibilities in a wide range of ways and allows courts to respond flexibly; presumptions about one designated arrangement being appropriate in most cases do not recognize variations or encourage flexibility. Individualized assessment protects the custody interests of any parent who had substantial involvement and a positive relationship with the child before divorce.

A thorough assessment of parenting patterns, focused on the child's relationship with each parent, can offer courts and families more options than the "primary caretaker" preference that has been adopted by a few states.[46] While that preference is seen by some as gender neutral,[47] others consider it "a thinly disguised variant of the maternal preference" that results in sole custody being awarded to mothers in most cases,[48] since continuing gender role divisions in many families make it more likely that mothers, rather than fathers, will be judged "primary." One of the difficult issues in custody decisions in is how to respond to concerned and loving fathers who limited involvement with their children during marriage because of the demands and structure of the workplace, their own concept of fatherhood, or their family's implicit or explicit decisions about how marital roles should be divided. After divorce many such fathers find a new need for their children, and the children, too, may benefit from a deepened relationship.[49] How can custody decisions based on the parenting patterns of the predivorce family respond to these needs?

The group of recommendations offered here provide several responses. First, in situations where there is a caring father who has been less involved than he might have been but who now, facing divorce, wants to change, mediation can help the family reach decisions about custody arrangements that promote the child's interests and are acceptable to everyone. When the desire for change does not hit home until some time later, postdivorce mediation can help families reach the same goal. When this mediation fails, it is because either the mother or the child has strong objections to a change in custody status. In that case, custody should remain as it is unless the dissatisfied parent brings the matter back into court for a hearing. In the absence of compelling circumstances, such as harm to the child, custody should not be relitigated frequently or soon after a custody arrangement has been established.[50] Courts must strike a difficult balance between providing stable custody arrangements for children and allowing access to parents who desire a change in custody.

From the standpoint of preventing parental kidnapping, it is important that custody decisions be perceived by parents as good for their children and as fair to themselves. It also is important that parents feel that legal avenues are available if they are dissatisfied with the outcome for themselves and for their children. Finally, custody decisions must not violate the emotional bonds between parent and child by limiting contact with a loved parent or forcing contact with a little-known or distrusted one. Either action can motivate one parent to abduct.

Recommendation 6: Courts can participate in expanding and encouraging systems that make tracking abducted children easier.

Earlier in this chapter we discussed why we believe widespread state record keeping on individuals and families should not be implemented as a device to counter the threat of parental kidnapping. However, there may be good reason to propose that when families come before a court to decide child custody, the state has a compelling enough interest in preserving the custody decisions it makes to justify certain preventive measures. Specifically, we recommend that in all custody cases courts make recent photographs of both parents and all children part of the court record at the time of the original custody decree and at any subsequent hearing to modify custody, visitation, or child support decisions. These could be provided by the parents, whenever possible, to reduce any possible stress or stigma of being photographed at the court. Fingerprints of the children and parents might also become part of the court record, along with social security and driver's license numbers and other identification. This approach could be useful in preventing abductions because it would convey to both parents the court's seriousness about preserving court-ordered custody arrangements and facilitating searches for abductors. Should an abduction occur, the searching parent could obtain release of the photographs and other documents if he or she wished to use them in search efforts. Finally, in situations where abduction has been attempted or threatened or where there are other indications of high risk, parents can be required to post bond money as a deterrent to abduction.

Recommendation 7: Courts should make available postdivorce mediation and counseling services.

The role of the court does not end when a child custody decision is made. The court retains continuing jurisdiction over the case, in accordance with state and federal laws, and any petitions for changes ordinarily come before the same court. It is in the interests of society and the court, as well as parents and children, that any changes be made by a cooperative process that will encourage both parents to abide by the amended order. Just as mediation can help parents reach an original custody decision that both agree promotes their children's interests, so too can it help parents resolve later disagreements in mutually satisfactory ways.[51]

In the context of preventing parental abductions, postdivorce mediation services can give dissatisfied parents a place to turn before they reach a point of desperation and act outside the law. Particularly for parents who are dissatisfied with a visitation agreement or who have serious disagreements about childrearing, mediation should be available on a nonmandatory basis to offer them hope that things can change.[52] Although this recommendation concerns the general availability of postdivorce mediation services, another helpful approach is mediation targeted specifically to potential abduction situations. One such program, operated by Child Find of America, has been reported in the literature and appears to have potential for preventing parental abductions.[53] (This mediation program is discussed in greater detail in the following chapter.)

APPLICATIONS AND DISCUSSION

Let us return for a moment to the case vignette that opened this chapter to see how that situation might evolve if the seven recommendations presented in this chapter are followed. Recall that George and Denise are on the verge of separation, owing in part to George's violence toward Denise. Another factor that suggests a high risk of parental abduction is George's recent layoff. He may believe he has little to lose by abducting the children. If George acts first, the result is abduction by a violent spouse who shares custody. If Denise leaves with the children, it is an abduction by a nonviolent partner who shares custody. In some states neither action would be a parental abduction in a criminal sense (although there might be other legal consequences, such as being sued for custodial interference); in other states both abductions would be criminal acts.

If Recommendation 1 (Courts should be accessible and prompt in response to parents seeking emergency custody orders) were in place, Denise could get an emergency protection order that would allow her and the children to remain at home while enjoining George to stay away from the family until there has been a hearing. Any visitation permitted in such a situation should be supervised closely. If Denise files for divorce, mediation would be considered inappropriate, because of the history of family violence, under Recommendation 2 (Courts should require mediation in disputed custody cases, unless there is cause to believe that domestic violence or child abuse has occurred). Once the divorce petition is filed, Recommendation 3 (In disputed custody cases that reach court, children should have their own court-appointed attorneys) would give the children legal counsel to represent their interests. Should George abduct at any time after the protection order, evidence of emergency custody and of George's violence might help her obtain help from law enforcement and missing children's organizations.[54] Her attorney, probably with the support of the children's counsel, could help her get a custody order to replace the emergency protection order. If George does not abduct before the custody proceeding, evidence of his battering would be admissible under Recommendation 4 (Courts should consider evidence of domestic violence in making child custody decisions). Because Denise left the house and sought help several times after being hit, the testimony of others would be available to establish the pattern of violence. Under Recommendation 5 (In disputed custody cases, courts seeking the least detrimental custody arrangement should weigh heavily the parenting patterns of the predivorce family) the court would award primary custody to Denise. If George threatened or attempted abduction up to this point, his visitation would probably be supervised and he could be required to post bond to deter such an action. Identifying photographs, documents, and fingerprints would be entered into the court record, further deterring abduction under Recommendation 6 (Courts can participate in expanding and encouraging systems that make tracking abducted children easier). Should a postdivorce abduction occur, Denise would be in an excellent position to obtain swift help to recover the children.

Denise and George's situation illustrates the way the recommendations work in the case of a violent shared custodial abductor, but what about a different kind of situation? Consider the following hypothetical case:

Gary and Nancy, married five years, are the parents of Elizabeth, age three. Both work the same hours, and Elizabeth is in day care during the week. The parents have divided the child care tasks between them so that the day looks something like this: Gary gives Elizabeth her breakfast while Nancy gets dressed; then Nancy takes her to day care and goes on to work while Gary gets ready; after work, Gary picks Elizabeth up while Nancy starts dinner. Each parent has a part in the routines of playtime, bath, bedtime, and weekend activities.

Although Gary and Nancy both are committed to Elizabeth, things are not good between them. They have little time for each other, and communication between them is poor. Each privately thinks the other is the less involved parent. Things come to a head when one begins an extramarital relationship and states an intention to divorce. The other, feeling angry and wronged, is determined to maintain custody of Elizabeth rather than suffer two losses. The idea of sharing their daughter with the partner's lover is unbearable.

If this situation proceeds into the win–lose environment that usually pervades the courtroom, the chances are poor that Elizabeth's interests will be protected and that both parents will be satisfied. The parent who feels closed out of Elizabeth's life may consider abduction, following the pattern of a nonviolent visitor parent who needs and wants to be with the child. Even if joint custody were ordered over the objections of one party, it is unlikely to be successful, given the level of anger and distrust between the parents. The recommendations in this chapter would work to change that scenario in a number of ways.

When one parent files for divorce, mediation can begin immediately to help work on problems during separation. Despite their anger and history of poor communication, Gary and Nancy are good candidates for mediation of child custody issues because they both care about their daughter and recognize the other parent's importance in her life. With the mediator available to help them talk things out and to keep them focused on Elizabeth's welfare, they may reach a mutually satisfactory custody agreement. If not, Elizabeth will have her own appointed attorney, and the judge will make a custody determination, based on the evidence presented by all parties, that seeks to follow the parenting patterns in the predivorce family. If that decision is joint custody, as appears likely, the court may still have a role, through postdivorce mediation, in helping Gary and Nancy make this arrangement work. Identifying photographs, documents, and fingerprints could be recorded by the court for possible use should either parent decide that the situation justified acting outside the law to gain sole control of the child. That might happen if, for example, either parent were convinced that Elizabeth was being maltreated by the other parent or by anyone in the other household. How parental abductions in joint legal custody situations and in those involving allegations of abuse should be handled are topics addressed in the next chapter, which includes recommendations concerning what should happen when parents kidnap.

CHAPTER 9

Resolving Parental Abductions and Reexamining Their Context

The preceding chapter considers how society might reduce the incidence of parental abduction and offers a number of recommendations about policies and services for those most at risk, particularly families in conflict and those disrupted by separation or divorce. This chapter addresses the question of how society should respond when parental abduction does occur. Resolving abductions, preventing their recurrence, and dealing with the people involved pose major challenges to social policy.

As we discussed in Chapter 1, the number of children estimated to be involved in parental abduction each year varies with the definition of abduction. The definition used in this study (which includes children taken from intact marriages and by single custodial parents) is similar to that used by Finkelhor and colleagues, who estimate that 350,000 abductions occur annually.[1] The target population for the recommendations made in this chapter is the group of children and families who actually experience abduction. The focus here is on how our laws can protect children from the worst outcomes of parental abduction after it has occurred.

The first part of this chapter gives an overview of some of the

240

policies that exist to combat parental kidnapping. The next section presents three overarching principles and a number of specific recommendations for dealing with abductions. In making these recommendations, we compare and contrast them with some of the policies that now exist in state and federal law. Later in the chapter is a discussion of how different abduction situations might by resolved with the recommendations in place. The chapter concludes with a summary that places some of the key conclusions of our work within the social context of parental kidnapping that we introduced in Chapter 1.

HOW ABDUCTIONS ARE HANDLED NOW[2]

Laws that shape society's response to parental abductions are found on different levels within the U.S. governmental system. The states have the authority to legislate in the field of family law, such as child custody. Most criminal law also is enacted on the state level. The federal government becomes involved in the civil and criminal aspects of a problem like parental kidnapping in a number of ways, such as by addressing the interstate aspects of law enforcement, by establishing a framework for resolving disputes between states, or by making an offense a federal crime.

To date, most federal efforts to combat parental kidnapping have emphasized primarily one approach: preventing abducting parents from going to another jurisdiction to obtain a custody order in their favor. Although the immediate goal of depriving abducting parents of a legal forum has been realized to a considerable extent, the ultimate goal of deterring parents from abducting children does not appear any closer. There is no evidence that parental kidnapping has become less common; the increase in organizations that assist searching parents and in underground networks that aid abductors[3] may be an indication that it is on the rise. This section outlines briefly some major legal initiatives in the field of parental abduction of children.

Uniform Child Custody Jurisdiction Act

The Uniform Child Custody Jurisdiction Act (UCCJA) was approved in 1968 by the National Conference of Commissioners on Uniform State Laws, a body that drafts model statutes for consideration by state legislatures.[4] States moved slowly to adopt the UCCJA, and it was not until 1979 that a majority of them had done so.[5] Now all states have adopted its provisions in some version, although there is variation among state statutes.

Prior to widespread adoption of the UCCJA, courts frequently refused to recognize custody decrees of out-of-state courts, which often led to conflicting custody awards being made in different jurisdictions. The UCCJA's main objective is to clarify which state's courts should have jurisdiction in interstate custody disputes, including situations involving parental abductions. A state that adopts the UCCJA is bound by its rules about the circumstances under which that state's courts have the authority to adjudicate custody cases.

The UCCJA provides ways of determining whether a state may assume custody jurisdiction over a child, one basis being that the child has lived in that state for at least six months immediately prior to the custody proceeding. Only one "home state" should be able to assume such initial jurisdiction. The UCCJA mandates recognition and enforcement of a prior valid custody order from another state and limits the authority of a court to modify a sister state's custody decree.[6]

Parental Kidnapping Prevention Act of 1980

Slow state movement toward adopting the UCCJA was one factor that influenced Congress to enact the Parental Kidnapping Prevention Act of 1980 (PKPA).[7] Like the UCCJA, its primary goals are to settle jurisdictional questions and promote the interstate enforcement of existing custody orders. However, as federal legislation binding on all states, it represents a stronger and more unified approach to the problem.

The PKPA makes it much more difficult for a parent to take an abducted child to a new state and obtain a custody order because it requires states to enforce and not modify existing decrees that conform to the PKPA. In addition, the PKPA includes several other provisions to support the enforcement of custody decrees, including allowing state authorities to search for abducting parents by utilizing their locator services for parents delinquent in child support payments and by accessing information from the federal parent locator service. The act also makes it possible for the FBI to become involved in searches under the Fugitive Felon Act when an abducting parent has violated a state felony abduction law.

To illustrate the workings of the PKPA, consider the following situation. In the course of marital difficulties, one parent leaves the state to visit relatives, taking the child along. When it becomes obvious that this spouse is not going to return, the other parent files for divorce and custody in the state where the couple had been residing. Meanwhile, the parent who left the state obtains a custody order in the new state. Which custody order was issued by the state with jurisdiction to decide the matter? Prior to the enactment of the PKPA, this was a common situation. Since the PKPA, the second state usually would decline to hear the case, since the original state had jurisdiction as the child's legal "home state," the jurisdictional basis preferred under the PKPA.[8]

Although it is now more difficult, it is still possible for more than one state to assume custody jurisdiction since enactment of the PKPA. This has raised the question of whether the federal courts have a role in resolving cases in which state courts have issued conflicting orders. That issue came before the courts in a case where divorced parents in California initially had joint custody of their son in 1978. Then the mother sought and gained a temporary order of sole custody to allow her to take the boy with her when she accepted a new job in Louisiana. Subsequently, and after the PKPA took effect, she obtained a sole custody order in the new state, while her ex-husband won sole custody in the final California hearing. The case of *Thompson v. Thompson* was appealed in the federal courts by the father, and the Supreme Court decided in 1988 that the PKPA "did not create an implied cause of action in federal court to determine which of two conflicting state custody decrees is valid."[9] As a result, parents are unable to resort to the federal courts to resolve conflicting awards of custody based on noncompliance with the PKPA.

Other Criminal and Civil Remedies to Parental Abduction

Apart from limited enforcement of the Fugitive Felon Act, there has been little federal involvement in criminal prosecution of abducting parents.[10] When kidnapping was made a federal offense in 1932 and a capital crime in 1934, largely in reaction to the

Lindbergh kidnapping, the question of including parental abductors was raised in Congressional committee debate.[11] As a result, parents were specifically excluded from prosecution under the Federal Kidnapping Act because they were presumed to act out of concern for the child rather than with criminal intent.[12]

Older state kidnapping laws frequently have been interpreted by courts as not applying to parents, even when parents are not clearly excluded.[13] However, by 1990 all 50 state legislatures had passed new laws making at least some parental kidnappings felonies, potentially allowing enforcement under the federal Fugitive Felons Act.[14]

Civil suits (torts) arising out of loss of physical custody also are possible.[15] Parents have sued successfully for civil damages in parental abduction situations, primarily on the basis of custodial interference or infliction of emotional distress.[16] However, when such a petition was heard by the Minnesota Supreme Court in 1990, that body ruled that allowing a parent to sue another parent did not serve the child's interests,[17] a ruling that runs counter to the national trend.[18] Some states have made special provisions in their statutes for civil suits in parental kidnapping cases,[19] and such legislation was introduced in Minnesota following the court case rejecting civil suits for damages.[20]

The Hague Convention on the Civil Aspects of International Child Abduction

The Hague Convention is discussed in some detail in Chapter 6, so only a brief overview is repeated here. The Hague Convention differs in approach from legislation designed to settle U.S. interstate custody disputes. Unlike the UCCJA and the PKPA, the Hague Convention provides for children under age 16 to be returned to their preabduction country of residence, regardless of whether a custody order is in effect. Circumstances covered by this convention include, in addition to abduction by a parent who lacks a sole custody order, abduction by any of the following: a married parent, a separated parent when there is no custody decree, or a parent with joint custody following divorce. The convention also includes provisions for promoting effective exercise of visitation rights across jurisdictions.

Although its goal is to avoid relitigation and to return children, there are several grounds on which the abducting parent may seek to have a court block return of a child. For example, if proceedings for return are begun more than a year after the child's removal to the new country and if the child has settled into his new environment, return may be denied. The grounds for blocking return are intended to be narrow and exceptional, but they may still allow local courts to prevent repatriation of abducted children. Enforcement of the convention also is hampered by the small number of countries (24 by summer of 1992) that have taken all the steps necessary to put it into effect.[21]

Despite model state statutes, federal legislation, and an international treaty, resolution of parental abductions continues to be problematic. Among the problems are lack of consensus in society about the right legal approach to parental abduction,[22] state laws that vary widely, uneven enforcement by police and other agencies, resolution of abductions based largely on jurisdictional issues, and criminal laws that sometimes do not distinguish among the many motivations for and effects of parental abduction. The balance of this chapter considers how our societal response to parental abduction could be improved.[23]

THREE PRINCIPLES CONCERNING PARENTAL ABDUCTION

Principle I: It is in the public interest and in the interest of children for parental abductions to be resolved.

Some abducting parents, particularly those protecting their children from abuse, receive a great deal of public sympathy. A few also obtain private assistance from underground safe-houses and from other people willing to aid abductors.[24] Others, particularly those thought likely to harm their children, are the objects of public loathing and professional zeal in tracking them down. Our work has led to some interesting conclusions, discussed thoroughly in Chapter 4, about patterns of abduction that are most likely to end in recovery of the child; that is, abductors who did not have primary custody, those with a history of family violence, and male abductors were less likely to be successful.

We find it disturbing that searching fathers are less likely to recover their children than mothers with the same right to custody or history of abuse. Moreover, it is unfortunate that public opinion and the enforcement system sometimes ignore the potential for harm of even seemingly benign abductions.[25]

Abduction is an undesirable and often ineffective way to deal with family and legal problems.[26] Life on the run takes a serious toll on children, regardless of the kind of life they are escaping. Fear of one parent, unanswered questions about the past, isolation from relatives and friends, and the need for secrecy and deceit are destructive to the normal growth and development of children. When a well-intentioned abductor is caught, children face further difficult changes and their relationship with the abducting parent sometimes ends.[27]

In examining prevention policy in the previous chapter, we advanced recommendations designed to give well-intentioned parents more confidence in the fact that working through the system produces results that are fair to themselves and are the least detrimental option for their children. If those recommendations are followed, we expect that abductions will be fewer. In any abduction, all concerned benefit from its rapid resolution. In saying that it is in the interests of the public and of children to resolve all abductions, we do not mean that it is desirable to resolve all of them in the same way, a point that is elaborated further in the additional principles and recommendations that appear in this chapter.

Principle II: When parental abductions end, custody should be resolved from a child-centered perspective with the objective of finding the least detrimental custody arrangement for the child.[28]

When an abduction is ended—by apprehension of the perpetrator, voluntary return of the child, or any other route—legal custody remains as decreed by a court before or during the abduction unless there is a custody hearing to modify that order. In the event that conflicting state custody decrees have been issued, the jurisdictional dispute will be resolved in favor of the state with the valid claim to jurisdiction over the child. If a former abductor tries to obtain a legal change in child custody or visitation from the court that previously had awarded custody to the left-behind parent, the history of abduction generally works against the former abductor getting custody.[29]

All abductions are not the same in motivation, means, or effect on the child.[30] Parents may abduct to protect or to abuse, with careful concern or with violence, for a brief time or for a lengthy one. Some children go with their abductors willingly or even plead to be taken out of intolerable situations. Indeed, custody status may be irrelevant to the way a child perceives events, one reason we have elected to define abduction as broadly as we have. For example, a child may have been too young at the time of an original abduction to have any memory of it, although that action may have violated laws against parental kidnapping; a later snatch-back by the custodial parent may be the one the child remembers and perceives as an abduction.[31]

Because of the range of circumstances that underlie abduction, a custody determination following the resolution of a abduction must be a child-centered decision, not one focused on prior parental claims. By child-centered we mean a decision that weighs carefully the child's interests, that is, one that takes into account the child's attachment to each parent, the parenting abilities of each parent, and any evidence of harm to the child by either parent as well as, among other factors, the child's preferences (depending on his or her age, maturity, and knowledge of both parents).

This principle of a child-centered custody decision following abduction requires courts to weigh the effect on the child of any change in residence. In many cases life with the abductor is harmful to the child, who should be returned to the other parent. In other cases, however, it is the parent left behind in the abduction who is a danger to the child, and the child should be placed in the custody of the abductor. Even when neither parent is abusive, there may be situations where return to the searching parent would be more detrimental than remaining with the abductor. Specific applications of this principle are discussed further in two of the recommendations that follow in this chapter.

Principle III: Society should respond differentially to the crime of parental abduction, depending on the motives or intent of the abductor and on the circumstances.

Just as the custody decision needs to take the child's welfare into consideration, so too must criminal laws differentiate between one type of abduction and another. This principle requires the drafters of criminal codes and the courts that enforce them to respond to abductions by considering motivation, harm, and extenuating circumstances. This sort of differential response is not unusual in criminal law. For example, the same action may result in a ruling of murder, manslaughter, or self-defense, depending in part on the killer's motives and the surrounding circumstances. Just as the law has evolved different responses to killing, it should develop different responses to parental abduction.

RECOMMENDATIONS CONCERNING PARENTAL ABDUCTION

Recommendation 1: Jurisdictions should work toward more uniform civil and criminal definitions of parental abduction.

Although examples of parental abduction go far back in history and mythology (see Chapter 1), kidnapping by parents was not addressed by federal law or the laws of most states until little more than 20 years ago. As recently as the 1970s, descriptions of cases were filled with a sense of frustration and futility, reflecting the belief that nothing could be done about parents taking unilateral charge of their own children and thereby depriving the other parent of custody or access.[32] When that belief began to change, it did so in part because of public concern about the larger problem of missing children, including runaways and victims of stranger abduction.[33]

After less than a quarter century of attention to the problem of parental abduction, public response is hindered by the many different definitions found in state, federal, and international legal codes. What is criminal parental abduction in one state may not be in another. The "unlawful flight to avoid prosecution (UFAP)" provisions of the federal PKPA rely on these variable state criminal definitions. Further, parental actions that are not proscribed at all in many states may be remedied under the Hague Convention if the child is taken abroad. Although it is not unusual for laws to vary a great deal from state to state, it is a particular problem in this situation because parental kidnapping is especially likely to involve multiple jurisdictions. In only about 3% of the families we studied were the children known or believed to have remained in state during the course of the abduction whereas 20% were known or thought to have left the country.

Enforcement of the PKPA depends in part on state criminal law, because the UFAP provisions apply only if a state felony has been committed. To illustrate some of the variation in criminal definitions, some brief examples follow.

In Maryland the misdemeanor offense of parental abduction applies to children under age 12 taken from a custodial parent; felony charges are involved only if the child is taken out of state.[34] In Texas interference with child custody is a third-degree felony applying to a parent who takes, retains, or entices a child younger than 18 away from a custodial parent in violation of a court order, even if the child remains in state.[35] Interference with child custody also includes situations where a parent removes a child from the court's jurisdiction after a petition for divorce or other custody proceeding has been initiated "with the intent to deprive the court of authority over the child."[36] It therefore applies to many children of separated parents who would not be considered abducted in some other states. California's definition of parental abduction, the broadest we have seen in a state statute, applies to any person having custody rights who "takes, detains, conceals, or entices away" a minor "with the intent to deprive the custody right of another person."[37] Under this statute a custodial parent who denies visitation may be guilty of the same offense as a noncustodial parent who disappears with the child. Abduction by married parents who share custody also is included.

In contrast to the range of approaches to parental abduction found in U.S. statutes, the Hague Convention uses a definition that is not tied to the criminal laws of any jurisdiction. In considering the "wrongful removal or retention" of a child under age 16, it emphasizes any breach of the custody rights of another, including an individual with joint custody, whether in marriage, separation, or after divorce.[38]

The United States should attempt to move toward a more unified civil definition of parental abduction to facilitate the search for and return of children. Any more uniform definition should emphasize a consensual view of when violation of parental rights to custody or access (i.e., visitation) constitutes parental abduction. We favor a broad definition that would enable law enforcement and other agencies to assist parents with limited parental rights and those with shared custody, in marriage or by court order, as well as those with primary custody. In essence, no parent should be able to deny the other parent custody or access without legal authority. Criminal definitions, discussed here because of their impact on search efforts for abducted children, also require changes (the topic of a later recommendation).

Recommendation 2: The services of the National Center for Missing and Exploited Children should be available to searching parents whose situations meet the more uniform definition.

It follows from Recommendation 1 that public services to searching parents should correspond to a more uniform definition of parental abduction. At this time the national center can assist only searching custodial parents. This places unmarried parents who may be unable to produce a custody order,[39] as well as parents with rights to visitation, at a disadvantage. In contrast, many private organizations do offer help to parents whose visitation rights have been interrupted by custodial parents who disappear with the children if, after investigation of the situation, it appears that the custodial parent and children are not in danger from the searching parent.[40]

Recommendation 3: Mediation services should be used more extensively to help resolve abductions.

Mediation, used in custody disputes to help prevent parental abductions, as explored in the preceding chapter, is also a promising tool to help resolve abductions.[41] It is at the center of a relatively new program of Child Find of America that uses media announcements to encourage abductors who would like to find a way to resolve an abduction to telephone a toll-free number.[42] After speaking with a counselor who determines if there is mutual interest in a mediated solution with no assurance of legal charges being dropped, both parents can be connected with a professional family mediator. There is no charge to parents for the time of the mediator, who works on a *pro bono* basis. This innovative program has had initial success in resolving situations where the abductor has second thoughts.[43]

As a program sponsored by a nongovernmental organization

funded by donations and grants, Child Find's parental abduction mediation service cannot reach and assist all abductors who might respond to mediation. If that approach continues to prove successful, public resources should be directed to mediation services so that they can benefit more children.

Recommendation 4: Professionals bound by legal standards of confidentiality should be permitted to divulge the whereabouts of an abducted child if they have reason to believe the child may be harmed.

Professionals who work with people—including social workers, mental health workers, doctors, nurses, teachers, clergy, and attorneys—come into contact with abducted children and their parents in the course of their work. They may be told of the abduction by a parent who requires their help to enroll a child in school, to attempt to obtain legal custody, or to enter a women's shelter or use other social services. If not told, such professionals may come to suspect abduction because of the behavior or statements of the child or because of such circumstances as missing medical or school records.

Professionals typically have an ethical obligation to keep their clients' or patients' statements and problems confidential. Depending on state laws and the particular profession, they also may have a legal duty to observe confidentiality and may be barred from revealing privileged information in court if the client withholds permission. In abduction situations where a child may be endangered if an adult client's confidences are respected, the helping person faces a dilemma. Which obligation takes priority? Medical, educational, and social service professionals, but not attorneys, are obligated by law in all states to report suspected child abuse or neglect, and in some instances that legal duty will help resolve the dilemma in favor of revealing the child's whereabouts to authorities.

Except in child abuse matters, the obligation of mental health professionals and social workers concerning client confidentiality is somewhat flexible in many jurisdictions where it is not regulated by law.[44] The code of ethics of the National Association of Social Workers states that clients' confidences should not be shared without consent except for "compelling professional reasons,"[45] a standard that appears broad enough to allow a social worker to act to prevent or reveal an abduction under a variety of circumstances. For example, if a client revealed plans to abduct in an interview with a social worker and if that person believed the child would be harmed, the ethical standard appears to allow the professional latitude to warn the other parent. Many states have statutes or precedent-setting court cases governing how professionals are to respond when their clients threaten people or show other evidence of dangerousness, and these also may provide guidance concerning when to break confidentiality to warn an intended victim.[46]

Attorneys are in a particularly difficult position when clients who are on the run with children come to them for help.[47] Although privileged communication between client and attorney is one of the foundations of our legal system, a number of court cases have considered the issue of whether an attorney can be compelled to reveal a client's whereabouts.[48] As a case in point, a superior court in Connecticut ruled in 1989 in a parental abduction case that when an attorney was ordered by the court to reveal a client's whereabouts, "attorney–client privilege did not apply to information imparted to an attorney by a client in the course of perpetrating a fraud on the court. Moreover, any claim of privilege must yield in these circumstances to the best interests of the children."[49]

The American Bar Association has included in its code of professional conduct for attorneys language that appears to allow disclosure in the most serious circumstances in order "to prevent the client from committing a criminal act that the lawyer believes is likely to result in death or substantial bodily harm."[50] California is one state that has considered adopting that rule.[51] It is important that professionals who come into contact with abducting parents and their children have the discretion through ethical codes, legal precedents, or other means legally to break confidence with clients if that is necessary to protect a child from substantial harm.[52]

Recommendation 5: Ways to find abducted children who may have entered foster care or been reported as abused or neglected should be expanded.

More than a third of the parents in our study whose children were recovered believed that their children had been physically or sexually abused while with the abductor. Although we do not know what proportion of these children were reported to child protection agencies while they were on the run, we do know of cases where abuse or neglect was serious enough for the children to have been removed from the abductor and placed in foster care. Although they were in the care of a state agency and no longer on the run with the abductor, none of these abducted children were located quickly or easily by the searching parent. Four to five percent of the parents whose children were recovered reported that child welfare agencies were involved in helping them locate or reclaim the children.

There are many barriers that keep child welfare agencies from knowing that children reported to them have been abducted. Abductors adopt assumed names for themselves and the children in many cases, and they contrive some plausible explanation for the absence of the other parent. Teachers, pediatricians, and child protection staff may be told, just as the children often are, that the searching parent is dead or has deserted. Without accurate information about names and former places of residence, it is virtually impossible for agencies to find and notify parents who may be searching for their children.

Systematic ways are needed to identify children who may have been abducted. One approach would be for foster children with missing, unknown, or unverifiably deceased parents to be fingerprinted and the prints cleared through FBI files to see if they have been registered by parents who feared abduction. More abducted children would be registered if children's fingerprints were made a requirement in the court records of child custody cases, one of the recommendations presented in Chapter 8.

There are difficulties with this approach to finding abducted children in foster care. The foster child's right to privacy might preclude routine fingerprinting, and the child's possible feelings of "being treated like a criminal" also must be considered. That feeling is a particular problem for children in foster care because they frequently blame themselves for the abuse they have received. However, in situations where the statements or behavior of the child or the known parent raise suspicion, the juvenile court judge who hears and reviews the foster care case could order fingerprinting of the child and possibly of the known parent. This could be undertaken in the interest of finding absent parents, a routine service obligation in all foster care cases.

Data bases listing information about foster children or about validated cases of abuse or neglect offer another possible avenue for locating abducted children, although there are a number of difficulties with this approach also. The data bases are state systems that contain only limited data, so it would be difficult to search them without knowing the names the child and abducting parent were using and the state where they might have had contact with a child welfare agency. The data bases are also highly confidential since they provide identifying information about parents and children, some of whom are in state custody. However, for all their limitations, data bases of child welfare clients should be accessible to law enforcement personnel searching for missing children (if necessary, by court order).

For children who may be known to child welfare agencies but who do not enter foster care, the options that could assist searching parents are fewer. In some jurisdictions it is routine for child protection staff to seek the help of law enforcement officials to clear the names of parents reported for child maltreatment through the National Crime Information Center (NCIC) data system. This computerized data base lists individuals with outstanding felony warrants, the charges against them, and the jurisdictions where charges are pending. If the correct identity of the parent reported for maltreatment is known, checking names against NCIC records would reveal any warrants for parental kidnapping. There also are suggestions in the literature that searching parents should request that abducted children be listed in NCIC.[53] If they do so, law enforcement officials are required to make the entry, thus assisting agencies that check the names of foster children to determine if they have been abducted. Single parents known to child welfare agencies also should be cleared through the parent locator service data system, another process that can provide a link to the searching parent.

Although only a very small proportion of abducted children are likely to enter foster care, a larger group may be reported as abused or neglected while on the run with the abductor. These children risk some of the worst outcomes of parental abduction. The state, which is charged with investigating child maltreatment and which assumes custody of children who cannot otherwise be protected, has a particular obligation to determine if victim children have parents searching for them who could capably assume their care. If they do, state custody and foster care placement may be unnecessary and unwarranted intrusions into the family. State child welfare agencies should review their procedures for keeping records and for accessing the records of other governmental agencies in order to find ways to locate the missing parents of children the agencies try to protect.

An abducted child who is in the process of being recovered is sometimes placed temporarily in foster care, usually after the abducting parent has been arrested and before the searching parent can be notified or arrive to claim the child. One way that the legal aspects of this kind of short-term placement, often lasting less than 48 hours, can be handled is for police to take the child into protective custody and then turn him or her over to a child welfare agency for care. An alternative is for state statutes to specify that the public child protection agency has a short grace period during which children can be held without the juvenile court issuing an emergency custody order. Once a juvenile court assumes jurisdiction and places children with an agency for foster care, the court or the agency may impose a host of requirements and timetables that can delay reunification of the child with the searching parent.[54]

Recommendation 6: Allegations of child abuse or neglect in custody disputes necessitate a prompt hearing in the court having custody jurisdiction to consider the evidence and to determine the least detrimental custody arrangement for the child.

Because allegations of abuse or neglect in a child custody dispute may be made before, during, or following an abduction, the recommendation for a prompt hearing in court has preventive as well as remedial aspects. Parents need to know that there is a forum for addressing their fears about abuse and neglect by the other parent and for taking action to protect children if the allegations are verified. In most cases that forum should be the court where the original custody hearing took place, but there are emergency situations that should qualify for a hearing before a different judge under that court's emergency jurisdiction. This recommendation concerns civil courts that hear child custody matters, not juvenile courts that act to protect children on behalf of the state.

Allegations of maltreatment that warrant a hearing to modify custody should, at minimum, meet the state definition of abuse and neglect that, if reported, would require an investigation by child protective services. As we note in Chapter 4, parents in abduction situations frequently disagree strongly about childrearing, and they sometimes couch their criticisms of each other in terms of emotional abuse or neglect. While emotional abuse and neglect can be very serious, parents should not be able to succeed in attaching that label to behaviors such as discouraging visitation, making disparaging remarks about the other parent, or occasionally yelling at the child. Serious cases of emotional maltreatment go far beyond the allegations typically made by competing parents.[55]

There are numerous problems with the ways some domestic relations or family courts respond to charges of abuse or neglect in disputed custody and parental kidnapping situations. Courts that place children with abusive parents or force visitation with them create some of the most compelling motivations for parental abduction.[56] These are children who have been failed, first by one parent, then by the system. The other parent may risk everything in an abduction attempt rather than fail them also.

One of the problems is that in some courts it is very difficult to prove allegations of abuse against a parent, especially when the allegations come from an ex-spouse.[57] This is exacerbated by the public and professional perception, despite evidence to the contrary,[58] that a large and growing proportion of custody disputes involve spurious allegations of child maltreatment, especially sexual abuse.[59] This perception can influence those in the court system to discourage or downplay such allegations lest they be overwhelmed by them. Another problem is that experts brought in to evaluate the family often disagree about whether abuse has occurred or, if it has, about how the child has been affected. In part, this is due to disagreements in the professional literature about the prevalence of false reports and of instances of children being coached into informing on innocent parents.[60]

Understandable as these problems are, they can combine to deprive children of proper consideration of their best interests. In custody hearings involving allegations of child maltreatment, the court should appoint an expert, or two independent experts if the parties request it, to evaluate all family members and to make custody recommendations.[61] The experts' fees, like other court costs, can be divided between the parties by the court, although there remains the problem that the costs of court contests are high for all parents and prohibitive for many.[62]

Although court appointment of an expert to evaluate family members does not affect the right of the parties to hire their own evaluators, it avoids the problem of all of the experts being "hired guns" for whichever side calls them as witnesses.[63] The problem with the competing experts model is not primarily that evaluators are biased but that they see only some of the actors in the family system, since litigants rarely consent to be evaluated by the expert for the "other side." This makes disagreements between experts not only possible but likely, leaving the court in doubt about the facts. The proposed appointment of an evaluator or evaluators who see the whole family also is consistent with the kinds of family-centered interventions we discuss in Chapter 7.

Another way to promote custody arrangements that serve the child's interests when abuse or neglect has been alleged was addressed in the last chapter: If children had their own appointed legal counsel, in postabduction custody hearings as well as in all others, their interests, views, and preferences could be protected more adequately. In representing a child client, though, attorneys should be cognizant of the tension between a broad view of the child's interests and a narrow view of the child's wishes. This is particularly important in cases involving abduction or alleged child abuse. In abduction cases there is risk of the child suffering from the hostage syndrome (see Chapter 5), which leads to overidentification with the abductor, just as in some abuse situations children occasionally want to live with an abuser because of a tangle of feelings that cannot be taken at face value. In Chapter 4 Dr. Ken Lewis describes how a *guardian ad litem* also can help the court with recommendations concerning the child's interests.

Recommendation 7: An abduction resolved after an extended period requires a prompt court hearing to consider the least detrimental custody and visitation arrangement for the child.

In elaborating Principle II we noted that when an abduction is resolved, legal custody ordinarily remains with the searching parent if that person had custody before the abduction or obtained it during the search. One situation that should result in a court hearing to determine whether the preabduction custody arrangement is appropriate is when allegations of child abuse or neglect are made against the custodial parent. A second situation is an extended abduction that has allowed the child time to settle in with the abducting parent and to develop and maintain a significant attachment within a healthy parent–child relationship.

Some legal approaches to parental abduction recognize the need for courts to consider the child's interests following a lengthy abduction rather than presume that return to the searching parent is always appropriate. Under the Hague Convention, in proceedings to recover children that are begun more than one year after the abduction, judges in the new country may use discretion in deciding whether to order a child returned; return may be denied if the court finds that the child has become settled into the new environment. The court also may take into account the wishes of a child who is considered mature enough to express a preference about being returned. There also are reports in the literature of countries that do not or formerly did not subscribe to the Hague Convention having used the test of the child's successful adaptation to decide whether to order the child's return to the preabduction country of residence.[64]

The one-year period that gives judges discretion under the Hague Convention is the same length of time that the psychiatric–legal team of Goldstein, Freud, and Solnit advocate as a conservative measure of how long it takes a child under age three who has experienced a change in custody or placement to form an attachment to a new psychological parent (older children ordinarily may be presumed to reattach within two years).[65] The child's sense of time, which varies by age, and the child's identification with a psychological parent are the principles on which Goldstein et al. base their influential child custody recommendations:[66]

From a child's point of view, no absence from his parents is temporary if it exceeds the period of time during which the child, always according to his age and stage of development, can preserve inner ties to them. . . . Once new psychological relationships form, separation from the substitute parents becomes no less painful and no less damaging to a child than his separation from natural or adoptive caretaking parents.[67]

In resolving the custody of children who have been in the long-term care of substitute parents, Goldstein, Freud, and Solnit recognize that there are situations where an older child will remain so attached to an absent parent that he or she resists bonding with anyone else. In that situation they recommend a hearing "to determine whether the child's absent parents are still his psychological parents and whether his return to them would be the least detrimental alternative."[68] We recommend a similar process of a court hearing to resolve custody and visitation issues following a long-term abduction.

Usually, hearings to modify custody decrees come about by petition of one of the parties. Unfortunately, that often is a slow and expensive process, and an expedited and more routine court review is desirable if a mechanism for that can be devised. If not, it might be most appropriate for the attorney who represented the child in the original custody hearing (in cases where there was one) to file the motion for a new hearing following a lengthy abduction. To a greater extent than either parent's counsel, the child's attorney is free to seek the custody arrangement that best serves the child's interests.

It is desirable for time guidelines to be available to courts concerning when to review an original custody decision following recovery of a child after an abduction of some length. The time frames in child placement situations advanced by Goldstein, Freud, and Solnit of one year for children less than three and two years for older children include a presumption that the new caretaker will have become the child's psychological parent within that time. We believe that such a presumption would be inappropriate in abduction situations, given that different patterns of parental kidnapping affect the experiences of the child. If no presumption is made, it is reasonable to suggest shorter time periods after which the court would review the appropriateness of preexisting child custody and visitation orders. We recommend such a court review after the resolution of any abduction of a child less than three years old that lasts for six months or longer and of any abduction of a child older than three that lasts for a year or longer.[69] Because each abduction situation is unique, this time frame is proposed as a guideline, not an invariable policy. Obviously, some shorter abductions may require review and some longer ones may not.

Recommendation 8: The response of criminal law to parental abduction should include a range of alternative charges, defenses, and penalties.

After being excluded from federal and many state criminal statutes for decades, parental kidnapping was criminalized in the 1970s and 1980s, often as a felony.[70] Despite this shift, it is obvious that parental kidnapping differs in motivation, risk of harm, and psychological effects from kidnapping by strangers and that cases of parental abduction also vary widely. The criminal law's response to parental kidnapping needs to be variable, based on the nature of the harm.

At present, many state criminal statutes for parental kidnapping make little or no distinction among abductions on the basis of considerations such as the use of force, harm done to the child, length of absence, or whether the child was concealed from the searching parent. Some state statutes do make important distinctions by defining first- and second-degree violations or aggravating circumstances. Unfortunately, many state laws use only criteria such as whether the child was taken out of state to define the more serious violations. Such criteria may be less relevant to the nature and effects of the abduction than issues such as concealment of the child or use of a weapon.[71]

One provision that is made in many state statutes and should be adopted in other jurisdictions provides for a defense against the charge of parental abduction if the abductor acted to prevent or avoid harm.[72] Maryland, for example, provides a defense if failure to take the child "would have resulted in a clear and present danger to the health, safety, or welfare of the child," and if the abductor seeks within 96 hours to "revise, amend, or clarify the custody order."[73] Thus, a parent who promptly seeks the court's assistance in protecting a child believed to be in danger has a defense against criminal charges. Wisconsin provides the well-motivated abducting parent with additional defenses if it can be established that the parent acted to "protect his or her child from imminent physical harm or sexual assault" or was "fleeing from imminent physical harm to himself or herself."[74] California provides protection for the parent who acts "to protect the child from immediate bodily injury or emotional harm" and who files a report explaining the circumstances with the law enforcement agency in the jurisdiction.[75] We support combining the positive features of these approaches and believe a defense against the charge of parental abduction should be provided for parents fleeing harm to themselves or their children if they turn to appropriate state authorities for help in protecting the child.

In addition to making actions to protect one's child or oneself from harm a defense against criminal charges, other changes need to be incorporated into criminal codes to differentiate among different types of abductions. Imagine the impact on a child of observing the abductor enter the home forcibly, of seeing the parent with whom the child lives threatened or hurt, and of being carried off unwillingly by another parent who may be unknown, feared, or distrusted. Imagine a child held unwillingly, not permitted to contact the parent who was last seen during the violent abduction. Abduction under these unusual circumstances may be treated no differently under state law than abduction that does not involve force or violence, such as when a noncustodial parent retains a child during visitation.

Where differential treatment of abductors does enter the system is through the decisions reached by prosecutors' offices about how to handle each criminal case. According to one judge and former prosecutor, factors such as the length of the abduction and whether the child was concealed or harmed routinely influence the decision to prosecute, the charges, and the sentence requested by prosecutors' offices.[76] Such flexibility is necessary and desirable, but greater consistency in the administration of justice might be obtained by the statutory recognition of mitigating and exacerbating circumstances.

Causing serious bodily harm or threatening harm with a weapon are circumstances that are widely recognized as adding to the seriousness of another offense and calling for more severe punishment.[77] In our study approximately one abduction in seven was accomplished with the use of force, and we know of situations (see, for example, Ava's story in Chapters 4 and 5) where one parent was knocked unconscious, tied up, or threatened with a gun in the course of abduction by the other parent.

These situations amount to "aggravated parental abduction," which should be a more serious class of felony than simple abduction, with more stringent penalties attached. Aggravation has been defined as "any circumstance attending the commission of a crime or tort which increases its guilt or enormity or adds to its injurious consequences, but which is above and beyond the essential constituents of the crime or tort itself."[78] In the case of abductions, a specific definition of aggravation might include violence or threats of violence against the other parent, another caretaker, or the child at the time of the abduction or against the child during the course of the abduction.

There is a final way in which criminal laws should respond differently to parental abductions. At the time of the abduction parents in our study had marital and custody arrangements reflecting the whole range of family situations found in society. They were unmarried and living together or no longer living together, married, separated, and divorced. They reported that custody was with the left-behind parent, with the abductor, or shared. Present criminal laws concerning child abduction do not respond adequately to some of these family circumstances.

One shortcoming in the legal system is that children of nonmarital relationships are not protected under many state laws. About one out of seven abductions in our study took place when the parents were not and had never been married to each other. In these situations there often is no court order establishing custody and no simple way to obtain one, so left-behind parents may find it particularly difficult to obtain assistance from police and other authorities.[79] Wisconsin, among the very few states to address this issue, explicitly includes abduction from "the child's mother in the case of a nonmarital child where parents do not subsequently intermarry."[80] Although there are many fewer unmarried fathers raising children than unmarried mothers, legal definitions also should protect their rights by including at least abductions from unmarried fathers whose paternity has been established by a court, who live with their children, or who are primary custodial parents.

Separated parents who have not yet been to court concerning custody and those with court-ordered joint custody also are inadequately protected in many jurisdictions. Some states, such as Texas and Wisconsin, include in their definitions of parental abduction the taking of children after receiving notice that a divorce action or other custody suit has been filed.[81] Wisconsin, by recent amendment, also explicitly covers children taken from parents with joint custody.[82] We support both of these provisions; the latter is particularly critical now that more divorces result in joint custody.

Children taken from intact marriages, who constitute less than a fifth of our study sample, are not considered to be abducted in the large majority of states until the left-behind parent obtains a custody order. California is an exception, including in its statute abductions by any person having a right to custody in the absence of a court order.[83] Penalties in that state for abductions when no court order exists recently were increased to equal penalties in other types of abductions.

Although this book uses a broad definition of abduction out of recognition that any unilateral taking of a child has serious consequences to which society needs to respond, it does not follow that the response to an abduction should always be the same. Just as the civil response of determining custody after an abduction must be flexible and child-centered, so too must the criminal response of prosecuting parents consider the context of the offense in terms of intent, use of violence, and harm to the child victim or others.

Recommendation 9: The complex nature of cases of parental abduction of children require special expertise and training of law enforcement personnel, investigators, prosecutors, and judges hearing juvenile, civil, and criminal matters.

Those who deal with cases of parental abduction of children within the legal system require special knowledge from many fields. Those who come into direct contact with abducted or recovered children need expertise in interviewing children of all ages about their experiences. Also needed is sensitivity to the diverse roles and styles assumed by parents and to different forms of gender bias. Abduction situations call for some of the same skills in communication and de-escalation that are needed to intervene in other domestic disputes and in cases of family violence. The high incidence of spouse abuse in families experiencing abduction suggests that serious attention must be paid to the dynamics of family violence and to the perceptions and behaviors of adults who have been victimized repeatedly. Familiarity with child abuse and neglect and its impact on children also is crucial.

There are groups that train professionals working in this area, among them the American Prosecutors Research Institute and various groups funded in part by the Office of Juvenile Justice and Delinquency Prevention, U.S. Department of Justice.[84] These efforts should be expanded in order to reach those in the jurisdictions that lack special expertise in intervening in cases of parental abduction of children.

APPLICATIONS AND DISCUSSION

This section considers how the principles and recommendations we have advanced might affect the resolution of different cases of parental abduction. Recall the case of Cathy, mother of Richard and Sarah, whose story is told in some detail in Chapter 3. Cathy lost custody to her ex-husband because of personal problems that she subsequently overcame. Feeling that her visitation rights as a noncustodial mother were too restrictive and unfair, she was distraught when they were cut further after she and her attorney missed a court hearing. When she discovered that her children were being told she did not love them, she planned an abduction. She settled them in a new community and confided in school officials rather than confuse the children with false identities. Thirteen months later, Cathy and her children were discovered. The children were returned to their father and a stepmother, and Cathy now sees them only under supervision in a small room in the courthouse.

This situation describes an abduction we hope would not happen at all if the recommendations discussed in Chapter 8 were in place. However, they are not, and parents who seek more contact with their children do abduct out of frustration and hopelessness with the child custody system. After an abduction like this one, how can the principles and recommendations in this chapter help? The primary recommendation that might alter the resolution of this abduction is Recommendation 7: An abduction resolved after an extended period necessitates a prompt court hearing to consider the least detrimental custody and visitation arrangement for the child.

It is not at all clear that the children's interests were served by their return to the primary custody of their father, with only severely limited visitation with their mother. A hearing following the resolution of the 13-month abduction might have concluded that joint custody or more liberal visitation might best meet the children's needs. That outcome might be especially likely if, as we recommend in Chapter 8, the children had their own legal counsel. Recommendation 7 is particularly helpful in resolving abductions that follow the nonviolent visitor pattern, which often involves a parent who is desperate for a greater role in the children's lives.

* * *

Ava's family story appears in Chapters 4 and 5, where we discuss recovery and the effects of abduction on children. She was a battered wife with two preschoolers when she attempted to separate from her husband, and her actions might have been considered an abduction under the laws of some states and under our recommendations for a broad definition of abduction. However, in an abduction following the pattern of the nonviolent shared custodian, Ava clearly acted to prevent serious harm to herself and her children, so she would have a defense against any charges under part of Recommendation 8: The response of criminal law to parental abduction should include a range of alternative charges, defenses, and penalties.

Ava's attempt to leave her abusive situation was followed by her husband forcibly taking the children from her in an abduction by a violent shared custodian. During its course, the children were seriously neglected, the boy was sexually abused, and the children ultimately entered foster care. It was only through one of the visions that we discuss in Chapter 4 that Ava contacted an old acquaintance who by chance had recently encountered the children. This is an example of a situation where a searching parent could benefit from Recommendation 5: Ways to find abducted children who may have entered foster care or been reported as abused or neglected should be expanded. For example, if the abductor and the children had been entered in the National Crime Information Center (NCIC) data base and if the child welfare agency had used police contacts to check that system routinely, the agency could have discovered that the children's mother was searching for them and Ava could have recovered her children several months earlier.

Following recovery, the abducting father was tried and sentenced, an unusual outcome in our experience. Despite his history of extreme violence toward Ava and the harm the children suffered while in his care, he was released from prison less than two years later. Ava might rest easier and the children might be safer if after his release he had been placed on probation or parole with frequent supervision and, possibly, restrictions on his ability to leave the state. This is another situation where the resolution could be affected by points made under Recommendation 8: The response of criminal law to parental abduction should include a range of alternative charges, defenses and penalties. Certainly, abductions in which there are aggravating conditions such as the use or threat of violence or harm done to the children during their course should carry longer prison sentences, larger payments in restitution or fines, and stricter post-release supervision than abductions that do not involve physical harm.

*   *   *

For a final illustration of the principles and recommendations set forth in this chapter, recall Ruth's story from Chapters 3 and 5. She was abducted by her noncustodial father at the age of six and did not see her mother again until she graduated from high school. Her father, Dan, following the pattern of the nonviolent visitor, devoted himself to her care, feeling both that he could bring her up better than her mother could and also that without his daughter his own life would be worthless. This is another abduction that we believe might not have happened if the recommendations for prevention elaborated in the last chapter had been implemented, particularly those that encourage custody decisions that recognize the need of most children for substantial involvement with both divorced parents.

Ruth's mother, Sandy, told us that it took months for her to get an arrest warrant issued, in part because in the 1970s it was difficult to interest authorities in conflicts over child custody. Prosecutors who help enforce custody decrees, as they do today in California, were unknown. Many important services that did not exist at that time, such as publicity, help coordinating a search, or mediation to resolve an abduction, now are available from the National Center for Missing and Exploited Children, from its affiliated state clearinghouses, or from independent missing children's organizations.

However, had Ruth been recovered after a lengthy abduction but prior to her 18th birthday, she would not have returned automatically to the sole custody of her searching mother. A court hearing, perhaps initiated by her own attorney or by her father's, would have considered modifying custody. Some of the factors considered at the hearing would have been the time spent with her father during the abduction, her attachment to him, and the care he had provided. When interviewed, Dan told us that he abducted in the first place to keep from being shut out of his daughter's life. That same result should not occur in the aftermath of the abduction, unless continued contact is considered more detrimental to the child than no contact. At the postabduction custody hearing, the result might be what was unavailable to this father at the time of his divorce, namely, joint legal and physical custody, with Ruth able to spend significant time with both her parents.

Penalties imposed for the abduction itself might have included making restitution to Ruth's mother for her search and legal expenses; and measures designed to deter another abduction, such as supervised probation and a posted cash bond, might have been instituted. Certainly, jail time would be inappropriate for this nonviolent abductor who called Ruth's mother immediately after the abduction and periodically for years afterward to let her know Ruth was safe.

The growing public and professional concern about parental abduction has changed the policy of neglect to one of serious attention to the problem. The UCCJA, the PKPA and the Hague Convention have given authorities some of the tools they need to tackle this multifaceted problem. That additional and refined tools are needed is obvious from the high rate of parental abduction, which is likely to increase further because of the changing social context in which families live.

REEXAMINING THE SOCIAL CONTEXT OF PARENTAL KIDNAPPING: CONCLUSIONS

In the first chapter of this book we considered parental abduction in the context of other social realities, including kidnapping in general and changing family patterns that lead more disrupted families to struggle over child custody and more children to spend part of their childhood in single-parent families. We also summarized what is known from other research about parental abduction of children and provided an overview of how our work may contribute to understanding the problem.

In subsequent chapters we viewed abduction of children by their parents through the lens of each participant in turn: parents left behind in abductions, parents who abduct, searching parents reunited with children, and the children themselves. We took in-depth looks at the special issues involved in international abductions, in helping the people involved in abduction cope with the personal and family problems they encounter, and in addressing abductions as social problems.

The central conclusion of our work is that parental abduction of children is not one phenomenon but several. The typology of five patterns that forms one theme of the book shows the range of family situations that can result in an abduction by one parent. The family stories retold throughout the book illustrate this core theme of varying motivations, differing events, and contrasting effects on the parents and children involved.

One facet of the parental abduction problem shows how it reflects the broader problem of family violence. More than half of the abductors in the families we dealt with were reported by the left-behind parent to have a history of violence within the marriage or relationship. Almost a third had been accused of child abuse before the abduction, and more than a third of the abducted children were believed by parents who recovered them to have been physically or sexually abused while on the run. When family violence is part of the picture, substance abuse and the use of force to bring about the abduction are also frequently present. Often the motivation for the abduction was to hurt an ex-partner further or to try to force that person to return to the relationship. Although abducting parents of both genders were reported to behave violently, it is consistent with the nature of our society that more men than women in our sample were seen as having these problems.

On the other side of the family violence equation, some abducting parents in our study were fleeing abuse of themselves or their children. Because our information came primarily from the left-behind parents, we expected to hear relatively few admissions of having been violent to a spouse or abusive toward a child. However, during telephone follow-up interviews, 30% of the left-behind parents did admit that they either had been accused of or had engaged in acts of family violence. What proportions of the allegations are false, we do not know. Yet we do know from other sources that many abducting parents are escaping what they see as an intolerable situation that they have been unable to resolve in any other way. Again, because of the larger social context that surrounds abduction, abducting mothers are more likely than fathers to be running to escape violence toward themselves and their children.

Then there are the abductions that seem unrelated to patterns of abuse, physical violence, or coercion. Some parents, feeling acute isolation from their children following the breakup of a marriage or relationship, ease their own emotional pain by abducting their children, irrespective of the pain caused to the other parent and the confusion and upset to the children. These abducting parents are not as much a part of their children's lives as they wish to be or as they believe would be good for their children. Some are distressed at the sense of having been replaced by stepparents in the households where their children are living. Some of the abducting mothers feel acute regret and guilt at having given up or lost custody of their children, feelings made more poignant by the disapproval directed at noncustodial mothers by family, friends, and society. Some of the abducting fathers chafe at the role of divorced father with visitation rights, and they despair of winning a greater place in their children's lives through the courts.

Some situations seem to cut across the patterns we have defined and are hard to summarize in simple terms. There are instances where both the abducting and the searching parent pose dangers to their children, as well as situations where both have been exploitive and hurtful in their relationships with each other. There also are parents who exhibit both violence and the same feelings of loss and need for the children that characterize the nonviolent patterns of abduction. While the typology of abductions introduced in this book can be a helpful tool for understanding the range of typical patterns, it is not a perfect reflection of all of the complex events and emotions that underlie abduction of children by parents.

The last chapters of this book deal with what can be done about parental kidnapping, both in professional practice with individual families and children and in social and legal efforts to prevent and resolve abductions on a larger scale. Efforts to intervene in the problem must be informed by recognition of its diversity. Not all abductions are alike. They are not motivated by the same factors, nor are they carried out under similar conditions. Although more equitable and consistent definitions of parental abduction are needed, society's response must include a range of options that reflect the fact that abductions differ in motivation and effect. The children and their welfare must be the center of concern when parents kidnap.

Appendix

Table A-1. Selected Demographic Characteristics of
Respondents and Abductors (male respondents, $n = 166$; female
respondents, $n = 205$)

	Respondents	Abductors*
	%	
Caucasian	92	85
American-born	93	87
Some education past high school	64	39
Employed in professional/managerial job	38	13
Unemployed	25	50
Had sole custody (vs. joint or visitation)	51	14
Income of $27,500 or less	66	unknown

*Data for abductors refer to status at time of abduction. Mean age at time of abduction
was 32 years old for respondents and 33 years old for abductors.

271

Table A-2.   Characteristics of Respondents' Marriage, and
Relative Frequency of Reasons Cited for Breakup, Abductor's
Visitation Arrangements, and Reasons for Abduction

Average length of marriage	**6 years**

Abducted child was product of marriage	87%
Violence present in marriage	54%

Reasons for breakup*

Incompatibility	31%
Victimized by physical/emotional abuse	26
Abductor's substance abuse	16
Abductor's emotional problems	15
Abductor's infidelity	11

Visitation patterns of abductors

Weekly	44%
Biweekly	22
Monthly or bimonthly	10
Infrequently or never	24

Reasons respondent thinks abduction occurred*

To hurt respondent	77%
Anger over breakup	23
Desire to be with child	16
Pressure from others to take child	13
Dissatisfaction with visitation	13
Other (write in)	23

*Respondents could give up to two responses.

NOTES

CHAPTER 1: Parental Kidnapping in Context

1. Finkelhor et al. (1990). A number of states keep track of their own statistics on missing children, including parental abductions. For example, in Ohio, according to the July 1, 1989, to June 30, 1990, Annual Report of the Missing Child Educational Program, there were 28,563 missing children reports entered during that time period. No breakdown was given as to the number that were parentally abducted or abducted by strangers or were runaways (Ohio Department of Education, 1990).

2. Fisher (1989).

3. Gillie (1990).

4. Agopian (1981); 1 Kings 3:16–28.

5. Feder (1964); Terr (1983).

6. *Richard III,* act III, scene 1, lines 31–34.

7. Alix (1978), pp. xvi–xvii.

8. "Charged with Kidnapping His Own Children," *New York Times,* 6 June 1875, p. 1.

9. "A Divorced Wife's Theft," *New York Times,* 24 October 1878, p. 1.

10. "The Blackstone Case," *New York Times,* 26 October 1878, p. 5.

11. Ernest Alix, Department of Sociology, University of Southern Illinois, personal communication, December 1990.

12. See "Judge Frees Woman" (1991) for a brief description of the case of a mother who placed her children in hiding after she believed the father was physically and sexually abusing them.

13. "Child Kidnapping," Hearing before the Subcommittee on Juvenile Justice of the Committee on the Judiciary, United States Senate, 98th Congress, February 2, 1983, Serial No. J–98–3.

14. *The World Almanac and Book of Facts* (1988).

15. Barrett (1981); Chu and Sciolino (1976); Gittelson (1976); Hewson (1979); Most (1977).

16. Best (1987).

17. "Child Kidnapping," Hearing before the Subcommittee on Juvenile Justice. Feb. 2, 1983.

18. Best (1987). See also Forst and Blomquist (1991).

19. Ibid.

20. Eric Foretich, in interviews given to the press over a one-year period through 1990 and in personal communications through March, 1992.

21. Long et al. (1991).

22. May (1980).

23. Phillips (1988).

24. Ibid.

25. Ibid.

26. Ibid.

27. Ibid.

28. U.S. Department of Commerce, *Statistical Abstract* (1990b).

29. Stone (1990).

30. Terr (1983).

31. U.S. Department of Commerce, *Statistical Abstract* (1990b).

32. Greif (1990).

33. Greif and Pabst (1988).

34. Agopian (1981); Schaefer (1984); Child Safe Products (1984).

35. Kline et al. (1991) found in their research on the emotional adjustment of 154 children that marital conflict was related to emotional and behavioral difficulties in the children.

36. Agopian (1980, 1981).

37. Agopian (1981).

38. Agopian (1984).

39. Janvier et al. (1990).

40. Sagatun and Barrett (1990).

41. Hatcher, Barton, and Brooks (1992). For other related federally funded

research, see Hatcher, Lippert, Barton, and Brooks (1992); also Girdner and Hoff (1992). The latter work examines the legal, policy, procedural, and practical obstacles to the location, recovery, and return of parentally abducted children.

42. Forehand, Long, Zogg, and Parrish (1989); Schetky and Haller (1983); Senior et al. (1982); and Terr (1983).

43. Finkelhor et al. (1990).

44. Finkelhor et al. (1990), p. 45.

45. Finkelhor et al. (1991). Whites were overrepresented in the sample of 142.

46. David Finkelhor, Director Family Research Laboratory, University of New Hampshire, personal communication, June 1991.

47. Gelles (1984).

48. Fisher (1989).

49. Hoff (1988). We attempted to contact at least one organization in every state that was included in this sourcebook. We targeted private organizations since those operated by local police or other law enforcement agencies have restrictions on divulging information owing to the need to maintain confidentiality. The 14 organizations that participated in the study were Missing Children of America, Inc., Anchorage; Find the Children, Los Angeles; Adam Walsh Resource Center, West Palm Beach; Missing Children Help Center, Tampa; Exploited Children's Help Organization, Louisville; Missing Children–Minnesota, Minneapolis; Services for the Missing, Gibbsboro, New Jersey; I.D. Resource Center of Albuquerque; Child Find of America, New Paltz, New York; National Missing Children's Locate Center, Gresham, Oregon; Children's Rights Northeast, Columbus; The Society for Young Victims (Massachusetts and Newport, Rhode Island); Childseekers, Rutland, Vermont; Operation Lookout, Mountlake Terrace, Washington; Child Find, Quebec, Montreal; and Missing and Exploited Children's Association, Lutherville, Maryland, which provided a sample for a pretest.

50. The design of the study makes the actual return rate difficult to determine because parents in contact with more than one organization received multiple copies of the survey. For example, a parent residing in Maryland who believes a child was taken to Pennsylvania would most likely contact organizations in Maryland and Pennsylvania. The actual rate of return is calculated to conservatively be between 15% (if no respondents received a second questionnaire) and 27% (if 85% received two, as was suggested by one director of a missing children's organization). In addition, many of the parents who contacted the missing children's organizations a number of years before may have moved and may no longer have mail forwarded by the post office. Thus, many more packets could have been lost in the mail. Further, at least one parent received three questionnaires, which means the return could be higher. No attempt was made to try to raise the return rate through follow-up, as we were reluctant to overburden the staff at many of the organizations.

51. We are unclear whether we had a more contentious group of respondents than in the general population. On the one hand, parents with an ax to grind might have been most interested in participating in the research, as they

would be the most interested in influencing the dialogue on the issues. On the other hand, those who were most helped by the missing children's organization, whether they were reunited with their children or not, may have wanted to assist because the request came in part from the organization. Many parents whom we interviewed reported wanting to help others as their motivation for participating.

52. Asking parents to report retrospectively about the earlier stages of their marriage also poses certain methodological problems.

53. See Agopian (1980), for example.

54. See Schetky and Haller (1983), Senior et al. (1982), and Terr (1983), for example.

55. Agopian (1981) and Forehand, Long, Zogg, and Parrish (1989), for example.

56. Kitson et al. (1985).

57. Greif (1985).

58. The mean number of years was 1.62.

59. The mean number of years children had been missing was 4.1.

CHAPTER 2:   Parents Whose Children Are Abducted

1. Jenkins and Norman (1972).

2. MacDonald et al. (1987); Stewart et al. (1986).

3. Agopian (1980, 1981, 1984, 1987).

4. Janvier et al. (1990).

5. Finkelhor et al. (1990, 1991).

6. Forehand, Long, Zogg, and Parrish (1989).

7. Agopian (1981), p. xvii.

8. Janvier et al. (1990), p. 6.

9. Forehand, Long, Zogg, and Parrish (1990).

10. In each case a level of statistical significance is noted that indicates the likelihood that the finding is due to chance. For example, .05 indicates five chances out of 100 that the difference reported is spurious.

11. Census Bureau data indicate that in 1970, 85% of all children under 18 lived with both parents and in 1980, 77% lived with both parents (U.S. Department of Commerce, 1982).

12. Gelles's (1980) review of family violence in the 1970s found a great variation in the reported incidence of acts of violence. One study documented that 16% of those interviewed reported some domestic violence within the previous year and 28% reported some violence during the course of the relationship. With about 20% of our sample reporting having witnessed family violence, the responses could be construed as being similar. Another study, according to Gelles, reported 3.8% of children as having been abused in a given year (with the probability for abuse at some point during childhood even higher). Again, our sample reports roughly comparable rates.

Some variation may be expected since most of our sample grew up in the 1960s.

13. Cases in which the abducted children were not the product of a marriage were not included in this particular analysis since there was no premarital period of time without children. DeMaris et al. (1992) note that men may underreport violence in their relationships.

14. Gelles and Cornell (1985).

15. Levinger (1966), pp. 89–97.

16. U.S. Department of Commerce (1987); Advance data from March–April 1986 current population surveys.

17. Greif and Pabst (1988); Greif (1990).

18. $\chi^2 = 40.21$, $df = 1$, $p < .0001$.

19. $\chi^2 = 7.436$, $df = 1$, $p < .05$.

20. $\chi^2 = 4.192$, $df = 1$, $p < .05$.

21. $\chi^2 = 5.662$, $df = 1$, $p < .05$.

22. $\chi^2 = 29.676$, $df = 1$, $p < .0001$.

23. $\chi^2 = 4.659$, $df = 1$, $p < .05$.

24. $\chi^2 = 13.458$, $df = 1$, $p < .001$.

25. $\chi^2 = 23.073$, $df = 1$, $p < .0001$.

26. $\chi^2 = 11.982$, $df = 1$, $p < .001$.

27. $\chi^2 = 5.354$, $df = 1$, $p < .05$.

28. $\chi^2 = 2.822$, $df = 1$, $p < .10$. *P* values of .1 indicate trends.

29. $\chi^2 = 2.823$, $df = 1$, $p < .10$.

30. $\chi^2 = 5.572$, $df = 1$, $p < .05$.

31. $\chi^2 = 3.425$, $df = 1$, $p < .07$.

32. $\chi^2 = 15.134$, $df = 1$, $p < .001$.

33. $\chi^2 = 3.023$, $df = 1$, $p < .10$.

34. $\chi^2 = 6.922$, $df = 1$, $p < .01$.

35. $\chi^2 = 6.507$, $df = 1$, $p < .05$.

36. $\chi^2 = 14.088$, $df = 1$, $p < .001$.

37. $\chi^2 = 30.526$, $df = 1$, $p < .0001$.

38. $\chi^2 = 18.714$, $df = 1$, $p < .0001$.

39. $\chi^2 = 2.83$, $df = 1$, $p < .10$.

40. $\chi^2 = 5.797$, $df = 1$, $p < .05$.

41. $\chi^2 = 8.519$, $df = 1$, $p < .001$.

42. $\chi^2 = 6.602$, $df = 1$, $p < .05$.

43. $\chi^2 = 2.76$, $df = 1$, $p < .10$.

44. $\chi^2 = 4.567$, $df = 1$, $p < .05$.

45. $\chi^2 = 5.589$, $df = 1$, $p < .05$.

46. $\chi^2 = 15.013$, $df = 1$, $p < .01$.

47. $\chi^2 = 2.718$, $df = 1$, $p < .10$.

48. $\chi^2 = 4.331$, $df = 1$, $p < .05$.

49. $\chi^2 = 3.927$, $df = 1$, $p < .05$.

50. $\chi^2 = 4.412$, $df = 1$, $p < .05$.

51. $\chi^2 = 16.407$, $df = 1$, $p < .0001$.

52. $\chi^2 = 5.589$, $df = 1$, $p < .05$.

53. $\chi^2 = 10.965$, $df = 1$, $p < .001$.

54. $\chi^2 = 3.139$, $df = 1$, $p < .10$.

55. $\chi^2 = 2.955$, $df = 1$, $p < .10$.

56. $\chi^2 = 4.499$, $df = 1$, $p < .05$.

57. $\chi^2 = 7.545$, $df = 1$, $p < .01$.

58. Brett et al. (1988).

59. $\chi^2 = 4.76$, $df = 1$, $p < .05$.

60. $\chi^2 = 13.12$, $df = 1$, $p < .001$.

61. $\chi^2 = 25.62$, $df = 1$, $p < .0001$.

62. $F = 8.97$, $df = 1$, $p < .01$.

63. $\chi^2 = 65.18$, $df = 1$, $p < .0001$.

64. $\chi^2 = 58.71$, $df = 1$, $p < .0001$.

65. $\chi^2 = 87.98$, $df = 1$, $p < .0001$.

66. $\chi^2 = 48.55$, $df = 1$, $p < .0001$.

67. $\chi^2 = 18.83$, $df = 1$, $p > .0001$.

68. See Hegar and Greif (1991a).

69. Janvier et al. (1990). It is possible that some respondents participated in both their study and ours.

70. Janvier et al. (1990).

71. Agopian (1981).

72. Ibid.

CHAPTER 3: Parents Who Abduct Their Children

1. Agopian (1981).

2. Janvier et al. (1990), p. 5.

3. Ibid., p. 6.

4. Data from the National Survey of Families and Households shows, by comparison, that the nonresidential fathers, according to the custodial mothers, visited much less frequently than this. According to Seltzer (1991), almost 60% saw their children at most a few times a year.

5. Greif and Pabst (1988).

6. Hegar and Yungman (1989).

7. $\chi^2 = 27.803$, $df = 3$, $p < .0001$.

8. $\chi^2 = 10.877$, $df = 3$, $p < .05$.

9. $\chi^2 = 11.667$, $df = 3$, $p < .01$.

10. $\chi^2 = 15.996$, $df = 3$, $p < .01$.

11. $r = .332$; $p < .001$ for all abductors; $r = .405$; $p < .001$ for male abductors.

12. $\chi^2 = 15.633$, $df = 3$, $p < .01$.

13. $\chi^2 = 16.831$, $df = 3$, $p < .001$.

14. $\chi^2 = 6.7$, $df = 3$, $p < .10$.

15. $\chi^2 = 12.16$, $df = 3$, $p < .01$.

16. $\chi^2 = 14.322$, $df = 3$, $p < .01$.

17. $\chi^2 = 4.777$, $df = 3$, $p < .10$.

18. $\chi^2 = 6.992$, $df = 3$, $p < .10$.

19. $\chi^2 = 14.088$, $df = 1$, $p < .001$.

20. $\chi^2 = 6.507$, $df = 1$, $p < .05$.

21. $\chi^2 = 9.942$, $df = 3$, $p < .05$.

22. $\chi^2 = 8.289$, $df = 3$, $p < .05$.

23. $\chi^2 = 13.29$, $df = 3$, $p < .005$.

24. These are actual quotes from a newspaper, but owing to other information given to us by the abductor, we have changed key identifying information from the newspaper article in order to protect the family's privacy.

25. Finkelhor et al. (1990, 1991).

26. Ibid.

27. Finkelhor et al. (1990).

28. Greif and Pabst (1988).

29. Personal communication with Detective Gregory Kovalenko, Baltimore County Police, September 21 and September 25, 1990.

30. Men also are battered in marriages, but because of societal sanctions against men seeking help for being beaten by a woman, they rarely seek help for this problem. In addition, it is our impression that they rarely leave a marriage with their children because of being battered.

31. Berliner (1990); Fisher (1990); Pennington (1990).

32. Gelles and Cornell (1985).

33. Pagelow (1990).

34. Applebome (1991); Junod (1992).

35. Berliner (1990).

36. Pennington (1990), pp. 6A3–4.

37. "Child's Location a Secret" (1987); Eig (1987); Moses (1991); Faye Yager was

found innocent in May 1992 of charges she was facing of kidnapping and child abuse (Applebome, 1992).

38. Moses (1991).

39. Lloyd (1990).

40. Eig (1987); Moses (1991); Pennington (1990).

41. Moses (1991).

42. Hoffman (1990); Junod (1991).

43. Nathan (1990a, 1990b).

44. Dart (1989); National Resource Center on Child Sexual Abuse (1989).

45. Long et al. (1991).

CHAPTER 4:   How Parents Recover Their Children

1. Finkelhor et al. (1990).

2. Forehand, Long, Zogg, and Parrish (1989).

3. Janvier et al. (1990).

4. Ibid.

5. Ibid, pp. 4-5.

6. $\chi^2 = 11.781$, $df = 1$, $p < .001$.

7. $\chi^2 = 19.377$, $df = 1$, $p < .0001$.

8. $\chi^2 = 5.297$, $df = 1$, $p < .05$. When the variable custody was examined with recovery controlling for sex, 65% of the female respondents who had custody recovered ($\chi^2 = 10.457$, $df = 1$, $p < .0012$) versus 48% of the male respondents ($\chi^2 = 4.788$, $df = 1$, $p < .05$).

9. Greif (1990).

10. Greif and Pabst (1988).

11. This interpretation was offered to us by the staff of the National Center for Missing and Exploited Children during our presentation of our data to them, 20 November, 1991.

12. The support of missing children's organizations, lawyers, and the local police were all significantly related to recovery while the other four variables showed trends in the same direction.

13. $\chi^2 = 5.017$, $df = 7$, $p =$ n.s. Even though the differences were not significant, the trend was in the direction noted in the text.

14. $\chi^2 = 4.433$, $df = 1$, $p < .05$.

15. $\chi^2 = 7.353$, $df = 1$, $p < .01$.

16. $\chi^2 = 8.425$, $df = 1$, $p < .01$.

17. $\chi^2 = 3.34$, $df = 1$, $p < .10$.

18. $\chi^2 = 1.552$, $df = 1$, $p =$ n.s.

19. $\chi^2 = 3.524$, $df = 1$, $p < .10$.

20. Hoff (1988). The pamphlet is available from the National Center for Missing and Exploited Children and lists many other helpful suggestions.

21. NCIC takes information on missing children and helps locate abductors who are criminally charged. In both instances, access is then sought through local law enforcement and not the parents.

22. Gill (1984).

23. Personal communication with Carolyn Zogg, 11 January 1991.

24. "ABA Study Identifies Key Legal Obstacles to the Recovery and Return of Parentally Abducted Children." ABA Press release concerning an interim report conducted by the American Bar Association Young Lawyers Division Center on Children and the Law, released by the Office of Juvenile Justice and Delinquency Prevention, January 1992. Chris Hatcher also cites a lack of funds on the part of the left-behind parent as an obstacle, personal communication, 8 June 1992.

25. $\chi^2 = 23.75$, $df = 7$, $p < .001$.

26. Maxwell and Gould (1989).

27. Waller (1991), p. 31.

28. Personal communications with Judy Feeney, 31 October 1991 and 5 June 1992.

29. Personal communication with Ernest Allen, president of the National Center for Missing and Exploited Children, 18 May 1991.

30. Prosecutors are under no obligation to drop charges, even after the parents have reached an agreement. (We thank our anonymous reviewers for clarifying this and other legal points.)

31. Greif (1990).

CHAPTER 5:   How Children Experience Abduction

1. Finkelhor et al. (1990) found in their national survey that 10% of abducted children are missing at least a month.

2. Wixom and Wixom (1987).

3. Cairns (1987); Rosenblatt (1983).

4. Luthar and Zigler (1991) present a review of the literature on resilience in childhood.

5. See, for example, Wallerstein and Kelly (1980).

6. Bowlby (1969).

7. Rutter (1972).

8. Ames and Ilg (1976).

9. Kagan (1984), p. 126.

10. Ames (1979).

11. Kagan (1984).

12. Kagan (1984); Rubenstein (1991) breaks down adolescence into early (ages

10 to 14), middle (15 to 17), and late (18 to 21) adolescence and discusses the cognitive development in each stage.

13. Senior et al. (1982).

14. Abrahms (1983).

15. Agopian (1984).

16. Abrahms (1983).

17. Children who are told about the death of a parent will often go through stages of mourning in coping with that loss. For tasks associated with a parent's death, see Baker et al. (1992).

18. Terr (1983).

19. Fuselier (1987); Ochberg (1980). The term comes from a hostage situation in Stockholm where the captives developed an affinity for their captors.

20. Sagatun and Barrett (1990) report that a few children were placed into foster care for months while custody and the adequacy of the searching parent were being established.

21. Janvier et al. (1990); Rotem (1991).

22. Finkelhor et al. (1991).

23. Faller (1991) found in a sample of 136 children where sexual abuse was at issue that false allegations were made in 14% of the cases and possibly false ones in another 8%.

24. $\chi^2 = .0316$, $df = 1$, $p < .05$.

25. There is great dispute among experts about what constitutes child abuse (Konker, 1992).

26. Agopian (1984).

27. Forehand, Long, Zogg, and Parrish (1989).

28. Schetky and Haller (1983).

29. Terr (1983).

30. Senior et al. (1982), p. 580.

31. We only used the preabduction scores of the children who were recovered so that meaningful comparisons could be drawn using the same children. There are potential problems in (1) relying on parental assessments of children's adjustment, (2) using retrospective assessments, and (3) being unable to attribute adjustment scores to particular children.

32. Finkelhor et al. (1991) found between 40% and 52%, depending on the definition, experienced some minor to serious mental harm.

33. $\chi^2 = 35.62$, $df = 1$, $p < .0001$.

34. $\chi^2 = 13.53$, $df = 1$, $p < .001$.

35. $\chi^2 = 11.02$, $df = 1$, $p < .001$.

36. $\chi^2 = 13.85$, $df = 1$, $p < .001$.

37. $\chi^2 = 13.65$, $df = 1$, $p < .001$.

38. $\chi^2 = 15.95$, $df = 1$, $p < .0001$.

39. $\chi^2 = 12.16$, $df = 1$, $p < .001$.

40. Finkelhor et al. (1990) found clear trends for abductions to occur in August and January.

41. Agopian (1980).

42. Straus et al. (1988).

43. Costin et al. (1991); Finkelhor (1984).

44. $\chi^2 = 3.34$, $df = 1$, $p < .10$. Data were taken at time of survey.

45. $\chi^2 = 35.62$, $df = 1$, $p < .0001$.

46. $\chi^2 = 9.18$, $df = 1$, $p < .02$.

47. $\chi^2 = 9.41$, $df = 1$, $p < .01$.

48. $\chi^2 = 6.06$, $df = 1$, $p < .02$.

49. Greif and Hegar (1991).

50. This number may go down over time, as suggested by our follow-up interviews over a two-year period.

51. $\chi^2 = 18.33$, $df = 1$, $p < .0001$.

52. $\chi^2 = 4.21$, $df = 1$, $p < .05$.

53. $\chi^2 = 7.96$, $df = 1$, $p < .05$.

54. $\chi^2 = 3.34$, $df = 1$, $p < .10$.

55. $\chi^2 = 7.15$, $df = 1$, $p < .01$.

56. $\chi^2 = 10.78$, $df = 1$, $p < .01$.

CHAPTER 6: International Abductions

1. Stevenson (1886, 1893). *The Compact Edition of the Oxford English Dictionary* (1971) traces use of the word *kidnapped* to 1682 and defines it as "originally, to steal or carry off (children or others) in order to provide servants or labourers for the American plantations; hence, in general use, to steal (a child), to carry off (a person) by illegal force."

2. U.S. Department of State (1989, 1991a, 1991b); "President Signs Law" (1988).

3. Hegar and Greif (1991b).

4. Janvier et al. (1990).

5. $\chi^2 = 11.64$, $df = 3$, $p < .01$.

6. $F = 10.80$, $df = 1,286$, $p < .001$.

7. $\chi^2 = 6.51$, $df = 1$, $p < .05$.

8. $\chi^2 = 12.85$, $df = 3$, $p < .005$.

9. $\chi^2 = 14.76$, $df = 3$, $p < .01$.

10. U.S. Department of Commerce (1989).

11. $\chi^2 = 3.93$, $df = 1$, $p < .05$.

12. $\chi^2 = 3.93$, $df = 1$, $p < .05$.

13. $\chi^2 = 6.47$, $df = 1$, $p < .05$.
    $\chi^2 = 8.11$, $df = 1$, $p < .01$.

14. U.S. Department of State (1991a) records reveal that the countries with the largest numbers of known active (unresolved) abductions of U.S. children are Greece (69 cases), Saudi Arabia (56 cases), Jordan (45 cases), Egypt (37 cases), Iran (33 cases), and Israel (31 cases). The country outside the Middle East having the highest number of active cases was Canada, with 30.

15. Mahmoody and Hoffer (1987).

16. U.S. Department of Commerce, *Marital Status and Living Arrangements* (1990a), p. 94.

17. U.S. Department of Commerce (1989).

18. Ibid.

19. Interracial/ethnic, $\chi^2 = 25.99$, $df = 1$, $p < .0001$.
    International, $\chi^2 = 43.10$, $df = 1$, $p < .0001$.

20. Cretser and Leon (1982).

21. $\chi^2 = 4.55$, $df = 1$, $p < .05$.

22. $\chi^2 = 3.85$, $df = 1$, $p < .05$.

23. Physical care, $\chi^2 = 8.93$, $df = 3$, $p < .05$.
    Supervision, $\chi^2 = 11.73$, $df = 3$, $p < .01$.

24. International, $\chi^2 = 7.76$, $df = 1$, $p < .01$.
    Interracial, $\chi^2 = 5.61$, $df = 1$, $p < .05$.

25. $\chi^2 = 5.29$, $df = 1$, $p < .05$.

26. U.S. Department of State (1989), p. 2.

27. See, for example, McGoldrick and Preto (1984).

28. Cretser and Leon (1982), pp. 10–11.

29. Ibid, p. 11.

30. Orthner and Bowen (1985).

31. Faulkner (1983).

32. Hoffman (1987); Strom et al. (1984).

33. Baptiste (1984), p. 375.

34. Bodzin (1989); Crawford (1990); Dyer (1987, 1991); Eekelaar (1982); McClean (1990); Nichols (1987); Rivers (1989). In addition to the Hague Convention, discussed here, relevant treaties include the European Convention on the Recognition and Enforcement of Custody Decrees and on Restoration of Custody (1980) and the Inter-American Convention on International Return of Children (1989); see Dyer (1991).

35. United Nations (1990), p. 17.

36. Bodzin (1989); Hoff (1986); McDonald (1988); Schwerin (1988).

37. Dyer (1991); Schwerin (1988).

38. The subsequent dissolution of Yugoslavia leaves its participation in doubt.

39. Rivers (1989).

40. Pfund (1990); "President Signs Law" (1988); Stotter (1986).

41. Janvier et al. (1990) report that recovery costs in international abductions were substantially higher than in domestic ones. One parent in our study reported legal fees of more than $100,000 for futile attempts to recover his child.

42. Janvier et al. (1990) also compared domestic and international abductions of children by parents. They report that children taken abroad were recovered more often than children who remained in the United States. The number of international abductions in that study was small ($n = 26$); that study, compared to ours, may have included abductions to different destinations or fewer abductors born in other countries. Either difference could help explain the contrasting findings about recovery.

43. $\chi^2 = 13.74$, $df = 1$, $p < .01$.

CHAPTER 7: Helping Parents Survive an Abduction:
Therapeutic Approaches

1. Lawson (1992).

2. Hegar and Greif (1991c).

3. Wallerstein (1990).

4. American Psychiatric Association (1987).

5. Stone (1992).

6. Brett et al. (1988).

7. Lindy (1986).

8. Figley (1986).

9. Marton (1988).

10. Figley (1986).

11. Ibid.

12. Wartel (1991).

13. Peterson et al. (1991).

14. Kalter et al. (1989) found children had a better chance of adjusting well after divorce if their parents were well-adjusted.

15. Patten et al. (1989).

16. Herndon and Law (1986).

17. Forehand, Long, Zogg, and Parrish (1989).

18. Terr (1983).

19. Schetky & Haller (1983).

20. Senior et al. (1982).

21. Ibid.

22. Sagatun and Barrett (1990).

23. See, for example, Faller (1991); Sgroi (1982); Spaulding (1987).

24. Glascoe and MacLean (1990).

25. Keshet (1990); Visher and Visher (1988).

26. Brown et al. (1990).

27. Kahn and Lewis (1988).

28. Camara and Resnick (1989).

CHAPTER 8: Before Parents Kidnap: Preventing Abductions

1. For a discussion of the levels of prevention, as well as the terms *primary, secondary,* and *tertiary prevention,* see Bloom (1981).

2. U.S. Department of Commerce (1989).

3. Mills (1959), p. 47.

4. Many of these policies and programs are advocated by Kamarck and Galston (1990).

5. Greif and Pabst (1988).

6. Czapanskiy (1989).

7. Personal communication (interview), Consular Affairs Office, U.S. State Department, 27 June 1990; personal communication (letter), A. P. Karpel, Jericho, N.Y., 29 May 1990.

8. Jana Singer, Esq., of the University of Maryland School of Law notes, "Recent federal efforts to enforce child support obligations make it quite likely that the government will soon have . . . personal information . . . for many divorcing (and never married) parents. For example, as of 1994, states will be required to institute mandatory wage withholding procedures every time a child support order is entered. (States are already required to do so for all support orders entered in AFDC [Aid to Families with Dependent Children] cases.) To implement this requirement, the government will need to have information about the employment and change of address status of many obligated parents." Personal communication (letter), 22 April 1991.

9. Hoff (1988); U.S. Department of State (1989)

10. These cases include *Meyer v. Nebraska,* 262 U.S. 390 (1923); *Pierce v. Society of Sisters,* 268 U.S. 510 (1925); *Griswold v. Connecticut,* 381 U.S. 479 (1965); *Wisconsin v. Yoder,* 406 U.S. 205 (1972); and *Roe v. Wade,* 410 U.S. 113 (1973).

11. U.S. Department of Commerce (1990a).

12. Ibid.

13. The "least detrimental alternative" is proposed as a more realistic test than seeking the "best interests of the child" in Goldstein, Freud, and Solnit, *Beyond the Best Interests of the Child* (1979b).

14. Krause (1986), p. 262.

15. In a few states, most notably California, flight by a custodial parent is included in state parental abduction statutes.

16. We learned recently that Philadelphia has started a program that makes

emergency court services, including access to a judge, available 24 hours a day. That is the kind of responsiveness that is necessary in all large jurisdictions.

17. Personal communication (interview) with Linda Girdner, Patricia Hoff, and Miriam Rollins of the American Bar Association Center on Children and the Law, 16 April 1991. The ABA Center's Parental Abduction Project is working to clarify this point.

18. We acknowledge and appreciate comments that helped clarify this point in an anonymous professional review (obtained by Free Press) of the draft manuscript.

19. Custody mediation has become quite common in the United States, and its use is growing in other countries. See Garwood (1991); Walker (1991); Zaidel (1991).

20. See, for example, Mnookin and Kornhauser (1979); Zemmelman et al. (1987).

21. Whether to include children in mediation depends on a number of factors, including their age. Saposnek (1991) discusses the issue from the perspective of different cultural backgrounds.

22. The qualifications for mediators specified in state statutes vary widely; see Dutenhaver (1988).

23. Bautz and Hill (1991); King (1982); Little et al. (1985); Pearson and Thoennes (1985); Zemmelman et al. (1985).

24. King and Thoennes (1984). But less conclusive results are reported in Pearson and Thoennes (1985).

25. See Bentch (1986).

26. Crites and Coker (1988); Girdner (1990); Hart (1990); Lerman (1984); Menard and Salius (1990). Note, however, that Geffner and Pagelow (1990) believe that mediation can be used in domestic violence situations under certain conditions: "Mediation with abusive couples can only be accomplished successfully with the consent of both parties, with a mediator who is trained in both family violence and mediation techniques, with the use of particular methods to balance the power differential and compensate for the automatic advantage of the abuser, and in conjunction with the abuser's participation in therapy. When conducted properly with certain types of cases, mediation can not only help couples arrive at mutually satisfactory arrangements but it can also help empower the battered woman" (p. 157).

27. *In re Gault,* 387 U.S. 1 (1967).

28. By 1984 a majority of states did allow judges to appoint counsel at their discretion for children in custody proceedings. See Guggenheim (1984).

29. Representation for children is encouraged in the Uniform Marriage and Divorce Act, section 310. Such uniform acts are model statutes developed by legal experts and available to state lawmakers. Legal counsel for children in custody hearings also is advocated by Goldstein, Freud, and Solnit, *Beyond the Best Interests of the Child* (1979b). However, other authors oppose the idea; see Guggenheim (1984).

30. When counsel is not appointed for children, for whatever reasons, then

parents' counselors should advocate for safeguards against abduction and for any other custody/visitation arrangements deemed to be in the child's best interests.

31. Hoff et al. (1990). See also Crites and Coker (1988); Keenan (1985); Lengyel (1990).

32. U.S. Congress, House (1990).

33. Ibid.

34. Crites and Coker (1988); Keenan (1985); Pagelow (1990).

35. Elkin (1987); Geffner and Pagelow (1990); Keenan (1985).

36. Davis and Carlson (1987); Pagelow (1990).

37. Krause (1986).

38. Atkinson (1984).

39. Mnookin and Weisberg (1988), p. 757.

40. As of 1987 these jurisdictions included California, Florida, Idaho, Kansas, Maine, New Mexico, and New Hampshire, according to Hagen (1987).

41. See, for example, Elkin (1987); Hagen (1987); Keenan (1985); Mobilia-Boumil (1987); Wallerstein and Blakeslee (1989).

42. Elkin (1987).

43. Goldstein, Freud, and Solnit, *Beyond the Best Interests of the Child* (1979b), who introduced the concept of psychological parent, maintain that all authority, including decisions about visiting the noncustodial parent, should rest with a single custodial parent after divorce. However, they do not contend that a relationship with both parents is not important for children in most cases.

44. This is the goal in mediation suggested by Samis and Saposnek (1987); see also Singer and Reynolds (1988).

45. Other commentators hold that joint custody should never be awarded over the objections of either parent. See Keenan (1985); Singer and Reynolds (1988).

46. For example, West Virginia and Minnesota. See Singer and Reynolds (1988).

47. Singer and Reynolds (1988).

48. Krause (1986), p. 18.

49. Greif (1985).

50. See Wexler (1985).

51. See Jacobs (1991).

52. Johnston and Campbell (1988) describe in detail the mediation of disputes within high-conflict divorcing families.

53. Long et al. (1991).

54. See note 17.

CHAPTER 9:   Resolving Parental Abductions and Reexamining
Their Context

1. Finkelhor et al. (1990).

2. Parts of this section are abstracted from Rebecca L. Hegar, "Parental Kidnapping and U.S. Social Policy," *Social Service Review* 64 (1990): 407–421. Used by permission of the copyright holder.

3. See discussions of the underground in Berliner (1990) and Pennington (1990).

4. Uniform Child Custody Jurisdiction Act, Uniform Laws Annotated, vol. 9, part 1 (St. Paul, Minn.: West, 1988).

5. "Uniform Child Custody Jurisdiction Act: Table of Jurisdictions Wherein Act Has Been Adopted," *Uniform Laws Annotated*, 9, pt. 1:115.

6. An excellent annotated bibliography of the legal literature pertaining to the UCCJA and other statutes affecting parental abduction has been prepared by Rollin, Hoff, and Girdner (1991).

7. Bentch (1986), p. 368; Parental Kidnapping Prevention Act, Public Law No. 96–611, sections 6–10, 94 Stat. 3568, 3569 (1980).

8. Coombs (1990).

9. *Thompson v. Thompson* 108 S.Ct. 513 (1988), p. 513; Wilson (1987).

10. For a detailed discussion of extradition in parental abduction cases, see LePori (1988).

11. See Agopian (1981), citing U.S. House Committee on the Judiciary, *Hearings on H.R. 5657,* 72nd Congress, 1st session, p. 5.

12. Federal Kidnapping Act, 18 U.S.C. section 1201 (1976); Lansing and Sherman (1983), citing 75 *Congressional Record* 13.286 (1932).

13. Lansing and Sherman (1983).

14. Agopian (1987); Hoff et al. (1990).

15. For a discussion of this issue in Wisconsin courts, see Hemming (1983).

16. Reynolds (1986).

17. *Lawson v. Dunn,* 460 N.W. 2d 39 (Minnesota 1990). See Hillebrand (1992).

18. Oberdorfer (1991).

19. Ibid.; Texas Codes Annotated, Family Code, Chapter 36.

20. Oberdorfer (1991).

21. They are Argentina, Australia, Austria, Belize, Canada, Denmark, Ecuador, France, Germany, Hungary, Ireland, Israel, Luxembourg, Mexico, the Netherlands, New Zealand, Norway, Portugal, Spain, Sweden, Switzerland, the United Kingdom, the United States, and Yugoslavia. Personal communication (telephone conversation), Consular Affairs Office, U.S. State Department, 3 June 1992.

22. Best (1987) reports that even after the passage of the PKPA, "only 64 percent of the respondents to a 1981 CBS/*New York Times* poll fully agreed that federal kidnapping laws should apply to [parental] child-snatching," p. 103.

23. See also Girdner et al. (1991).

24. Berliner (1990); Fisher (1990); Pennington (1990).

25. Lloyd (1990).

26. Ibid.

27. Patricia Hoff, Esq., legal director, American Bar Association Parental Abduction Research Project, notes: "Once a child is returned to a lawful custodian, the court with jurisdiction (consistent with the UCCJA and PKPA) may hear a petition for modification based on changed circumstances. Surely, the court will not look favorably upon an abduction (barring compelling justification, i.e., domestic violence/child abuse), but ultimately the court will weigh the petitioner-abductor's conduct along with all other evidence concerning the child's best interests in deciding whether a change of custody or visitation is warranted." Personal communication (note), 17 April 1991.

28. "Least detrimental alternative" is the language used by Goldstein et al. (1979b) in place of the more familiar legal standard "the best interests of the child." They write: "The traditional standard does not, as does the phrase 'least detrimental,' convey to the decisionmaker that the child in question is already a victim of his environmental circumstances, that he is greatly at risk, and that speedy action is necessary to avoid further harm being done to his chances of healthy psychological development. . . . Moreover, . . . many decisions are 'in-name-only' for the best interests of the specific child who is being placed. They are fashioned primarily to meet the needs and wishes of competing adult claimants . . ." (p. 54).

29. This is part of the "clean hands doctrine," which holds that individuals should not benefit from illegal acts. See, for example, Anderson (1988). Also see note 15. Something of a parallel to our recommendation arises in custody disputes involving surrogate mothers that have been resolved based on the best interests of the child, not the principle of holding people to their contracts. See *In re Baby M.,* 109 N.J. 396, A.2d 1227 (1988).

30. We acknowledge and appreciate the contribution to our thinking about this point made by Carol Alexander, director, House of Ruth, Baltimore, MD.

31. Terr (1983).

32. See, for example, Demeter (1977); Gill (1981); Goldstein et al. (1979b), pp. 113–133.

33. Best (1987).

34. Annotated Code of Maryland, Family Law Article 9–304, 9–305.

35. Texas Codes Annotated, Sec. 25.03.

36. Texas Codes Annotated, Sec. 25.03(a)(2).

37. California Penal Code, Title 9, Chapter 4, Sec. 277.

38. Hague Convention on the Civil Aspects of International Child Abduction, Article 3.

39. Erickson (1988).

40. Personal communication (interview) with Carolyn Zogg, director, Child Find of America, Inc., of New Paltz, NY, 11 January 1991.

41. Hegar (1990).

42. The number is 1–800–A WAY OUT. Personal communication (interview) with Carolyn Zogg, director, Child Find of America, Inc., of New Paltz, NY, 11 January 1991.

43. Forehand, Long, and Zogg (1989).

44. Note that some states do have statutes governing the confidentiality of conversations between social workers and clients. See, for example, Annotated Code of Maryland, Sec. 9–121.

45. *National Association of Social Workers Policy Statements 1: Code of Ethics* (1990), p. 6.

46. See, for example, Annotated Code of Maryland, Courts and Judicial Proceeding Article, Sec. 5–316. The major court case in this area is *Tarasoff v. Regents of University of California, et al* 551 P 2d 334 (1976), a California Supreme Court decision that also has been influential in other jurisdictions; see Stone (1986).

47. Pennington (1990).

48. Several such cases are discussed in Martin (1987). A more recent case is *Bersani v. Bersani* 565 A.2d 1368 (Conn. Super. 1989).

49. *Bersani v. Bersani,* 565 A.2d 1368 (Conn. Super. 1989), 1371–72.

50. American Bar Association, *Model Rules* (1989).

51. Rule 4–102 (C) (3) (a), cited in Martin (1987), p. 22.

52. The degree of harm required to outweigh client confidentiality is, of course, difficult to define. The ABA standard of "death or substantial bodily harm" is helpful in its specificity, but it is perhaps too restrictive.

53. Marks (1990).

54. We are indebted to Linda Girdner, Esq., director, Parental Kidnapping Project, ABA National Legal Resource Center of Child Advocacy and Protection, for being the first to bring this problem to our attention. Personal communication (interview), 16 April 1991.

55. For a discussion and review of the literature concerning emotional neglect, see Hegar and Yungman (1989).

56. Fisher (1990) and Pennington (1990) relate poignant cases of abduction to avoid abuse when repeated efforts to modify the visitation rights of noncustodial fathers had failed.

57. Berliner (1990); Fisher (1990). Also see Fahn (1991) for a general discussion of sexual abuse allegations in custody disputes.

58. Berliner (1990); Quinn (1988); Thoennes (1988).

59. See Gardner (1987).

60. Gardner (1987); Quinn (1988).

61. White and Quinn (1988).

62. Many of the parents and professionals we interviewed noted the prohibitively high costs of legal representation and court costs for those involved in child custody disputes and abduction cases. Legal services need to be more

accessible in these and many other kinds of disputes. Although the solution to lack of access to legal services is beyond the scope of this book, a partial answer may lie in a combination of alternative forms of dispute resolution, expanded legal services for low-income people, more *pro bono* work by attorneys, and additional public funding for court-appointed counsel and other court services.

63. Thoennes (1988), p. 18.

64. For example, Rosen-Zvi (1989/90) reports that in Israel (before adoption of the Hague Convention there): "The court examines with particular care the best interests of the child at the time of the hearing. In quite a few cases the court has refrained from issuing an order for return of the child when it was clear that the child had become accustomed to his Israeli surroundings" (p. 539).

65. Goldstein et al. (1979a).

66. Goldstein et al. (1979b).

67. Goldstein et al. (1979a), pp. 40–41.

68. Ibid., p. 48.

69. This recommendation and the preceding one raise a number of legal questions that are beyond the scope of this book to resolve. One of these concerns the legal standard that would be applied in hearings following abductions. According to Jana B. Singer, Esq., University of Maryland School of Law: "If courts were to use a straight best interests/least detrimental alternative standard, this might well result in the abductor retaining custody in many, if not most, cases that trigger a hearing [following a lengthy abduction]. If, on the other hand, the hearing is treated as a traditional modification [of custody] proceeding, then a higher standard (such as a change of custody only if necessary to protect the child) would apply and a change in the pro-abduction custody arrangements is less likely. Both standards are arguably child centered, but I think they would produce substantially different results, at least in the aggregate." Personal communication (letter), 22 April 1991.

It occurs to us that the reason for a higher standard in most hearings to modify custody is to preserve the child's stability in the home of the custodial parent (see Wexler, 1985). In cases of prolonged abduction, the child's interest in stability may no longer be served by making it more difficult to modify the original custody decree. This suggests that the least detrimental alternative standard is the appropriate one.

70. Not all authorities see this trend as desirable. See, for example, Dyer (1991).

71. For example, Maryland's statute makes parental abduction a felony only if the child is taken out of state. Abductors who remain within the state face a maximum misdemeanor penalty of a $250 fine or 30 days in jail. Annotated Code of Maryland, Family Law Article, Section 9–307.

72. One important issue to be addressed when this type of defense is incorporated into statute concerns whether it is based on sincere belief, which is a subjective interpretation, or on ability to prove that the belief was reasonable, which is a more objective interpretation. We thank our colleague Jana B. Singer, Esq., of the University of Maryland Law School for drawing our

attention to this distinction, although it is beyond the scope of these recommendations to resolve this and similar technical questions.

73. Annotated Code of Maryland, Family Law Article 9–306(b).

74. Wisconsin Statutes Annotated, Section 948.31 (4) (a, 1–2).

75. California Penal Code, Title 9, Chapter 4, Section 277.

76. Cole (1991).

77. "In all jurisdictions statutes punish such aggravated assaults as assaults with intent to murder (or rob or kill or rape) and assault with a dangerous (or deadly) weapon more severely than 'simple' assaults" (Black, 1979, p. 60).

78. Ibid.

79. Erickson (1988).

80. Wisconsin Statutes Annotated, Section 948.31 (2).

81. Texas Codes Annotated, Title 6, Chapter 25.03 (a) (2); Wisconsin Statutes Annotated, Section 948.31 (3) (b).

82. Wisconsin Statutes Annotated, Section 948.31 (1) (a) 2.

83. California Penal Code, Title 9, Chapter 4, Section 277.

84. NPRI's (National Prosecutors Research Institute) National Center of Prosecution of Child Abuse sponsored a major conference for law enforcement personnel, prosecutors, court personnel, and others; Parental Abduction: A Crime Against the Family in Denver, 17–18 May 1991. They also publish *National Directory of Parental Abduction Prosecutors* (1990). The Reunification of Missing Children Project at the University of California Center for the Study of Trauma began offering training to law enforcement and other personnel in a number of cities in 1991. The authors participated in both programs by presenting the research on which this book is based.

STATUTES AND COURT CASES

Annotated Code of Maryland, Family Law Article 9–304, 9–305, 9–307.
Bersani v. Bersani, 565 A.2d 1368 (Conn. Super. 1989).
California Penal Code, Title 9, Chapter 4, Sec. 277.
Federal Kidnapping Act, 18 U.S.C. section 1201 (1976).
Griswold v. Connecticut, 381 U.S. 479 (1965).
Hague Convention on the Civil Aspects of International Child Abduction, 25 October 1980, 19 I.L.M. 1501.
In re Baby M., 109 N.J. 396, A.2d 1227 (1988).
In re Gault, 387 U.S. 1 (1967).
Lawson v. Dunn, 460 N.W. 2d 39 (Minn. 1990).
Meyer v. Nebraska, 262 U.S. 390 (1923).
Parental Kidnapping Prevention Act, Public Law No. 96–611, sections 6–10, 94 Stat. 3568, 3569 (1980).
Pierce v. Society of Sisters, 268 U.S. 510 (1925).
Roe v. Wade, 410 U.S. 113 (1973).
Tarasoff v. Regents of the University of California, et al. 551 P 2d 334 (Calif. 1976).
Texas Codes Annotated, Section 25.
Texas Codes Annotated, Family Code, Chapter 36.
Thompson v. Thompson 108 S.Ct. 513 (1988).
Uniform Child Custody Jurisdiction Act, Uniform Laws Annotated, vol. 9, part 1 (St. Paul, Minn.: West, 1988).

"Uniform Child Custody Jurisdiction Act: Table of Jurisdictions Where-
in Act Has Been Adopted," *Uniform Laws Annotated,* 9, pt. 1:115.
Uniform Marriage and Divorce Act, Uniform Laws Annotated (St. Paul,
Minn.: West, 1988).
Wisconsin Statutes Annotated, Section 948.31.
Wisconsin v. Yoder, 406 U.S. 205 (1972).

BIBLIOGRAPHY

Abrahms, Sally. *Children in the Crossfire: The Tragedy of Parental Kidnapping.* New York: Atheneum, 1983.

Abram, Marian C. "The Parental Kidnapping Prevention Act: Constitutionality and Effectiveness." *Case Western Reserve Law Review* 33 (Fall 1982): 89–115.

Agopian, Michael W. "Parental Child Stealing: Participants and the Victimization Process." *Victimology: An International Journal* 5, nos. 2–4 (1980): 263–273.

———. *Parental Child-Stealing.* Lexington, MA: Lexington Books, 1981.

———. "The Impact on Children of Abduction by Parents." *Child Welfare* 63, no. 6 (Nov./Dec. 1984): 511–519.

———. "International Abduction of Children: The United States Experience." *International Journal of Comparative and Applied Criminal Justice* 11 (Spring/Winter 1987): 231–239.

Agopian, Michael W. and Gretchen L. Anderson. "Legislative Reforms to Reduce Parental Child Abduction." *Journal of Juvenile Law* 6 (1982): 1–26.

Alix, Ernest Kahlar. *Ransom Kidnapping in America/1874–1974: The Creation of a Capital Crime.* Carbondale, IL: Southern Illinois University Press, 1978.

Alvarez, Julia. "Hold the Mayonnaise." *New York Times Magazine,* 12 January 1992, pp. 14, 24.

American Bar Association. *Model Rules of Professional Conduct and Code of Judicial Conduct.* Chicago: Author, 1989.

American Prosecutors Research Institute, National Center for Prosecution of Child Abuse. *National Directory of Parental Abduction Prosecutors.* Alexandria, VA: Author, 1990.

———. *Parental Abduction: A Crime Against the Family-Training Manual.* Alexandria, VA: Author, 1991.

American Psychiatric Association. *Diagnostic and Statistical Manual of Mental Disorders (DSM III-R),* 3rd ed., rev. Washington, DC: Author, 1987.

Ames, Louise B. *Your Six Year Old.* New York: Delta Books, 1979.

Ames, Louise B. and Frances L. Ilg. *Your Two Year Old.* New York: Delta Books, 1976.

Anderson, Cerisse. "Mother Loses Custody of Child for Plotting his Kidnapping." *New York Law Journal* 199 (April 1988): 1.

Applebome, Peter. "Founder of a Network for Abused Children Is Acquitted of Cruelty." *New York Times,* 16 May 1992, A6.

Atkinson, Jeff. "Criteria for Deciding Child Custody in the Trial and Appellate Courts." *Family Law Quarterly* 18 (1984): 1–42.

Baker, John E., Mary Sedney, and Esther Gross. "Psychological Tasks for Bereaved Children." *American Journal of Orthopsychiatry* 62 (January 1992): 105–116.

Baptiste, David A., Jr. "Marital and Family Therapy with Racially/Culturally Intermarried Stepfamilies: Issues and Guidelines." *Family Relations* 33 (1984): 373–380.

Barber, Michael E. "Soldiers, Sailors and the Law." *Family Advocate* 9, no. 4 (Spring 1987): 38–41.

Barrett, K. "I Always Knew You'd Find Me, Mom." *Ladies' Home Journal,* August 1981, p. 86.

Bautz, Barbara J. and Rose M. Hill. "Mediating the Breakup: Do Children Win?" *Mediation Quarterly* 8, no. 3 (1991): 199–210.

Bentch, Sue T. "Court-Sponsored Custody Mediation to Prevent Parental Kidnapping: A Disarmament Proposal." *St. Mary's Law Journal* 18 (Winter 1986): 361–393.

Berliner, L. "Protecting or Harming: Parents Who Flee with Their Children." *Journal of Interpersonal Violence* 5 (1990): 119–120.

Best, Joel. "Rhetoric in Claims-Making: Constructing the Missing Children Problem." *Social Problems* 34, no. 2 (April 1987): 101–121.

Black, Henry Campbell. *Black's Law Dictionary,* 5th ed., edited by Joseph R. Nolan and M. J. Connolly. St. Paul, MN: West, 1979.

Bloom, Martin. *Primary Prevention: The Possible Science.* Englewood Cliffs, NJ: Prentice-Hall, 1981.

Bodenheimer, Brigitte M. "The International Kidnapping of Children: The United States Approach." *Family Law Quarterly* 11, no. 1 (Spring 1977): 83–100.

Bodzin, Martin I. "International Parental Child Abduction: The Need for Recognition and Enforcement of Foreign Custody Decrees."

Emory Journal of International Dispute Resolution 3 (1989): 205–219.

Bowlby, John. *Attachment and Loss: Vol. 1. Attachment.* New York: Basic Books, 1969.

Brett, Elizabeth A., Robert L. Spitzer, and Janet B. W. Williams. "DSM-III-R Criteria for Post-Traumatic Stress Disorder." *American Journal of Psychiatry* 145 (1988): 1232–1235.

Brown, Anne C., Robert Jay Green, and Joan Druckman. "A Comparison of Step-Families with and Without Child-Focused Problems." *American Journal of Orthopsychiatry* 60, no. 4 (1990): 556–566.

Cairns, Ed. *Caught in Crossfire: Children and the Northern Ireland Conflict.* Belfast: Appletrees Press, 1987.

Camara, Kathleen A. and Gary Resnick. "Styles of Conflict Resolution and Cooperation Between Divorced Parents: Effects on Child Behavior and Adjustment." *American Journal of Orthopsychiatry* 59, no. 4 (1989): 560–575.

Child Safe Products. *My Child Is Not Missing.* Plantation, Fl: Author, 1984.

"Child's Location a Secret: Fugitive Mom Dies in New Orleans Hospital." *Hattiesburg American* (Mississippi), 16 October 1987, pp. A1, A12.

Chu, Daniel and Elaine Sciolino. "Family Affair: Child Snatching." *Newsweek,* 18 October 1976, p. 24.

Cleveland, Gaines H. "The Uniform Child Custody Jurisdiction Act and the Parental Kidnapping Prevention Act: Dual Response to Interstate Child Custody Problems." *Washington and Lee Law Review* 39 (Winter 1982): 149–163.

Cole, Paul C. "Case Evaluation and Charging Decisions: Making the Hard Choices." Paper presented at American Prosecutors' Research Institute's conference "Parental Abduction: A Crime Against the Family," Denver, 18 May 1991.

The Compact Edition of the Oxford English Dictionary, Vol. 1. Oxford: Oxford University Press, 1971.

Coombs, Russell M. "Progress Under the PKPA." *Journal of the American Academy of Matrimonial Lawyers* 6 (1990): 59–102.

Costin, Lela B., Cynthia J. Bell, and Susan W. Downs. *Child Welfare: Policies and Practice.* 4th ed. New York: Longman, 1991.

Crawford, Elizabeth. "International Child Abduction." *Journal of the Law Society of Scotland* 35 (Summer 1990): 277–282.

Cretser, Gary A. and Joseph J. Leon. "Intermarriage in the U.S.: An Overview of Theory and Research." *Marriage and Family Review* 5, no. 1 (1982): 3–15.

Crites, Linda and Donna Coker. "What Therapists See That Judges May Miss: A Unique Guide to Custody Decisions When Spouse Abuse Is Charged." *Judges' Journal* 27, no. 2 (1988): 9–13, 40–43.

Crouch, Richard Edelin. "Effective Measures Against International

Child Snatching." *New Law Journal* 131, no. 6004 (June 1981): 592–594.

———. "International Child-Snatching." *Family Advocate* 9, no. 4 (Spring 1987): 16–19, 46–47.

Czapanskiy, Karen. *Report of the Special Joint Committee on Gender Bias in the Courts.* Annapolis, MD: Administrative Office of the Courts, 1989.

Dart, John. "Scholars Find No Evidence of Spreading Occult Cults." *New York Times,* 29 October 1989, pp. A3, A30.

Davis, L. V. and Bonnie E. Carlson. "Observation of Spouse Abuse: What Happens to the Children?" *Journal of Interpersonal Violence* 2 (1987): 278–291.

DeHart, Gloria F. "Getting the Child Back." *Family Advocate* 9, no. 4 (Spring 1987): 20–23, 47.

———. "Getting Support—Over There." *Family Advocate* 9, no. 4 (Spring 1987): 34–37.

DeMaris, Alfred, Meredith D. Pugh, and Erika Harman. "Sex Differences in the Accuracy of Recall of Witnesses of Portrayed Dyadic Violence." *Journal of Marriage and the Family* 54 (1992): 335–345.

Demeter, Anna. *Legal Kidnapping.* Boston: Beacon Press, 1977.

Dickens, Scott T. "The Parental Kidnapping Prevention Act: Application and Interpretation." *Journal of Family Law* 23 (April 1985): 419–436.

Dutenhaver, Katheryn M. "Qualifications of Family Mediators." *Mediation Quarterly* 19 (1988): 3–11.

Dyer, Adair. "Recognition and Enforcement—Abroad." *Family Advocate* 9, no. 4 (1987): 5–8.

———. "Childhood's Rights in Private International Law." *Australian Journal of Family Law* 5 (1991): 103–119.

Eekelaar, John M. "International Child Abduction by Parents." *University of Toronto Law Journal* 32 (1982): 281–325.

Eig, Jonathan. "Missing Girl's Secret Safe with Witnesses." *Times-Picayune* (New Orleans), 10 November 1987, pp. A1, A4.

Elkin, Meyer. "Joint Custody: Affirming That Parents and Families Are Forever." *Social Work* 32 (1987): 18–24.

Erickson, Nancy S. "The Parental Kidnapping Prevention Act: How Can Non-Marital Children Be Protected?" *Golden Gate University Law Review* 18 (1988): 529–537.

Esterle, Mark D. "Parental Kidnapping Prevention Act: Troubles under *Thompson.*" *Clearinghouse Review* 22, no. 6 (Nov. 1988): 584–587.

Fahn, Meredith S. "Allegations of Child Sexual Abuse in Custody Disputes: Getting to the Truth of the Matter." *Family Law Quarterly* 25, no. 2 (Summer 1991): 193–216.

Faller, Kathleen C. "Possible Explanations for Child Sexual Abuse Allegations in Divorce." *American Journal of Orthopsychiatry* 61, no. 1 (1991): 86–91.

Faulkner, Janette. "Women in Interracial Relationships." *Women and Therapy* 2, no. 2/3 (1983): 191–203.

Feder, Lillian. *Crowell's Handbook of Classical Literature.* New York: Lippincott & Crowell, 1964.

Figley, Charles R. "Traumatic Stress: The Role of the Family and Social Support System." In *Trauma and Its Wake,* edited by C. R. Figley, Vol. 2, pp. 39–54. New York: Brunner/Mazel, 1986.

Finkelhor, David. *Child Sexual Abuse: New Theory and Research.* New York: Free Press, 1984.

Finkelhor, David, Gerald Hotaling, and Andrea Sedlak. *Missing, Abducted, Runaway and Throwaway Children in America: First Report: Numbers and Characteristics.* Washington, DC: Department of Justice, 1990.

———. "Children Abducted by Family Members: A National Household Survey of Incidence and Episode Characteristics." *Journal of Marriage and the Family* 53 (1991): 805–817.

Fisher, Deborah. "Why Parents Run." *Journal of Interpersonal Violence* 5 (1990): 123–125.

Fisher, Joan. *Missing Children Research Project: Vol. 1. Findings of the Study.* Ottawa: Solicitor General of Canada, 1989.

Forehand, Rex, Nicholas Long, and Carolyn Zogg. "Parental Child Abduction: The Problem and Possible Solution." In *Advances in Clinical Child Psychology,* edited by B. B. Lahey and A. E. Kazdin, Vol. 12, pp. 113–137. New York: Plenum, 1989.

Forehand, Rex, Nicholas Long, Carolyn Zogg, and Elizabeth Parrish. "Child Abduction: Parent and Child Functioning Following Return." *Clinical Pediatrics* 28, no. 7 (1989): 311–316.

Forst, Martin L. and Martha-Elin Blomquist. *Missing Children: Rhetoric and Reality.* New York: Lexington Books, 1991.

Fox, Greer Litton. "Noncustodial Fathers." In *Dimensions of Fatherhood,* edited by Shirley M. H. Hanson and Frederick W. Bozett, pp. 393–415. Beverly Hills, CA: Sage, 1985.

Frank, Robin Jo. "American and International Responses to International Child Abductions." *International Law and Politics* 16 (1984): 415–474.

Friedman, Susan M. and Vaughn Taus. "Kidnapping your Child: Is There a Defense?" *Trial* 20 (Oct. 1984): 46–48.

Fuselier, G. Dwayne. "Hostage Negotiation Consultant: Emerging Role for the Clinical Psychologist." *Professional Psychologist* 19 (1987): 175–179.

Gardner, Richard A. *The Parental Alienation Syndrome and the Differentiation Between Fabricated and Genuine Child Sex Abuse.* Cresskill, NJ: Creative Therapeutics, 1987.

Garwood, Fiona. "Divorce and Conciliation in Sweden and Scotland." *Mediation Quarterly* 8, no. 4 (Summer 1991): 293–301.

Gaw, Monica A. "When Uncle Sam Needs to Come to the Rescue." *Family Advocate* 9, no. 4 (Spring 1987): 24–27, 37.

Geffner, Robert and Mildred D. Pagelow. "Mediation and Child Custody Issues in Abusive Relationships." *Behavioral Sciences and the Law* 8 (1990): 151–159.

Gelles, Richard. "Violence in the Family: A Review of Research in the Seventies." *Journal of Marriage and the Family* 42 (Nov. 1980): 873–887.

———. "Parental Child Snatching: A Preliminary Estimate of the National Incidence." *Journal of Marriage and the Family* 46 (August 1984): 735–739.

Gelles, Richard J. and Claire P. Cornell. *Intimate Violence in Families.* Beverly Hills, CA: Sage, 1985.

Gill, John E. *Stolen Children.* New York: Seaview Books, 1981.

———. "Tracking Missing Children." *The Single Parent* 27 (April 1984): 1245.

Gillie, Oliver. "Abducted Children Leave Painful Trail of Legal Confusion." *The Independent* (London), 28 December 1990, p. 4.

Girdner, Linda K. "Mediation Triage: Screening for Spouse Abuse in Divorce Mediation." *Mediation Quarterly* 4, no. 7 (1990): 365–376.

Girdner, Linda K. and Patricia M. Hoff (editors). *Obstacles to the Recovery and Return of Parentally Abducted Children: Final Report.* Washington, DC: Office of Juvenile Justice and Delinquency Prevention, U.S. Department of Justice, 1992.

Girdner, Linda K., Patricia M. Hoff, and Miriam Rollin. *Obstacles to the Recovery and Return of Parentally Abducted Children* (Congressional Report, OJJDP Grant 90-MC-CX-K001). Washington, DC: American Bar Association Center on Children and the Law, 1991.

Gittelson, Natalie. "Parents as Kidnappers." *McCalls,* August 1976, p. 103.

Glascoe, Frances P. and William E. MacLean. "How Parents Appraise Their Child's Development." *Family Relations* 39, no. 3 (1990): 280–283.

Goldstein, Joseph, Anna Freud, and Albert J. Solnit. *Before the Best Interests of the Child.* New York: Free Press, 1979a.

———. *Beyond the Best Interests of the Child,* rev. ed. New York: Free Press, 1979b.

Greif, Geoffrey L. *Single Fathers.* Lexington, MA: Lexington Books, 1985.

———. *The Daddy Track and the Single Father.* Lexington, MA: Lexington Books, 1990.

Greif, Geoffrey L. and Rebecca L. Hegar. "Parents Whose Children are Abducted by the Other Parent: Implications for Treatment." *American Journal of Family Therapy* 19 (1991): 215–225.

Greif, Geoffrey L. and Mary Pabst. *Mothers Without Custody.* Lexington, MA: Lexington Books, 1988.

Groner, Jonathan. *Hilary's Trial.* New York: Simon & Schuster, 1991.

Grossberg, Scott Jay. "Children in the Crossfire: Parental Kidnapping and Custodial Interference." *Journal of Juvenile Law* 9 (Winter 1985): 138–142.

Guggenheim, Martin. "The Right to be Represented but Not Heard: Reflections on Legal Representation of Children." *New York University Law Review* 59 (1984): 76–155.

Hagen, Jan L. "Proceed with Caution: Advocating Joint Custody." *Social Work* 32 (1987): 26–30.

Hanson, Shirley M. H. "Single Custodial Fathers." In *Dimensions of Fatherhood,* edited by Shirley M. H. Hanson and Frederick W. Bozett, pp. 369–392. Beverly Hills, CA: Sage, 1985.

Hart, Barbara J. "Gentle Jeopardy: The Further Endangerment of Battered Women and Children in Custody Mediation." *Mediation Quarterly* 4, no. 7 (1990): 317–330.

Hatcher, Chris, Cole Barton, and Loren Brooks. *Families of Missing Children: Psychological Consequences.* Washington, DC: Office of Juvenile Justice and Delinquency Prevention, U.S. Department of Justice, 1992.

Hatcher, Chris, Joann Lippert, Cole Barton, and Loren Brooks. *Reunification of Missing Children Project: Final Report.* Washington, DC: Office of Juvenile Justice and Delinquency Prevention, U.S. Department of Justice, 1992.

Hegar, Rebecca L. "Parental Kidnapping and U.S. Social Policy." *Social Service Review* 64 (1990): 407–421.

Hegar, Rebecca L. and Geoffrey L. Greif. "Abduction of Children by Parents: A Survey of the Problem." *Social Work* 36 (1991a): 421–426.

———. "Bicultural Marriages and Parental Abduction." Paper presented at the Council on Social Work Education Annual Program Meeting, New Orleans, 15 March 1991(b).

———. "Parental Kidnapping across International Borders." *International Social Work* 34 (1991c): 353–363.

Hegar, Rebecca L., John G. Orme, and Geoffrey L. Greif. "Self-Esteem in Parents of Children Abducted by the Other Parent." *Children and Youth Services Review* 14 (1992): 465–482.

Hegar, Rebecca L. and Jeffrey J. Yungman. "Toward a Causal Typology of Child Neglect." *Children and Youth Services Review* 11 (1989): 203–220.

Hemming, Robert B. "Parental Kidnapping, Child Stealing, and the Parental Kidnapping Prevention Act (PKPA)." *Journal of Juvenile Law* 7 (Spring 1983): 246–257.

Herndon, Angie D. and Joseph G. Law. "Post-Traumatic Stress and the Family: A Multimethod Approach to Counseling." In *Trauma and Its Wake,* edited by C. R. Figley, Vol. 2, pp. 264–279. New York: Brunner/Mazel, 1986.

Hewson, M. "When Parents Kidnap Their Own." *McCalls,* December 1979, pp. 54–55.

Hillebrand, Joseph R. "Parental Kidnapping and the Tort of Custodial Interference: Not in a Child's Best Interests." *Indiana Law Review* 25, no. 3 (1992): 893–940.

Hoff, Patricia M. *Legal Remedies in Parental Kidnapping Cases: A Collection of Materials.* Washington, DC: National Legal Resource Center for Child Advocacy and Protection, 1986.

——. *Parental Kidnapping: How to Prevent an Abduction and What to Do If Your Child Is Abducted,* 3rd ed. Washington, DC: National Center for Missing and Exploited Children, 1988.

Hoff, Patricia M., Joanne Schulman, and Adrienne E. Volenik. *Interstate Child Custody Disputes and Parental Kidnapping: Policy, Practice and Law.* New York: American Bar Association/Legal Services Corporation, 1982, and National Center on Women and Family Law, 1990 Supplement.

Hoffman, Jan. "The Devil and Faye Yager." *Village Voice,* 12 June 1990, p. 39.

Hoffman, Lois Wladis. "The Value of Children to Parents and Childrearing Patterns." *Social Behavior* 2 (1987): 123–141.

Hughes, Honore M. "Psychological and Behavioral Correlates of Family Violence in Child Witnesses and Victims." *American Journal of Orthopsychiatry* 58 (1988): 77–90.

Jacobs, Lynn C. "Mediating Postdecree Disputes." *Mediation Quarterly* 8, no. 3 (Spring 1991): 171–183.

Janvier, Rosemary F., Kathleen McCormick, and Rose Donaldson. "Parental Kidnapping: A Survey of Left-Behind Parents." *Juvenile and Family Court Journal* 41 (1990): 1–8.

Jenkins, Shirley and Elaine Norman. *Filial Deprivation and Foster Care.* New York: Columbia University Press, 1972.

——. *Beyond Placement: Mothers View Foster Care.* New York: Columbia University Press, 1975.

Johnston, Janet R. and Linda E. G. Campbell. *Impasses of Divorce.* New York: Free Press, 1988.

"Judge Frees Woman in Fight for Custody with Ex-Spouse." *New York Times,* 14 April 1991, p. A29.

Junod, Tom. "The Last Angry Woman." *Life,* April 1991, pp. 64–76.

Kagan, Jerome. *The Nature of the Child.* New York: Basic Books, 1984.

Kahn, Michael and Karen Gail Lewis, Eds. *Siblings in Therapy.* New York: Norton, 1988.

Kalter, Neil, Amy Kloner, Shelly Schreier, and Kathleen Okla. "Predictors of Children's Post-Divorce Adjustment." *American Journal of Orthopsychiatry* 59, no. 4 (1989): 605–612.

Kamarck, Elaine Ciulla and William A. Galston. *Putting Children First: A Progressive Family Policy for the 1990s.* Washington, DC: Progressive Policy Institute, 1990.

Katz, Sanford N. *Child Snatching: The Legal Response to the Abduction of Children.* Chicago: American Bar Association Press, 1981.

Keenan, Linda R. "Domestic Violence and Custody Litigation: The Need for Statutory Reform." *Hofstra Law Review* 13 (1985): 407–441.

Keshet, Jamie K. "Cognitive Remodeling of the Family: How Remarried People View Stepfamilies." *American Journal of Orthopsychiatry* 60, no. 2 (1990): 196–203.

King, Donald B. "Handling Custody and Visitation Disputes Under the New Mandatory Mediation Law." *California Lawyer* 2, no. 1 (1982): 40–41.

King, Jessica Pearson and Nancy Thoennes. "Mediating and Litigating Custody Disputes: A Longitudinal Evaluation." *Family Law Quarterly* 17 (1984): 497–524.

Kitson, Gay, Karen Babri, and Mary J. Roach. "Who Divorces and Why: A Review." *Journal of Family Issues* 6 (1985): 255–293.

Kline, Marsha, Janet R. Johnson, and Jeanne M. Tschann. "The Long Shadow of Marital Conflict: A Model of Children's Postdivorce Adjustment." *Journal of Marriage and the Family* 53 (1991): 293–309.

Konker, Claudia. "Rethinking Child Sexual Abuse: An Anthropological Perspective." *American Journal of Orthopsychiatry* 62 (Jan. 1992): 147–153.

Krause, Harry D. *Family Law in a Nutshell,* 2nd ed. St. Paul, MN: West, 1986.

Lansing, Paul and Gerald M. Sherman. "The Legal Response to Child Snatching." *Journal of Juvenile Law* 7 (1983): 16–29.

Lawrence, Bobbi and Olivia Taylor-Young. *Child Snatchers.* Boston: Charles River Books, 1982.

Lawson, Carol. "Requiring Classes in Divorce." *New York Times,* 23 January 1992, p. C1.

Lengyel, Linda B. "Survey of State Domestic Violence Legislation." *Legal Reference Services Quarterly* 10 (1990): 59–82.

LePori, Suzanne Y. "The Conflict Between the Parental Kidnapping Prevention Act and the Extradition Act: Naming the Custodial Parent Both Legal Guardian and Fugitive." *St. Mary's Law Journal* 19 (Spring 1988): 1047–1082.

Lerman, Lisa G. "Mediation of Wife Abuse Cases: The Adverse Impact of Informal Dispute Resolution on Women." *Harvard Women's Law Journal* 7 (1984): 57–113.

Levinger, George. "Sources of Marital Dissatisfaction Among Applicants for Divorce." *American Journal of Orthopsychiatry* 26 (1966): 89–97.

Lewis, Karen Gail. "Sibling Therapy with Children in Foster Homes." In *Treating Young Children in Family Therapy,* edited by James C. Hansen and Lee Combrinck-Graham, pp. 52–61. Rockville, MD: Aspen, 1986a.

———. "Sibling Therapy with Multiproblem Families." *Journal of Marital and Family Therapy* 12, no. 3 (1986b): 291–300.

Libby, Lee. "Investigation of Parental Abductions." In *Missing Children: The Law Enforcement Response,* edited by Martin L. Forst, pp. 107–125. Springfield, IL: Thomas, 1990.

Lindy, Jacob D. "An Outline for the Psychoanalytic Psychotherapy of Post-Traumatic Stress Disorder." In *Trauma and Its Wake,* edited by C. R. Figley, pp. 195–212. New York: Brunner/Mazel, 1986.

Little, Margaret, Nancy Thoennes, Jessica Pearson, and Robin Appleford. "A Case Study: The Custody Mediation Services of the Los Angeles Conciliation Court." *Conciliation Courts Review* 23, no. 2 (1985): 1–13.

Lloyd, David W. "Disobedience to a Judicial Order: An Inappropriate Action." *Journal of Interpersonal Violence* 5 (1990): 120–123.

Long, Nicholas, Rex Forehand, and Carolyn Zogg. "Preventing Parental Child Abduction: Analysis of a National Project." *Clinical Pediatrics* 30, no. 9 (Sept. 1991): 549–554.

Luthar, Suniya S. and Edward Zigler. "Vulnerability and Competence: A Review of Research on Resilience in Childhood." *American Journal of Orthopsychiatry* 61, no. 1 (1991): 6–22.

MacDonald, Nancy E., Patricia D. Ebert, and Susan E. Mason. "Marital Status and Age As Related to Masculine and Feminine Personality Dimensions and Self-Esteem." *Journal of Social Psychology* 127 (1987): 289–298.

Mahmoody, Betty and William Hoffer. *Not Without My Daughter.* New York: St. Martin's Press, 1987.

Marks, Evan R. "Fighting Back: The Attorney's Role in a Parental Kidnapping Case," *Florida Bar Journal* 64, no. 4 (June 1990): 23–26.

Martin, Barry S. "To Tell or Not To Tell: A Dilemma for Lawyers Whose Clients Kidnap Their Own Children." *California Lawyer* 7 (Sept. 1987): 21–24, 109.

Marton, Frances K. "Defenses: Invincible and Vincible." *Clinical Social Work Journal* 16, no. 2 (1988): 143–155.

Maxwell, Colin and Allan Gould. *Child Finder: Canada's #1 Tracker of Missing Children.* Scarborough, Ontario: Prentice-Hall Canada, 1989.

May, Elaine Tyler. *Great Expectations: Marriage and Divorce in Post-Victorian America.* Chicago: University of Chicago Press, 1980.

McClean, David. "'Return' of Internationally Abducted Children." *Law Quarterly Review* (England) 106 (July 1990): 375–379.

McDonald, Elizabeth C. "More Than Mere Child's Play: International Parental Abduction of Children." *Dickinson Journal of International Law* 6 (1988): 283–312.

McGoldrick, Monica and Nydia Garcia Preto. "Ethnic Intermarriage: Implications for Therapy." *Family Process* 23 (1984): 347–364.

Menard, Anne E. and Anthony J. Salius. "Judicial Response to Family Violence: The Importance of Message." *Mediation Quarterly* 7 (1990): 293–302.

Mills, C. Wright, *The Sociological Imagination.* Oxford: Oxford University Press, 1959. (Reprinted in *Perspectives on Social Welfare: An Introductory Anthology,* edited by Paul E. Weinberger, pp. 46–47. New York: Macmillan, 1969.)

Mnookin, Robert H. and Lewis Kornhauser. "Bargaining in the Shadow of the Law: The Case of Divorce." *Yale Law Journal* 88 (1979): 950–997.

Mnookin, Robert H. and D. Kelly Weisberg. *Child, Family and State: Problems and Materials on Children and the Law,* 2nd ed. Boston: Little, Brown, 1988.

Mobilia-Boumil, M. "Joint Custody: In Whose Best Interest?" *Suffolk University Law Review* 21 (1987): 1–31.

Morgan, Elizabeth. *Custody.* Boston: Little, Brown, 1985.

Moses, Jonathan M. "Child's Rights Are Broadened in Custody Case." *Wall Street Journal,* 10 December 1991, pp. B1, B11.

Most, Bruce W. "Parent Against Parent: The Child Stealing Epidemic." *Nation,* 7 May 1977, pp. 559–561.

Nathan, Debbie. "Homegrown Hysteria." *The Texas Observer* 82, no. 25 (21 December 1990a): 11.

————. "The Ritual Sex Abuse Hoax." *Village Voice,* 12 June 1990b, pp. 36–43.

National Center on Women and Family Law. *State Custody Laws with Respect to Domestic Abuse.* New York: Author, 1991.

National Resource Center on Child Sexual Abuse. "Think Tank Report: Investigation of Ritualistic Abuse Allegations." Proceedings for the 8th National Conference on Child Abuse and Neglect, Salt Lake City, 22 October 1989.

"Native of Iran Denied Custody for Fleeing Country with Sons." *Pennsylvania Law Journal-Reporter* 11 (1988): 9.

Nichols, John F. "American Courts Look at Foreign Decrees." *Family Advocate* 9, no. 4 (1987): 9–14.

Nobel, Dorinda N. "How to Divide and Reassemble a Child." *Social Casework* 64, no. 7 (Sept. 1983): 406–413.

Oberdorfer, Daniel. *"Larson v. Dunn:* Toward a Reasoned Response to Parental Kidnapping." *Minnesota Law Review* 75 (1991): 1701–1730.

Ochberg, Frank M. "What Is Happening to the Hostages in Iran?" *Psychiatric Annals* 10 (May 1980): 23–29.

Ohio Department of Education. *Missing Child Educational Program: 1989–1990 Annual Report.* Columbus: Author, 1990.

Orthner, Dennis K. and Gary L. Bowen. "Fathers in the Military." In *Dimensions of Fatherhood,* edited by Shirley M. H. Hanson and Frederick W. Bozett, pp. 307–326. Beverly Hills, CA: Sage, 1985.

Pagelow, Daley. "Effects of Domestic Violence on Children and Their Consequences for Custody and Visitation Agreements." *Mediation Quarterly* 7, no. 4 (1990): 347–363.

Patten, Sylvia B., Yvonne K. Gatz, Berlin Jones, and Deborah L. Thomas. "Posttraumatic Stress Disorder and the Treatment of Sexual Abuse." *Social Work* 34 (1989): 197–203.

Pearson, Jessica and Nancy Thoennes. "Divorce Mediation: An Overview of Research Results." *Columbia Journal of Law and Social Problems* 19 (1985): 451–484.

Pennington, H. Joan. "Representing Women Who Conceal or Who Are Considering Concealing Their Children: The Underground Movement." In *Women and the Law,* edited by Carol H. Lefcourt, pp. 6A1–6A36. New York: Clark Boardman, 1990.

Peterson, Kirtland C., Maurice F. Prout, and Robert A. Schwarz. *Post-Traumatic Stress Disorder: A Clinician's Guide.* New York: Plenum Press, 1991.

Pettenati, Jeanne L. "The Effect of the Parental Kidnapping Prevention Act of 1980 on Child Snatching." *New England Law Review* 17 (Spring 1982): 499–526.

Pfund, Peter H. "The Hague Convention on International Child Abduction, The International Child Abduction Remedies Act, and the Need for Availability of Counsel for All Petitioners." *Family Law Quarterly* 24 (1990): 35–51.

Phillips, Roderick. *Putting Asunder: A History of Divorce in Western Society.* Cambridge: Cambridge University Press, 1988.

"President Signs Law Implementing International Child Abduction Treaty." *ABA Juvenile & Child Welfare Law Reporter* 7, no. 4 (1988): 62.

Quinn, Kathleen M. "The Credibility of Children's Allegations of Sexual Abuse." *Behavioral Sciences and the Law* 6 (1988): 181–199.

Reynolds, Sheila. "Parental Kidnapping: A Proposed Act for Expanding Tort Remedies." *Washburn Law Journal* 25 (Winter 1986): 242–263.

Rivers, Dana. "The Hague International Child Abduction Convention and the International Child Abduction Remedies Act: Closing Doors to the Parent Abductor." *The Transnational Lawyer* 2 (1989): 589–640.

Rollin, Miriam, Patricia M. Hoff, and Linda Girdner. *Parental Child Abduction: An Annotated Legal Bibliography.* Washington, DC: American Bar Association Center on Children and the Law, 1991.

Rosenblatt, Roger. *Children of War.* Garden City, NJ: Anchor Books, 1983.

Rosen-Zvi, Ariel. "Israel: Inter-Family Agreements and Parent–Child Relationships." *Journal of Family Law* 28 (1989/90): 526–541.

Rotem, Michael. "Boy, Kidnapped by Father, Found Dead on Beach." *Jerusalem Post,* 13 April 1991.

Rubenstein, Elaine. "An Overview of Adolescent Development, Behavior, and Clinical Intervention." *Families in Society* 72, no. 4 (1991): 220–225.

Rutter, Michael. *Maternal Deprivation Reassessed.* London: Penguin Books, 1972.

Sagatun, Inger J. and Lin Barrett. "Parental Child Abduction: The Law, Family Dynamics, and Legal System Responses." *Journal of Criminal Justice* 18 (1990): 433–442.

Samis, Michell D. C. and Donald Saposnek. "Parent–Child Relationships in Family Mediation: A Synthesis of Views." *Mediation Quarterly* 14/15 (Winter 1986/Spring 1987): 23–37.

Saposnek, Donald T. "The Value of Children in Mediation: A Cross-Cultural Perspective." *Mediation Quarterly* 8, no. 4 (Summer 1991): 325–342.

Schaefer, Michael W. *Child Snatching: How to Prevent It from Happening to Your Child.* New York: McGraw-Hill, 1984.

Schetky, Diane H. and Lee H. Haller. "Child Psychiatry and Law: Parental Kidnapping." *Journal of the American Academy of Child Psychiatry* 22, no. 3 (1983): 279–285.

Schwartz, Philip. "Obtaining Evidence Overseas." *Family Advocate* 9, no. 4 (Spring 1987): 28–33, 45.

Schwerin, Barbara Ullman. "The Hague Convention on International Child Abduction: A Practical Application." *Loyola of Los Angeles International and Comparative Law Journal* 6 (Winter 1988): 163–195.

Seltzer, Judith A. "Relationships Between Fathers and Children Who Live Apart: The Father's Role After Separation." *Journal of Marriage and the Family* 53, no. 1 (1991): 79–101.

Senior, Neil, Toba Gladstone, and Barry Nurcombe. "Child Snatching: A Case Report." *Journal of the American Academy of Child Psychiatry* 21, no. 6 (1982): 579–583.

Sgroi, Suzanne M. *Handbook of Clinical Intervention in Child Sexual Abuse.* Lexington, MA: Heath, 1982.

Singer, Jana B. and William L. Reynolds. "A Dissent on Joint Custody." *Maryland Law Review* 47, no. 2 (1988): 497–523.

Spangler, Susan E. "Snatching Legislative Power: The Justice Department's Refusal to Enforce the Parental Kidnapping Prevention Act." *Journal of Criminal Law and Criminology* 73, no. 3 (1982): 1176–1203.

Spaulding, William. *Interviewing Child Victims of Sexual Exploitation.* Washington, DC: National Center for Missing and Exploited Children, 1987.

Stevenson, Robert Lewis. *Kidnapped.* London: Oxford University Press, 1964 (original work published 1886).

——. *David Balfour.* New York: Scribner, 1925 (original work published 1893).

Stewart, James R., Andrew I. Schwebel, and Mark Fine. "The Impact of Custodial Arrangements on the Adjustment of Recently Divorced Fathers." *Journal of Divorce* 9 (1986): 55–65.

Stone, Alan A. "Vermont Adopts *Tarasoff:* A Real Barn-Burner." *American Journal of Psychiatry* 143 (1986): 352–355.

Stone, Andrew M. "The Role of Shame in Post-Traumatic Stress Disorder." *American Journal of Orthopsychiatry* 62 (Jan. 1992): 131–136.

Stone, Lawrence. *Road to Divorce: England 1530–1987.* Oxford: Oxford University Press, 1990.

Stotter, Lawrence H. "The Light at the End of the Tunnel: The Hague Convention on International Child Abduction Has Reached Capitol Hill." *Hastings International and Comparative Law Review* 9 (1986): 285–328.

Straus, Murray A., Richard J. Gelles, and Suzanne K. Steinmetz. *Behind Closed Doors: Violence in the American Family.* Newbury Park, CA: Sage, 1988.

Strom, Robert, Stanley Wurster, M. Austin Betz, Susan Daniels, Peter Graf, and Louise Jansen. "A Comparison of West German and Guestworker Parents' Childrearing Attitudes and Expectations." *Journal of Comparative Family Studies* 15 (1984): 427–440.

Terr, Lenore C. "Child Snatching: A New Epidemic of an Ancient Malady." *Journal of Pediatrics* 103 (July 1983): 151–156.

Thoennes, Nancy. "Child Sexual Abuse: Whom Should a Judge Believe: What Should a Judge Believe?" *The Judges Journal* 27, no. 3 (Summer 1988): 14–18, 48.

United Nations. *Convention on the Rights of the Child: Fact Sheet 10.* Geneva: Author, 1990.

U.S. Congress, House. *Hearings on H.R. 5657.* 72nd Congress, 1st Session, 1957.

U.S. Congress, House. *Sense of Congress Regarding Child Custody, House Concurrent Resolution 172,* 1990.

U.S. Congress, Senate, Committee on the Judiciary, Subcommittee on Juvenile Justice. *Child Kidnapping: Hearing (Serial No. J-98-3).* 98th Congress, 2 February 1983.

U.S. Department of Commerce, Bureau of the Census. *Characteristics of American Children and Youth: 1980* (Series p-23, no. 114). Washington, DC: U.S. Government Printing Office, 1982.

———. *Child Support and Alimony: 1985 (Series P-23, No. 152).* Washington, DC: U.S. Government Printing Office, 1987.

———. *Statistical Abstract of the United States: 1989.* Washington, DC: U.S. Government Printing Office, 1989.

———. *Marital Status and Living Arrangements: March 1989 (Series P-20, No. 433).* Washington, DC: U.S. Government Printing Office, 1990a.

———. *Statistical Abstract of the United States: 1990.* Washington, DC: U.S. Government Printing Office, 1990b.

———. *Marital Status and Living Arrangements: March 1990 (Series P-20, No. 450).* Washington, DC: U.S. Government Printing Office, 1991.

U.S. Department of State, Bureau of Consular Affairs. *International Parental Child Abduction,* 3rd ed. Washington: Author, 1989.

————. *International Parental Child Abduction Case Statistics.* Washington: Author, 1991a.

————. *Statistical Report of the United States Central Authority for the Hague Convention on the Civil Aspects of International Child Abduction.* Washington, DC: Author, 1991b.

Visher, Emily and John Visher. *Stepfamilies: Old Loyalties, New Ties.* New York: Brunner/Mazel, 1988.

Walker, Janet. "Family Mediation in England: Strategies for Gaining Acceptance." *Mediation Quarterly* 8, no. 4 (Summer 1991): 253–264.

Waller, Douglas. "Rent-a-Rescue Commandos: Ex-Delta Force Operatives Hunt for Abducted Kids." *Newsweek,* 8 July 1991, p. 31.

Wallerstein, Judith. "Transference and Countertransference in Clinical Intervention with Divorcing Families." *American Journal of Orthopsychiatry* 60, no. 3 (1990): 337–345.

Wallerstein, Judith and Sandra Blakeslee. *Second Chances: Men, Women and Children a Decade After Divorce.* New York: Ticknor & Fields, 1989.

Wallerstein, Judith and Joan B. Kelly. *Surviving the Breakup.* New York: Basic Books, 1980.

Walters, Lynda Henley and Audrey Wagner Elam. "The Father and the Law." *American Behavioral Scientist* 29, no. 1 (Sept./Oct. 1985): 78–111.

Wartel, Stephen G. "Clinical Considerations for Adults Abused as Children." *Families in Society* 72, no. 3 (1991): 157–163.

Wexler, Joan. "Rethinking the Modification of Child Custody Decrees." *Yale Law Journal* 94 (1985): 757–820.

White, Sue and Kathleen M. Quinn. "Investigatory Independence in Child Sexual Abuse Evaluations: Conceptual Considerations." *Bulletin. American Academy of Psychiatry and the Law* 16, no. 3 (1988): 269–278.

Wilson, Ann T. "The Parental Kidnapping Prevention Act: Is There an Enforcement Role of the Federal Courts?" *Washington Law Review* 62 (Oct. 1987): 841–862.

Wixom, Hartt and Judene Wixom. *Trial by Terror: The Child Hostage Crisis in Cokeville, Wyoming.* Bountiful, Utah: Horizon Books, 1987.

World Almanac and Book of Facts. Cleveland: Pharos Books, 1988.

Zaidel, Susan. "Challenges Facing the Development of Family Mediation in Israel." *Mediation Quarterly* 8, no. 4 (Summer 1991): 281–291.

Zemmelman, Steven E., Susan B. Steinman, and Thomas M. Knoblauch. "A Study of Parents Who Sought Joint Custody Following Divorce: Who Reaches Agreement and Sustains Joint Custody and Who

Returns to Court." *Journal of the American Academy of Child Psychiatry* 24 (1985): 554–562.

————. "A Model Project on Joint Custody for Families Undergoing Divorce." *Social Work* 32 (1987): 32–37.

INDEX